CW00662711

COLLECTION

OF

BRITISH AUTHORS

TAUCHNITZ EDITION.

VOL. 1730.

A THOUSAND MILES UP THE NILE
BY
AMELIA B. EDWARDS.

IN TWO VOLUMES.

VOL. I.

———

A THOUSAND MILES UP THE NILE.

BY

AMELIA B. EDWARDS,

AUTHOR OF

"BARBARA'S HISTORY," "UNTRODDEN PEAKS," ETC.

COPYRIGHT EDITION.

IN TWO VOLUMES.

VOL. I.

LEIPZIG

BERNHARD TAUCHNITZ

1878.

The Right of Translation is reserved.

PREFACE.

"Un voyage en Égypte, c'est une partie d'ânes et une promenade en bateau entremêlées de ruines."—AMPÈRE.

AMPÈRE has put Egypt in an epigram. "A donkey-ride and a boating-trip interspersed with ruins" does, in fact, sum up in a single line the whole experience of the Nile traveller. Apropos of these three things—the donkeys, the boat, and the ruins—it may be said that a good English saddle and a comfortable Dahabeeyah add very considerably to the pleasure of the journey; and that the more one knows about the past history of the country, the more one enjoys the ruins.

Of the comparative merits of wooden boats, iron boats, and steamers, I am not qualified to speak. We, however, saw one iron Dahabeeyah aground upon a sandbank, where, as we afterwards learned, it remained for three weeks. We also saw the wrecks of three steamers between Cairo and the First Cataract. It certainly seemed to us that the old-fashioned wooden Dahabeeyah—flat-bottomed, drawing little water, light in hand, and easily poled off when stuck—was the one vessel best constructed for the navigation of the Nile.

Other considerations, as time and cost, are, of course, involved in this question. The choice between Dahabeeyah and steamer is like the choice between travelling with post-horses and travelling by rail. The one is expensive, leisurely, and delightful; the other is swift, less expensive, and less luxurious. Those who are content to snatch but a glimpse of the Nile will doubtless prefer the steamer. I may add that the whole cost of the "Philæ"—food, dragoman's wages, boat-hire, cataract, everything included except wine—was about £10 per day.

With regard to temperature, we found it cool—even cold, sometimes—in December and January; mild in February; very warm in March and April. The climate of Nubia is simply perfect. It never rains; and once past the limit of the tropic, there is no morning or evening chill upon the air. Yet even in Nubia, and especially along the forty miles that divide Aboo-Simbel from Wady Halfeh, it is cold when the wind blows strongly from the north. I had hoped to add here a little table of average temperatures, compiled from notes taken by a fellow-traveller who carefully registered the variations of the thermometer from day to day. But the Idle Man has only too well carried out the promise of his sobriquet; and I am still without the necessary data.

In giving the names of places, I have adhered to the spelling adopted in Murray's *Handbook for Egypt*. There are perhaps instances in which I should have preferred a different rendering; but it seemed to me

that in following Murray, I best consulted the convenience of the general reader.

Touching the title of this book, it may be objected
that the distance from the port of Alexandria to the
Second Cataract falls short of a thousand miles. It is,
in fact, calculated at $964\frac{1}{2}$ miles. But from the Rock
of Abooseer, five miles above Wady Halfeh, the traveller
looks over an extent of country far exceeding the thirty
or thirty-five miles necessary to make up the full tale
of a thousand. We distinctly saw from this point the
summits of mountains which lie about 145 miles to the
southward of Wady Halfeh, and which look down upon
the Third Cataract.

It will be seen by those who do not weary of my
companionship before reaching the eighteenth Chapter,
that I had the great good fortune to be one of a party,
which, in the month of February 1874, discovered and
excavated an extremely interesting group of ruins at
Aboo-Simbel in Nubia. If an apology were needed for
the writing of another book about the Nile, this circum-
stance would alone furnish sufficient reason for the pro-
duction of the present volumes. I do not feel, however,
that such apology is called for; but rather that there
has long been a distinct opening for some such work
as I have now endeavoured to write. The published
literature of the subject, it is true, is already ample,
and would fill a small library; but it is singularly the
reverse of homogeneous. Egyptologists, for instance,
absorbed in study, rarely travel. Nile travellers, on the
other hand, though they frequently excel as observers,

are as a rule but slightly acquainted with the true meaning and history of the things and places they describe. It seemed, therefore, to both author and publishers, that a book about the Nile which should be written from both these points of view was yet wanted, and would be acceptable to readers at home and abroad. To bring the Nile, its scenery, its people, its associations ancient and modern, before the mind's eye of those who have never visited Egypt or the East; to recall all these things, and perhaps sometimes to make them clearer, to those who already know the river and its banks, have been my aim and hope from the beginning to the end of a long, and sometimes a laborious undertaking. When I say that every description which the book contains was written on the spot, and that every sketch engraved in the original edition was likewise made and finished on the spot, it will be seen that I spared no pains of pen or pencil to ensure such picturesque accuracy as lay in my power. The illustrations, in accordance with the prevailing rule of the Tauchnitz Series, are, however, with some few exceptions, unavoidably omitted from the present issue.

Of the charm of the Nile, of the unexpected and surpassing beauty of the desert, of the ruins which are the wonder of the world, I have said enough elsewhere. I must, however, add that I brought home with me an impression that things and people are much less changed in Egypt than we of the present day are wont to suppose. I believe that the physique and life of the modern Fellah is almost identical with the physique and life of that ancient Egyptian labourer whom we know so well in the wall-paintings of the tombs. Square in the shoulders, slight but strong in the limbs, full-lipped, brown-skinned, we see him wearing the same loin-cloth, plying the same shadoof, ploughing with the same plough, preparing the same food in the same way, and eating it with his fingers from the same bowl, as did his forefathers of six thousand years ago. The household life and social ways of even the provincial gentry are little changed. Water is poured on one's hands before going to dinner from just such a ewer and into just such a basin as we see pictured in the festival-scenes at Thebes. Though the lotus-blossom is missing, a bouquet is still given to each guest when he takes his place at table. The head of the sheep killed for the banquet is still given to the poor. Those who are helped to meat or drink touch the head and breast in acknowledgment, as of old. The musicians still sit at the lower end of the hall; the singers yet clap their hands in time to their own voices; the dancing-girls still dance, and the buffoon in his high cap still performs his uncouth antics, for the entertainment of the guests. Water is brought to table in the same jars manufactured at the same town as in the days of Cheops and Chephren; and the mouths of the bottles are filled in precisely the same way with fresh leaves and flowers. The cucumber stuffed with minced-meat was a favourite dish in those times of old; and I can testify to its excellence in 1874. Little boys in Nubia yet wear the side-lock

that graced the head of Rameses in his youth; and
little girls may be seen in a garment closely resembling
the girdle worn by young princesses of the time of
Thothmes the First. A Sheykh still walks with a long
staff; a Nubian belle still plaits her tresses in scores of
little tails; and the pleasure-boat of the modern
Governor or Moodeer, as well as the Dahabeeyah hired
by the European traveller, reproduces in all essential
features the painted galleys represented in the tombs
of the kings.

In these, and in a hundred other instances, all of
which came under my personal observation and have
their place in the following pages, it seemed to me
that any obscurity which yet hangs over the problem
of life and thought in ancient Egypt originates most
probably with ourselves. Our own habits of life and
thought are so complex that they shut us off from the
simplicity of that early world. So it was with the
problem of hieroglyphic writing. The thing was so
obvious that no one could find it out. As long as the
world persisted in believing that every hieroglyph was
an abstruse symbol, and every hieroglyphic inscription
a profound philosophical rebus, the mystery of Egyptian literature remained insoluble. Then at last came
Champollion's famous letter to Dacier, showing that
the hieroglyphic signs were mainly alphabetic and syl-
labic, and that the language they spelt was only Coptic
after all.

If there were not thousands who still conceive that
the sun and moon were created, and are kept going,

for no other purpose than to lighten the darkness of our little planet; if only the other day a grave gentleman had not written a perfectly serious essay to show that the world is a flat plain, one would scarcely believe that there could still be people who doubt that ancient Egyptian is now read and translated as fluently as ancient Greek. Yet an Englishman whom I met in Egypt—an Englishman who had long been resident in Cairo, and who was well acquainted with the great Egyptologists attached to the service of the Khedive—assured me of his profound disbelief in the discovery of Champollion. "In my opinion," said he, "not one of these gentlemen can read a line of hieroglyphics." As I then knew nothing of Egyptian, I could say nothing to controvert this speech. Since that time, however, and while writing this book, I have been led on step by step to the study of hieroglyphic writing; and though still but the veriest beginner, I now know that Egyptian can be read, for the simple reason that I find myself able to read an Egyptian sentence. The testimony of a tyro may not be of much value; but I give it for the little that it is worth.

In these days of Egyptian grammars, dictionaries, reading-books and classes, there is, in fact, no reason why the educated traveller who passes a winter on the Nile should not decipher for himself an ancient Egyptian inscription written in hieroglyphic characters, as easily as he reads an epitaph on the Eleusian Way at Athens, or the dedication of a triumphal arch in Rome.

The study of Egyptian literature has advanced of late years with rapid strides. Papyri are found less frequently than they were some thirty or forty years ago; but the translation of those contained in the museums of Europe goes on now more diligently than at any former time. Religious books, variants of the Ritual, moral essays, maxims, private letters, hymns, epic poems, historical chronicles, accounts, deeds of sale, medical, magical, and astronomical treatises, geographical records, travels, and even romances and tales, are brought to light, photographed, facsimiled in chromo-lithography, printed in hieroglyphic type, and translated in forms suited both to the learned and to the general reader. It must be admitted, however, that the more intimately we penetrate into the secrets of this extinct civilisation, the more it becomes apparent that much yet remains, and must always remain, unexplained. Of the Gods of ancient Egypt, of their curious genealogies and adventures, of the intricate network of myths into which the religion gradually developed, we know, for instance, almost as much as did the most learned hierogrammate of Ptolemaic times; but we know next to nothing of the phases and fluctuations of faith throughout the ages that lie between Menes and Theodosius. Possessing, as we now do, copies and translations of every line of the tens of thousands of hieroglyphic texts sculptured all over the great Temples of Denderah and Edfoo, we have still but the dimmest idea of the kind of service that was performed within those walls. We do know that the ancient Egyptians, with their pompous festivals and their all-powerful priesthood, had no kind of public worship in the modern sense of the phrase; but we do not actually know for certain whether the Fellah class of old received any kind of religious instruction, or had even any glimmering of religious belief. As in theological matters, so is it also in matters political and social. Much has been discovered; but much remains hidden. Thus the old mystery hangs over Egypt to the last, and it seems as if we should never pluck out the heart of it. It is as a haze which closes in upon the one horizon as it lifts upon the other. Hence the lasting fascination of Egyptian study; hence the undying novelty of Egyptian travel. We are always learning, and there is always more to be learned; we are always seeking, and there is always more to find. Every year brings to the surface some long-buried inscription or papyrus. Each successive traveller has some new thing to tell. The work of discovery and interpretation goes on apace. Old truths receive unexpected corroboration: old histories are judged by the light of new readings; fresh wonders are disclosed wherever the Egyptologist or the excavator strikes new ground. The interest never flags—the subject never stales—the mine is never exhausted.

Let me add in conclusion that whenever, in the course of the present book, I have found occasion to quote from the published works of previous writers, I have been careful to give full and satisfactory references. These references, in order to leave the thread of the narrative unbroken, have been added in the form of foot-notes; and every extract so presented is accompanied by the name of the author, the title, chapter, and page of the work, as well as the place and date of publication. Where authorities differ, the leading opinions on both sides have been given. The convenience of those who may care to pursue the subject farther is thus consulted; while the general reader, who is not especially concerned in Egyptological subjects, need only read the narrative, if he is so minded.

AMELIA B. EDWARDS.

Westbury on Trym,
Gloucestershire, Sept. 1877.

CONTENTS

OF VOLUME L

A THOUSAND MILES
UP THE NILE.

***

CHAPTER I.

Cairo and the Great Pyramid.

It is the traveller's lot to dine at many table-d'hôtes in the course of many wanderings; but it seldom befalls him to make one of a more miscellaneous gathering than that which overfills the great dining-room at Shepherd's Hotel in Cairo during the beginning and height of the regular Egyptian season. Here assemble daily some two to three hundred persons of all ranks, nationalities, and pursuits; half of whom are Anglo-Indians homeward or outward bound, European residents, or visitors established in Cairo for the winter. The other half, it may be taken for granted, are going up the Nile. So composite and incongruous is this body of Nile-goers, young and old, well-dressed and ill-dressed, learned and unlearned, that the new-comer's first impulse is to inquire from what motives so many persons of dissimilar tastes and training can be led to embark upon an expedition which is, to say the least of it, very tedious, very costly, and of an altogether exceptional interest.

His curiosity, however, is soon gratified. Before two days are over, he knows everybody's name and everybody's business; distinguishes at first sight between a Cook's tourist and an independent traveller; and has discovered that nine-tenths of those whom he is likely to meet up the river are English or American. The rest will be mostly German, with a sprinkling of Belgian and French. So far *en bloc;* but the details are more heterogeneous still. Here are invalids in search of health; artists in search of subjects; sportsmen keen upon crocodiles; statesmen out for a holiday; special correspondents alert for gossip; collectors on the scent of papyri and mummies; men of science with only scientific ends in view; and the usual surplus of idlers who travel for the mere love of travel, or the satisfaction of a purposeless curiosity.

Now in a place like Shepherd's, where every fresh arrival has the honour of contributing, for at least a few minutes, to the general entertainment, the first appearance of L. and the Writer, tired, dusty, and considerably sun-burned, may well have given rise to some of the comments in usual circulation at those crowded tables. People asked each other, most likely, where these two wandering Englishwomen had come from; why they had not dressed for dinner; what brought them to Egypt; and if they also were going up the Nile—to all which questions it would have been easy to give satisfactory answers.

We came from Alexandria, having had a rough passage from Brindisi followed by forty-eight hours of quarantine. We had not dressed for dinner because, having driven on from the station in advance of dragoman and luggage, we were but just in time to take seats with the rest. We intended, of course, to go up the Nile; and had any one ventured to inquire in so many words what brought us to Egypt, we should have replied:—"Stress of weather."

For in simple truth we had drifted hither by accident, with no excuse of health, or business, or any serious object whatever; and had just taken refuge in Egypt as one might turn aside into the Burlington Arcade or the Passage des Panoramas—to get out of the rain.

And with good reason. Having left home early in September for a few weeks' sketching in central France, we had been pursued by the wettest of wet weather. Washed out of the hill-country, we fared no better in the plains. At Nismes it poured for a month without stopping. Debating at last whether it were better to take our wet umbrellas back at once to England, or push on farther still in search of sunshine, the talk fell upon Algiers—Malta—Cairo; and Cairo carried it. Never was distant expedition entered upon with less premeditation. The thing was no sooner decided than we were gone. Nice, Genoa, Bologna, Ancona flitted by, as in a dream; and Bedreddin Hassan when he woke at the gates of Damascus was scarcely more surprised than the writer of these pages, when she found herself on board the "Simla," and steaming out of the port of Brindisi.

Here, then, without definite plans, outfit, or any kind of Oriental experience, behold us arrived in Cairo on the 29th of November 1873, literally and most prosaically in search of fine weather.

But what had memory to do with rains on land, or storms at sea, or the impatient hours of quarantine, or anything dismal or disagreeable, when one woke at sunrise to see those grey-green palms outside the win-

dow solemnly bowing their plumed heads towards each
other, against a rose-coloured dawn? It was dark last
night, and I had no idea that my room overlooked an
enchanted garden, far-reaching and solitary, peopled
with stately giants beneath whose tufted crowns hung
rich clusters of maroon and amber dates. It was a
still, warm morning. Grave grey and black crows flew
heavily from tree to tree, or perched, cawing medi-
tatively, upon the topmost branches. Yonder, between
the pillared stems, rose the minaret of a very distant
mosque; and here where the garden was bounded by
a high wall and a windowless house, I saw a veiled
lady walking on the terraced roof in the midst of a
cloud of pigeons. Nothing could be more simple than
the scene and its accessories; nothing, at the same
time, more Eastern, strange, and unreal.

But in order thoroughly to enjoy an overwhelming,
ineffaceable first impression of Oriental out-of-doors
life, one should begin in Cairo with a day in the
native bazaars; neither buying, nor sketching, nor seeking information, but just taking in scene after scene
with its manifold combinations of light and shade,
colour, costume, and architectural detail. Every shop-
front, every street-corner, every turbaned group is a
ready-made picture. The old Turk who sets up his
cake-stall in the sculptured recess of a Moorish doorway; the donkey-boy with his gaily caparisoned ass,
waiting for customers; the beggar asleep on the steps
of the mosque; the veiled woman filling her water-jar
at the public fountain—they all look as if they had
been put there expressly to be painted.

Nor is the background less picturesque than the
figures. The houses are high and narrow. The upper

stories project; and from these again jut windows of
delicate turned lattice-work in old brown wood, like
big birdcages. The street is roofed in overhead with
long rafters and pieces of matting, through which a
dusty sunbeam straggles here and there, casting patches
of brilliant light upon the moving crowd. The unpaved thoroughfare—a mere narrow lane, full of ruts
and watered profusely twice or thrice a day—is lined
with little wooden shop-fronts, like open cabinets full
of shelves, where the merchants sit cross-legged in the
midst of their goods, looking out at the passers-by and
smoking in silence. Meanwhile the crowd ebbs and
flows unceasingly—a noisy, changing, restless, parti-*
coloured tide, half European, half Oriental, on foot, on
horseback, and in carriages. Here are Syrian dragomans in baggy trousers and braided jackets; bare-
footed Egyptian fellaheen in ragged blue shirts and
felt skull-caps; Greeks in absurdly stiff white tunics,
like walking penwipers; Persians with high, mitre-like
caps of dark woven stuff; swarthy Bedouins in flowing
garments, creamy-white with chocolate stripes a foot
wide, and head-shawl of the same bound about the
brow with a fillet of twisted camel's hair; Englishmen
in palm-leaf hats and knickerbockers, dangling their
long legs across almost invisible donkeys; native women
of the poorer class, in black veils that leave only the
eyes uncovered, and long trailing garments of dark
blue and black striped cotton; dervishes in patchwork
coats, their matted hair streaming from under fantastic
head-dresses; blue-black Abyssinians with incredibly
slender, bowed legs, like attenuated ebony balustrades;
Armenian priests, looking exactly like Portia as the
Doctor, in long black gowns and high, square caps;

majestic ghosts of Algerine Arabs all in white; mounted
Janissaries with jingling sabres and gold-embroidered
jackets; merchants, beggars, soldiers, boatmen, labourers,
workmen, in every variety of costume, and of every
shade of complexion from fair to dark, from tawny to
copper-colour, from deepest bronze to bluest black.

Now a water-carrier goes by, bending under the
weight of his newly-replenished goatskin, which (having
the hair left on, the legs tied up, and the neck fitted
with a brass cock) looks horribly bloated and life-like.
Now comes a sweetmeat-vendor with a tray of that
gummy compound known to English children as
"Lumps of Delight;" and now an Egyptian lady on a
large grey donkey led by a servant with a showy sabre
at his side. The lady wears a rose-coloured silk dress
and white veil, besides a black silk outer garment,
which, being cloak, hood, and veil all in one, fills out
with the wind as she rides, like a balloon. She sits
astride; her naked feet, in their violet velvet slippers,
just resting on the stirrups. She takes care to display
a plump brown arm laden with massive gold bracelets,
and, to judge by the way in which she uses a pair of
liquid black eyes, would not be sorry to let her face
be seen also. Nor is the steed less well dressed than
his mistress. His close-shaven legs and hind-quarters
are painted in blue and white zigzags picked out with
bands of pale yellow; his high-pomelled saddle is
resplendent with velvet and embroidery; and his head-
gear is all tags, tassels, and fringes. Such a donkey
as this is worth from sixty to a hundred pounds sterling.
Next passes an open barouche full of laughing Englishwomen; or a grave provincial sheykh all in black, riding a handsome bay Arab, *demi-sang;* or an Egyptian

gentleman in European dress and Turkish fez, driven by an English groom in an English phaeton. Before him, wand in hand, barelegged, eager-eyed, in Greek skull-cap and gorgeous gold-embroidered waistcoat and fluttering white tunic, flies a native Saïs, or running footman. No person of position drives in Cairo without one or two of these attendants. The Saïs (strong, light, and beautiful, like John of Bologna's Mercury), are said to die young. The pace kills them. Next passes a lemonade-seller with his tin jar in one hand and his decanter and brass cups in the other; or an itinerant slipper-vendor with a bunch of red and yellow morocco shoes dangling at the end of a long pole; or a London-built miniature brougham containing two ladies in transparent Turkish veils, preceded by a Nubian outrider in semi-military livery; or, perhaps, a train of camels, ill-tempered and supercilious, craning their scrannel necks above the crowd, and laden with canvas bales scrawled over with Arabic addresses.

But the Egyptian, Arab, and Turkish merchants, whether mingling in the general tide or sitting on their counters, are the most picturesque personages in all this busy scene. They wear ample turbans, for the most part white; long vests of striped Syrian silk reaching to the feet; and an outer robe of braided cloth or cashmere. The vest is confined round the waist by a rich sash; and the outer robe, or *gibbeh*, is generally of some beautiful degraded colour, such as maize, mulberry, olive, peach, sea-green, salmon-pink, sienna-brown, and the like. That these stately beings should vulgarly buy and sell, instead of reposing all their lives on luxurious divans and being waited upon by beautiful Circassians, seems altogether contrary to the eternal fitness of things. Here, for instance, is a Grand Vizier in a gorgeous white and amber satin vest, who condescends to retail pipe-bowls,—dull red clay pipe-bowls of all sizes and prices. He sells nothing else, and has not only a pile of them on the counter, but a binful at the back of his shop. They are made at Siout in middle Egypt, and may be bought at the Algerian shops in London almost as cheaply as in Cairo. Another majestic Pasha deals in brass and copper vessels, drinking-cups, basins, ewers, trays, incense-burners, chafing-dishes, and the like; some of which are exquisitely engraved with Arabesque patterns or sentences from the poets. A third sells silks from the looms of Lebanon, and gold and silver tissues from Damascus. Others, again, sell old arms, old porcelain, old embroideries, second-hand prayer-carpets, and quaint little stools and cabinets of ebony inlaid with mother-of-pearl. Here, too, the tobacco-merchant sits behind a huge cake of Latakia as big as his own body; and the sponge-merchant smokes his long chibouk in a bower of sponges.

Most amusing of all, however, are those bazaars in which each trade occupies its separate quarter. You pass through an old stone gateway or down a narrow turning, and find yourself amid a colony of saddlers stitching, hammering, punching, riveting. You walk up one alley and down another, between shop-fronts hung round with tasselled head-gear and humpbacked saddles of all qualities and colours. Here are ladies' saddles, military saddles, donkey-saddles, and saddles for great officers of state; saddles covered with red leather, with crimson and violet velvet, with maroon, and grey, and purple cloth; saddles embroidered with gold and silver, studded with brass-headed nails, or trimmed with braid.

Another turn or two, and you are in the slipper bazaar, walking down avenues of red and yellow morocco slippers, the former of home manufacture, the latter from Tunis. Here are slippers with pointed toes, turned-up toes, and toes as round and flat as horse-shoes; walking slippers with thick soles, and soft yellow slippers to be worn as inside socks, which have no soles at all. These absurd little scarlet bluchers with tassels are for little boys; the brown morocco shoes are for grooms; the velvet slippers embroidered with gold and beads and seed-pearls are for wealthy hareems, and are sold at prices varying from five shillings to five pounds the pair.

The carpet-bazaar is of considerable extent, and consists of a network of alleys and counter-alleys opening off to the right of the Moskee, which is the Regent Street of Cairo. The houses in most of these alleys are rich in antique lattice-windows and Saracenic doorways. One little square is tapestried all round with Persian and Syrian rugs, Damascus saddle-bags, and Turkish prayer-carpets. The merchants sit and smoke in the midst of their goods: and up in one corner an old "Kahwegee," or coffee-seller, plies his humble trade. He has set up his little stove and hanging-shelf beside the doorway of a dilapidated Khan, the walls of which are faced with Arabesque pannellings in old carved stone. It is one of the most picturesque "bits" in Cairo. The striped carpets of Tunis; the dim grey and blue, or grey and red fabrics of Algiers; the shaggy rugs of Laodicea and Smyrna; the rich blues and greens and subdued reds of Turkey; and the wonderfully varied, harmonious patterns of Persia, have each their local habitation in the neighbouring alleys. One is never tired of traversing these half-lighted avenues, all aglow with gorgeous colour and peopled with figures that come and go like the actors in some Christmas piece of Oriental pageantry.

In the As Siàgha, the place of the gold and silver smiths' bazaar, there is found, on the contrary, scarcely any display of goods for sale. The alleys are so narrow in this part that two persons can with difficulty walk in them abreast; and the shops, tinier than ever, are mere cupboards with about three feet of frontage. The back of each cupboard is fitted with tiers of little drawers and pigeon-holes, and in front is a kind of matted stone step, called a mastabah, which serves for seat and counter. The customer sits on the edge of the mastabah; the merchant squats, cross-legged, inside. In this position he can, without rising, take out drawer after drawer; and thus the space between the two becomes piled with gold and silver ornaments. These differ from each other only in the metal, the patterns being identical; and they are sold by weight, with a due margin for profit. In dealing with strangers who do not understand the Egyptian system of weights, silver articles are commonly weighed against rupees or five-franc pieces, and gold articles against napoleons or sovereigns. The ornaments made in Cairo consist chiefly of chains and ear-rings, anklets, bangles, necklaces strung with coins or tusk-shaped pendants, amulet-cases of filigree or repoussé work, and penannular bracelets of rude execution, but rich and ancient designs. As for the merchants, their civility and patience are inexhaustible. One may turn over their whole stock, try on all their bracelets, go away again and again without buying, and yet be always welcomed and dismissed with smiles. L. and the Writer spent many an hour practising Arabic in the As Siàgha, without, it is to be feared, a corresponding degree of benefit to the merchants.

There are many other special bazaars in Cairo, as the Sweetmeat Bazaar; the Hardware Bazaar; the Tobacco Bazaar; the Sword-mounters' and Coppersmiths' Bazaars; the Moorish Bazaar, where Fez caps, and burnouses, and Barbary goods are sold; and some extensive bazaars for the sale of English and French muslins and Manchester cotton goods; but these last are, for the most part, of inferior interest. Among certain fabrics manufactured in England expressly for the Eastern market, we observed a most hideous printed muslin representing small black devils capering over a yellow ground, and learned that it was much in favour for children's dresses.

But the bazaars, however picturesque, are far from being the only sights of Cairo. There are mosques in plenty; grand old Saracenic gates; ancient Coptic churches; the museum of Egyptian antiquities; and, within driving distance, the tombs of the Caliphs, Heliopolis, the Pyramids, and the Sphinx. To remember in what order the present travellers saw these things would now be impossible; for they lived in a dream, and were at first too bewildered to catalogue their impressions very methodically. Some places they were obliged to dismiss for the present with only a glance *en passant;* and others had to be wholly deferred till their return to Cairo.

In the meanwhile our first business was to look at dahabeeyahs; and the looking at dahabeeyahs compelled us constantly to turn our steps and our thoughts in the direction of Boulak—a desolate place by the river where some two or three hundred Nile-boats lay moored for hire. Now most persons know something of the miseries of house-hunting; but only those who have experienced them know how much keener are the miseries of dahabeeyah-hunting. It is more bewildering and more fatiguing, and is beset with its own special and peculiar difficulties. The boats, in the first place, are all built on the same plan, which is not the case with houses; and except as they run bigger or smaller, cleaner or dirtier, are as like each other as twin oysters. The same may be said of their captains, with the same differences; for to a person who has been only a few days in Egypt, one black or copper-coloured man is exactly like every other black or copper-coloured man. Then each Reïs, or captain, displays the certificates given to him by former travellers; and these certificates, being apparently in active circulation, have a mysterious way of turning up again and again on board different boats and in the hands of different claimants. Nor is this all. Dahabeeyahs are given to changing their places, which houses do not do; so that the boat which lay yesterday alongside the eastern bank may be over at the western bank to-day, or hidden in the midst of a dozen others half-a-mile lower down the river. All this is very perplexing; yet it is as nothing compared with the state of confusion one gets into when attempting to weigh the advantages or disadvantages of boats with six cabins and boats with eight; boats provided with canteen

and boats without; boats that can pass the cataract,
and boats that can't; boats that are only twice as dear
as they ought to be, and boats with that defect five or
six times multiplied. Their names, again—Ghazal,
Sarawa, Fostat, Dongola—unlike any names one has
ever heard before, afford as yet no kind of help to the
memory. Neither do the names of their captains; for
they are all Mohammeds or Hassans. Neither do their
prices; for they vary from day to day, according to the
state of the market as shown by the returns of arrivals
at the principal hotels.

Add to all this the fact that no Reïs speaks anything but Arabic, and that every word of inquiry or
negotiation has to be filtered, more or less inaccurately,
through a dragoman; and then perhaps those who have
not yet tried this variety of the pleasures of the chase
may be able to form some notion of the weary, hopeless, puzzling work that lies before the dahabeeyah
hunter in Cairo.

Thus it came to pass that for the first ten days or
so, some three or four hours had to be devoted every
morning to the business of the boats; at the end of
which time we were no nearer a conclusion than at
first. The small boats were too small for either com-
fort or safety, especially in what Nile-travellers call "a
big wind." The medium-sized boats (which lie under
the suspicion of being used in summer for the transport
of cargo) were for the most part of doubtful cleanliness. The largest boats, which alone seemed unexceptionable, contained from eight to ten cabins, besides two saloons, and were obviously too large for a
party consisting of only L., the writer, and a maid.
And all were exorbitantly dear. Encompassed by these

manifold difficulties; listening now to this and now to
that person's opinion; deliberating, haggling, comparing,
hesitating, we vibrated daily between Boulak and Cairo,
and led a miserable life. Meanwhile, however, we met
some former acquaintances; made some new ones; and
when not too tired or down-hearted, saw what we
could of the sights of Cairo—all of which helped a
little to soften the asperities of our lot.

One of our first excursions was, of course, to the
Pyramids, which lie within an hour-and-a-half's easy
drive from the hotel door. We started immediately
after an early luncheon, followed an excellent road all
the way, and were back in time for dinner at half-past
six. But it must be understood that we did not go to
see the Pyramids. We went only to look at them.
Later on (having, meanwhile, been up the Nile and
back, and gone through months of training), we came
again, not only with due leisure, but also with some
practical understanding of the manifold phases through
which the arts and architecture of Egypt had passed
since those far-off days of Cheops and Chephren. Then,
only, we can be said to have *seen* the Pyramids; and
till we arrive at that stage of our pilgrimage it will be
well to defer everything like a detailed account of them
or their surroundings. Of this first brief visit, enough
therefore a brief record.

The first glimpse that most travellers now get of
the Pyramids is from the window of the railway carriage as they come in from Alexandria; and it is not
impressive. It does not take one's breath away, for instance, like a first sight of the Alps from the high
level of the Neufchâtel line, or the outline of the
Acropolis at Athens as one first recognises it from the

sea. The well-known triangular forms look small and shadowy, and are too familiar to be in any way startling. And the same, I think, is true of every distant view of them,—that is, of every view which is too distant to afford the means of scaling them against other objects. It is only in approaching them and observing how they grow with every foot of the road, that one begins to feel they are not so familiar after all.

But when at last the edge of the desert is reached, and the long sand-slope climbed, and the rocky platform gained, and the Great Pyramid in all its unexpected bulk and majesty towers close above one's head, the effect is as sudden as it is overwhelming. It shuts out the sky and the horizon. It shuts out all the other Pyramids. It shuts out everything but the sense of awe and wonder.

Now, too, one discovers that it was with the forms of the Pyramids, and only their forms, that one had been acquainted all these years past. Of their surface, their colour, their relative position, their number (to say nothing of their size), one had hitherto entertained no kind of definite idea. The most careful study of plans and measurements, the clearest photographs, the most elaborate descriptions, had done little or nothing, after all, to make one know the place beforehand. This undulating table-land of sand and rock pitted with open graves and cumbered with mounds of shapeless masonry, is wholly unlike the desert of our dreams. The Pyramids of Cheops and Chephren are bigger than we had expected; the Pyramid of Mycerinus is smaller. Here, too, are nine Pyramids, instead of three. They are all entered in the plans and mentioned in the guide-books; but somehow, one is unprepared to find them there, and cannot help looking upon them as intruders. These six extra Pyramids are small and greatly dilapidated. One, indeed, is little more than a big cairn.

Even the Great Pyramid puzzles us with an unexpected sense of unlikeness. We all know, and have known from childhood, that it was stripped of its outer blocks some five hundred years ago to build Arab mosques and palaces; but the rugged, rock-like aspect of that giant staircase takes us by surprise, nevertheless. Nor does it look like a partial ruin either. It looks as if it had been left unfinished, and as if the workmen might be coming back to-morrow morning.

The colour, again, is a surprise. Few persons can be aware beforehand of the rich tawny hue that Egyptian limestone assumes after ages of exposure to the blaze of an Egyptian sky. Seen in certain lights, the Pyramids look like piles of massy gold.

Having but one hour and forty minutes to spend on the spot, we resolutely refused on this first occasion to be shown anything, or told anything, or to be taken anywhere,—except, indeed, for a few minutes to the brink of the sand-hollow in which the Sphinx lies couchant. We wished to give our whole attention, and all the short time at our disposal, to the Great Pyramid only. To gain some impression of the outer aspect and size of this enormous structure,—to steady our minds to something like an understanding of its age, —was enough, and more than enough, for so brief a visit.

For it is no easy task to realise, however imperfectly, the duration of six or seven thousand years; and the Great Pyramid, which was some four thousand two hundred and odd years old at the time of the birth of Christ, is now in its seventh millennary. Standing there close against the base of it; touching it; measuring her own height against one of its lowest blocks; looking up all the stages of that vast, receding, rugged wall that leads upward like an Alpine buttress and seems almost to touch the sky, the writer suddenly became aware that these remote dates had never presented themselves to her mind until this moment as anything but abstract numerals. Now for the first time they resolved themselves into something concrete, definite, real. They were no longer figures, but years, with their changes of season, their high and low Niles, their seed-times and harvests. The consciousness of that moment will never, perhaps, quite wear away. It was as if one had been snatched up for an instant to some vast height overlooking the plains of Time, and had seen the centuries mapped out beneath one's feet.

To appreciate the size of the Great Pyramid is less difficult than to apprehend its age. No one who has walked the length of one side, climbed to the top, and learned the dimensions from Murray, can fail to form a tolerably clear idea of its mere bulk. The measurements given by Sir Gardner Wilkinson, are as follows: —length of each side, 732 feet; perpendicular height, 480 feet, 9 inches; area, 535,824 square feet.* That is to say, it stands 115 feet 9 inches higher than the cross on the top of St. Paul's, and about 20 feet lower than Box Hill in Surrey, and if transported bodily to

* Colonel Howard Vyse gives the Great Pyramid 14 feet more in the length of the side, and 10 feet 9 inches more in perpendicular height. It is difficult to understand how two such careful observers can have arrived at such different results.

London, would a little more than cover the whole area of Lincoln's Inn Fields. These are sufficiently matter-of-fact statements, and sufficiently intelligible; but, like most calculations of the kind, they diminish rather than do, justice to the dignity of the subject.

More impressive by far than the weightiest array of figures or · the most striking comparisons was the shadow cast by the Great Pyramid as the sun went down. That mighty Shadow, sharp and distinct, stretched across the stony platform of the desert and over full three-quarters of a mile of the green plain below. It divided the sunlight where it fell, just as its great original divided the sunlight in the upper air; and it darkened the space it covered, like an eclipse. It was not without a thrill of something approaching to awe that one remembered how this self-same Shadow had gone on registering not only the height of the most stupendous gnomon ever set up by human hands, but the slow passage, day by day, of more than sixty centuries of the world's history.

It was still lengthening over the landscape as we went down the long sand-slope and regained the carriage. Some six or eight Arabs in fluttering white garments ran on ahead to bid us a last good-bye. That we should have driven over from Cairo only to sit quietly down and look at the Great Pyramid had filled them with unfeigned astonishment. With such energy and despatch as the modern traveller uses, we might have been to the top, and seen the temple of the Sphinx, and done two or three of the principal tombs in the time.

"You come again!" said they. "Good Arab show you everything. You see nothing this time!"

So, promising to return ere long, we drove away; well content, nevertheless, with the way in which our time had been spent.

The Pyramid Bedouins have been plentifully abused by travellers and guide-books, but we found no reason to complain of them now or afterwards. They neither crowded round us, nor followed us, nor importuned us in any way. They are naturally vivacious and very talkative, yet the gentle fellows were dumb as mutes when they found we wished for silence. And they were satisfied with a very moderate backsheesh at parting.

As a fitting sequel to this excursion, we went, I think next day, to see the mosque of Sultan Hassan, which is one of those mediæval structures built with the casing stones of the Great Pyramid.

CHAPTER II.

Cairo and the Mecca Pilgrimage.

THE mosque of Sultan Hassan, confessedly the most beautiful in Cairo, is also perhaps the most beautiful in the Moslem world. It was built at just that happy moment when Arabian art in Egypt, having ceased merely to appropriate or imitate, had at length evolved an original architectural style out of the heterogeneous elements of Roman and early Christian edifices. The mosques of a few centuries earlier (as, for instance, that of Tooloon, which marks the first departure from the old Byzantine model) consisted of little more than a courtyard with colonnades leading to a hall supported on a forest of pillars. A little more than a century later, and the national style had already experienced the beginnings of that prolonged

3*

eclipse which finally resulted in the bastard Neo-Byzantine Renaissance, represented by the mosque of Mehemet Ali. But the mosque of Sultan Hassan, built just ninety-seven years before the taking of Constantinople, may justly be regarded as the highest point reached by Saracenic art in Egypt after it had used up the Greek and Roman material of Memphis, and before its new-born originality became modified by influences from beyond the Bosphorus. Its pre-eminence is due neither to the greatness of its dimensions nor to the splendour of its materials. It is neither so large as the great mosque at Damascus, nor so rich in costly marbles as Saint Sophia in Constantinople, but in design, proportion, and a certain lofty grace impossible to describe, it surpasses these, and every other mosque, whether original or adapted, with which the writer is acquainted.

The whole structure is purely national. Every line and curve in it and every inch of detail is in the best style of her best period of the Arabian school. And, above all, it was designed expressly for its present purpose. The two famous mosques of Damascus and Constantinople having, on the contrary, been Christian churches, betray evidences of adaptation. In Saint Sophia the space once occupied by the figure of the Redeemer may be distinctly traced in the mosaic-work of the apse, filled in with gold tesseræ of later date; while the magnificent gates of the great mosque at Damascus are decorated, among other Christian emblems, with the sacramental chalice. But the mosque of Sultan Hassan, built by the En Nasir Hassan in the high and palmy days of the Memlook rule, is marred by no discrepancies. For a mosque it was designed,

añd a mosque it remains.   Too soon it will be only a
beautiful ruin.

A number of small streets having lately been demolished in this quarter, the approach to the mosque
lies across a desolate open space littered with débris,
but destined to be laid out as a public square.   With
this desirable end in view some half-dozen workmen
were lazily loading as many camels with rubble, which
is the Arab way of carting rubbish.   If they persevere,
and the Minister of Public Works continues to pay their
wages with due punctuality, the ground will perhaps
get cleared in eight or ten years' time.

Driving up with some difficulty to the foot of the
great steps, which were crowded with idlers smoking
and sleeping, we observed a long and apparently fast-
widening fissure reaching nearly from top to bottom of
the main wall of the building, close against the minaret.
It looked just such a rent as might be caused by a
shock of earthquake, and, being still new to the East,
we wondered the government had not set to work to
mend it.   We had yet to learn that nothing is ever
mended in Cairo.   Here, as in Constantinople, new
buildings spring up apace, but the old, no matter how
venerable, are allowed to moulder away, inch by inch,
till nothing remains but a heap of ruins.

Going up the steps and through a lofty hall, up
some more steps and along a gloomy corridor, we came
to the great court, before entering which, however, we
had to take off our boots and put on slippers brought
for the purpose.   The first sight of this court is an
architectural surprise.   It is like nothing one has ever
seen before, and its beauty equals its novelty. Imagine
an immense marble quadrangle open to the sky and

enclosed within lofty walls, at each side of which is a
vast recess framed in by a single arch. The quadrangle
is more than 100 feet square, and the walls are more
than 100 feet high. Each recess forms a spacious hall
for rest and prayer, and all are matted; but that at the
eastern end is wider and considerably deeper than the
other three, and the noble arch that encloses it like the
proscenium of a splendid stage, measures, according to
Fergusson, 69 feet 5 inches in the span. It looks much
larger. This principal hall, the floor of which is raised
one step at the upper end, measures 90 feet in depth
and 90 in height. The dais is covered with prayer-
rugs, and contains the holy niche and the pulpit of the
preacher. We observed that those who came up here
came only to pray. Having prayed, they either went
away or turned aside into one of the other recesses to
rest. There was a charming fountain in the court, with
a dome roof as light and fragile-looking as a big bubble,
at which each worshipper performed his ablutions on
coming in. This done, he left his slippers on the matting and trod the carpeted dais barefoot.

This was the first time we had seen Muslims at
prayer, and we could not but be impressed by their
profound and unaffected devotion. Some lay prostrate,
their foreheads touching the ground; others were kneeling; others bowing in the prescribed attitudes of prayer.
So absorbed were they, that not even our unhallowed
presence seemed to disturb them. We did not then
know that the pious Moslem is as devout out of the
mosque as in it; or that it is his habit to pray when
the appointed hours come round, no matter where he
may be, or how occupied. We soon became so familiar,
however, with this obvious trait of Mahommedan life,

that it seemed quite a matter of course that the camel-driver should dismount and lay his forehead in the dust by the roadside; or the merchant spread his prayer-carpet on the narrow mastabah of his little shop in the public bazaar; or the boatman prostrate himself with his face to the east, as the sun went down behind the hills of the Libyan desert.

While we were admiring the spring of the roof and the intricate Arabesque decorations of the pulpit, a custode came up with a big key, and invited us to visit the tomb of the founder. So we followed him into an enormous vaulted hall a hundred feet square, in the centre of which stood a plain, railed-off tomb, with an empty iron-bound coffer at the foot. We afterwards learned that for five hundred years—that is to say ever since the death and burial of Sultan Hassan—this coffer had contained a fine copy of the Koran, traditionally said to have been written by Sultan Hassan's own hand; but that the Khedive, who is collecting choice and antique Arabic MSS., had only the other day sent an order for its removal.

Nothing can be bolder or more elegant than the proportions of this noble sepulchral hall, the walls of which are covered with tracery in low relief incrusted with discs and tesseræ of turquoise-coloured porcelain; while high up, in order to lead off the vaulting of the roof, the corners are rounded by means of recessed clusters of exquisite Arabesque wood-work, like pendent stalactites. But the tesseræ are fast falling out, and most of their places are vacant; and the beautiful wood-work hangs in fragments tattered and cobwebbed, like timeworn banners which the first touch of a brush would bring down.

Going back again from the tomb to the courtyard, we observed everywhere traces of the same dilapidation. The fountain, once a miracle of Saracenic ornament, was fast going to destruction. The rich marbles of its basement were cracked and discoloured, its stuccoed cupola was flaking off piecemeal, its enamels were dropping out, its lace-like wood-tracery shredding away by inches.

Presently a tiny brown and golden bird perched with pretty confidence on the brink of the basin, and having splashed and drunk, and preened its feathers, like a true believer at his ablutions, flew up to the top of the cupola and sang deliciously. All else was profoundly still. Large spaces of light and shadow divided the quadrangle. The sky showed overhead as a square opening of burning solid blue; while here and there, reclining, praying, or quietly occupied, a number of turbaned figures were picturesquely scattered over the matted floors of the open halls around. Yonder sat a tailor cross-legged, making a waistcoat; near him, stretched on his face at full length, sprawled a basket-maker with his half-woven basket and bundle of rushes beside him; and here, close against the main entrance, lay a group of tattered mendicants asleep. It was, as I have said, our first mosque, and I well remember the surprise with which we saw that tailor sewing on his buttons, and the sleepers lying about in the shade. We did not then know that a Mahommedan mosque is as much a place of rest and refuge as of prayer, or that the houseless Arab may take shelter there by night or day, as freely as the birds may build their nests in the cornice.

Driving away, we looked up again at that ominous

fissure which is slowly severing the minaret from the mosque, and caught a glimpse of the noble external dome that covers the hall of the tomb of Sultan Hassan. And then we found ourselves speculating on what might happen a hundred years hence or so, when the minaret had fallen, and the dome had caved in, and the beautiful mosque had become a shapeless ruin. Would it then perchance occur to the *savants* of the future to investigate the stones of which it is built? And if so, will it be possible to reconstruct from them any of those lost hierogylphic legends that once covered the entire surface of the Great Pyramid? The builders of the mosque would scarcely have wasted labour on effacing that ancient writing which no man could then understand. They would naturally have been content to imbed that side of each stone in the thickness of the walls; and there, no doubt, pages of precious history, —the history of the dynasties before Cheops and Chephren—lie buried.

From the mosque of this Memlook sovereign it is but a few minutes' uphill drive to the mosque of Mehemet Ali, by whose orders the last of that royal race were massacred just sixty-six years ago. This mosque, built within the precincts of the citadel on a spur of the Mokattam Hills overlooking the city, is the most conspicuous object in Cairo. Its attenuated minarets and clustered domes show from every point of view for miles around, and remain longer in sight, as one leaves or returns to Cairo, than any other landmark. It is a spacious, costly, gaudy, commonplace building, with nothing really beautiful about it, except the great marble courtyard and fountain. The inside, which is entirely built of Oriental alabaster, is carpeted

with magnificent Turkey carpets and hung with innumerable cut-glass chandeliers, so that it looks like a
huge vulgar drawing-room from which the furniture
has been cleared out for dancing.

The view from the outer platform is, however,
magnificent. We saw it on a hazy day, and could not
therefore distinguish the point of the Delta, which
ought to have been visible on the north; but we could
plainly see as far southward as the Pyramids of Sakkarah, and trace the windings of the Nile for many
miles across the plain. The Pyramids of Geezeh, on
their dais of desert rock about twelve miles off, looked,
as they always do look from a distance, small and un-
impressive; but the great alluvial valley dotted over
with mud villages and intersected with canals and
tracts of palm forest; the shining river specked with
sails; and the wonderful city, all flat roofs, cupolas,
and minarets, spread out like an intricate model at
one's feet, were full of interest and absorbed our whole
attention. Looking down upon it from this elevation,
it is as easy to believe that Cairo contains four hundred mosques, as it is to stand on the brow of the
Pincio and believe in the three hundred and sixty-five
churches of modern Rome.

As we came away, they showed us the place in
which the Memlook nobles, four hundred and seventy *
in number, were shot down like mad dogs in a trap,
that fatal first of March, A.D. 1811. We saw the upper
gate which was shut behind them as they came out

---

* One only is said to have escaped—a certain Emeem Bey, who leaped
his horse over a gap in the wall, alighted safely in the piazza below, and gal-
loped away into the desert. The place of this famous leap continued to be
shown for many years, but there are no gaps in the wall now, the citadel being
the only place in Cairo that is kept in thorough repair.

from the presence of the Pasha, and the lower gate which was shut before them to prevent their egress. The walls of the narrow roadway in which the slaughter was done, are said to be pitted with bullet-marks; but we would not look for them.

I have already said that I do not very distinctly remember the order of our sight-seeing in Cairo, for the reason that we saw some places before we went up the river; some after we came back; and some (as for instance the museum at Boulak) both before and after, and indeed as often as possible. But I am at least quite certain that we witnessed a performance of howling dervishes and the departure of the caravan for Mecca, before starting.

Of all the things that people do by way of pleasure, the pursuit of a procession is surely one of the most wearisome. They generally go a long way to see it; they wait a weary time; it is always late; and when at length it does come, it is over in a few minutes. The present pageant fulfilled all these conditions in a superlative degree. We breakfasted uncomfortably early, started soon after half-past seven, and had taken up our position outside the Báb-en-Nasr, on the way to the desert, by half-past eight. Here we sat for nearly three hours, exposed to clouds of dust and a burning sun, with nothing to do but to watch the crowd and wait patiently. All Shepherd's Hotel was there, and every stranger in Cairo; and we all had smart open carriages drawn by miserable screws and driven by bare-legged Arabs. These Arabs, by the way, are excellent whips, and the screws get along wonderfully; but it seems odd at first and not a little humiliating to be whirled along behind a coachman whose only

livery consists of a rag of dirty white turban, a scant
tunic just reaching to his knees, and the top-boots with
which Nature has provided him.

Here, outside the walls, the crowd increased momentarily. The place was like a fair with provision-stalls,
swings, story-tellers, serpent-charmers, cake-sellers, sweet-
meat-sellers, sellers of sherbet, water, lemonade, sugared
nuts, fresh dates, hard-boiled eggs, oranges and sliced
water-melon. Veiled women carrying little bronze
Cupids of children astride upon the left shoulder,
swarthy Egyptians, coal-black Abyssinians, Arabs and
Nubians of every shade from golden-brown to chocolate, Fellahs, dervishes, donkey-boys, street urchins, and
beggars with every imaginable deformity, came and
went; squeezed themselves in and out among the carriages; lined the road on each side of the great towered
gateway; swarmed on the top of every wall; and filled
the air with laughter, a babel of dialects, and those
odours of Araby that are inseparable from an Eastern
crowd. A harmless, unsavoury, good-humoured, in-
offensive throng, one glance at which was enough to
put to flight all one's preconceived notions about
Oriental gravity of demeanour! For the truth is that
gravity is by no means an Oriental characteristic. Take
a Mahommedan at his devotions, and he is a model
of religious abstraction; bargain with him for a carpet,
and he is as impenetrable as a judge; but see him in
his hours of relaxation, or on the occasion of a public
holiday, and he is as garrulous and full of laughter as
a big child. Like a child, too, he loves noise and
movement for the mere sake of noise and movement,
and looks upon swings and fireworks as the height of
human felicity. Now swings and fireworks are Arabic

for bread and circuses, and our pleb's passion for them is insatiable. He not only indulges in them upon every occasion of public rejoicing, but calls in their aid to celebrate the most solemn festivals of his religion. It so happened that we afterwards came in the way of several Mahommedan fêtes both in Egypt and Syria, and we invariably found the swings at work all day and the fireworks going off every evening.

To-day, the swings outside the Báb-en-Nasr were never idle. Here were creaking Russian swings hung with little painted chariots for the children; and plain rope swings, some of them as high as Haman's gallows, for the men. For my own part, I know no sight much more comic and incongruous than the serene enjoyment with which a bearded, turbaned, middle-aged Egyptian squats upon his heels on the tiny wooden seat of one of these enormous swings, and, holding on to the side-ropes for dear life, goes careering up forty feet high into the air at every turn.

At a little before midday, when the heat and glare were becoming intolerable, the swings suddenly ceased going, the crowd surged in the direction of the gate, and a distant drumming announced the approach of the procession. First came a string of baggage-camels laden with tent-furniture; then some two hundred pilgrims on foot, chanting passages from the Koran; then a regiment of Egyptian infantry, the men in a coarse white linen uniform consisting of coat, baggy trousers and gaiters, with cross-belts and cartouche-boxes of plain black leather, and the red fez, or tarboosh, on the head. Next after these came more pilgrims, followed by a body of dervishes carrying green banners embroidered with Arabic sentences in white and yellow; then a native cavalry regiment headed by a general and four colonels in magnificent gold embroidery and preceded by an excellent military band; then another band and a second regiment of infantry; then more colonels, followed by a regiment of lancers mounted on capital grey horses and carrying lances topped with small red and green pennants. After these had gone by there was a long stoppage, and then, with endless breaks and interruptions, came a straggling irregular crowd of pilgrims, chiefly of the Fellah class, beating small darabookahs or native drums. Those about us estimated their number at two thousand. And now, their guttural chorus audible long before they arrived in sight, came the howling dervishes—a ragged, wild-looking, ruffianly set, rolling their heads from side to side, and keeping up a hoarse incessant cry of "Allàh! Allàh! Allàh!" Of these there may have been a couple of hundred. The Sheykhs of the principal orders of Dervishes came next in order, superbly dressed in robes of brilliant colours embroidered with gold, and mounted on magnificent Arabs. Finest of all, in a green turban and scarlet mantle, rode the Sheykh of the Hasaneyn, who is a descendant of the Prophet; but the most important, the Sheykh el Bekree, who is a sort of Egyptian Archbishop of Canterbury and head of all the Dervishes, came last, riding a white Arab with gold-embroidered housings. He was a placid-looking old man, and wore a violet robe and an enormous red and green turban.

This very reverend personage was closely followed by the chief of the carpet-makers' guild—a handsome man sitting sidewise on a camel.

Then happened another break in the procession—

an eager pause—a gathering murmur. And then, riding
a gaunt dromedary at a rapid trot, his fat sides shaking
and his head rolling in a stupid drunken way at every
step, appeared a bloated, half-naked Silenus, with long
fuzzy black locks and a triple chin, and no other
clothing than a pair of short white drawers and red
slippers. A shiver of delight ran through the crowd
at sight of this holy man—the famous Sheykh of the
Camel (Sheykh el-Gemel), the "great, good Priest"—
the idol of the people. We afterwards learned that
this was his twentieth pilgrimage, and that he was
supposed to fast, roll his head, and wear nothing but
this pair of loose drawers, all the way to and from
Mecca.

But the crowning excitement was yet to come, and
the rapture with which the crowd had greeted the
Sheykh el-Gemel was as nothing compared with their
ecstasy when the Mahmal, preceded by another group
of mounted officers and borne by a gigantic camel,
was seen coming through the gateway. The women
held up their children; the men swarmed up the scaf-
foldings of the swings and behind the carriages. They
screamed; they shouted; they waved handkerchiefs
and turbans; they were beside themselves with excitement. Meanwhile the camel, as if conscious of the
dignity of his position and the splendour of his trap-
pings, came on slowly and ponderously with his nose
in the air, and passed close before our horses' heads.
We could not possibly have had a better view of the
Mahmal; which is nothing but a sort of cage, or
pagoda, of gilded tracery very richly decorated. In
the days of the Memlooks, the Mahmal * went empty,

* It is related that the Sultan Ez-Zahir Beybars, King of Egypt, was the

like a royal carriage at a public funeral; but we were told that it now carried the tribute-carpet sent annually by the carpet-makers of Cairo to the tomb of the Prophet.

This closed the procession. As the camel passed the crowd surged in, and everything like order was at an end. The carriages all made at once for the Gate, so meeting the full tide of the outpouring crowd and causing unimaginable confusion. Some stuck in the sand half-way—our own among the number; and all got into an inextricable block in the narrow part just inside the gate. Hereupon the drivers abused each other, and the crowd got impatient, and some Europeans got pelted.

Coming back, we met two or three more regiments. The men, both horse and foot, seemed fair average specimens, and creditably disciplined. They rode better than they marched, which was to be expected. The uniform is the same for cavalry and infantry throughout the service; the only difference being that the former wear short black riding boots, and the latter, Zouave gaiters of white linen. They are officered up to a certain point by Egyptians; but the commanding officers and the staff (among whom are enough colonels and generals to form an ordinary regiment) are chiefly Europeans and Americans.

first who sent a Mahmal with the caravan of Pilgrims to Mekkeh, in the year of the flight 670 (A.D. 1272) or 675; but this custom, it is generally said, had its origin a few years before his accession to the throne. Sheger-ed-Durr, a beautiful Turkish female slave, who became the favorite wife of the Sultan Es-Sáleh Negm-ed-Deen, and on the death of his son (with whom terminated the dynasty of the house of the Eiyoob) caused herself to be acknowledged as Queen of Egypt, performed the pilgrimage in a magnificent "hódag", or covered litter, borne by a camel; and for several successive years her empty "hódag" was sent with the caravan merely for the sake of state. Hence succeeding princes of Egypt sent, with each years' caravan of pilgrims, a kind of "hódag" (which received the name of Mahmal) as an emblem of royalty. *The modern Egyptians* by *E. W. Lane.* Chap. XXIV. London, 1860.

It had seemed, while the procession was passing, that the proportion of pilgrims was absurdly small when compared with the display of military; but this, which is called the departure of the caravan, is in truth only the procession of the sacred carpet from Cairo to the camp outside the walls; and the troops are present merely as part of the pageant. The true departure takes place two days later. The pilgrims then muster in great numbers; but the soldiery is reduced to a small escort. It was said that seven thousand souls went out this year from Cairo and its neighbourhood.

The procession took place on Thursday the 21st day of the Mohammedan month of Showwál, which was our 11th of December. The next day, Friday, being the Mohammedan Sabbath, we went to the Convent of the Howling Dervishes, which lies beyond the walls in a quiet nook between the river-side and the part known as Old Cairo.

We arrived a little after two, and passing through a courtyard shaded by a great sycamore, were ushered into a large, square, whitewashed hall with a dome roof and a neatly matted roof. The place in its arrangements resembled none of the Mosques that we had yet seen. There was, indeed, nothing to arrange—no pulpit, no holy niche, no lamps, no prayer-carpets; nothing but a row of cane-bottomed chairs at one end, some of which were already occupied by certain of our fellow-guests at Shepherd's Hotel. A party of some forty or fifty wild-looking Dervishes were squatting in a circle at the opposite side of the hall, their outer caftans and queer pyramidal hats lying in a heap close by.

Being accommodated with chairs among the other

spectators, we waited for whatever might happen. More Dervishes and more English dropped in from time to time. The new Dervishes took off their caps and sat down among the rest, laughing and talking together at their ease. The English sat in a row, shy, uncomfortable, and silent; wondering whether they ought to behave as if they were in church, and mortally ashamed of their feet. For we had all been obliged to take off or cover our boots before going in, and those who had forgotten to bring slippers had their feet tied up in pocket-handkerchiefs.

A long time went by thus. At last, when the number of Dervishes had increased to about seventy, and every one was tired of waiting, eight musicians came in—two trumpets, two lutes, a cocoa-nut fiddle, a tambourine, and two drums. Then the Dervishes, some of whom were old and white-haired, and some mere boys, formed themselves into a great circle shoulder to shoulder. The band struck up a plaintive discordant air. And a grave middle-aged man, placing himself in the centre of the ring and inclining his head at each repetition, began to recite the name of Allah.

Softly at first, and one by one, the Dervishes took up the chant:—"Allàh! Allàh! Allàh!" Their heads and their voices rose and fell in unison. The dome above gave back a hollow echo. There was something strange and solemn in the ceremony.

Presently, however, the trumpets brayed louder— the voices grew hoarser—the heads bowed lower—the name of Allah rang out faster and faster, fiercer and fiercer. The leader, himself cool and collected, began sensibly accelerating the time of the chorus; and it became evident that the performers were possessed by a growing frenzy. Soon the whole circle was madly rocking to and fro; the voices rose to a hoarse scream; and only the trumpets were audible above the din. Now and then a Dervish would spring up convulsively some three or four feet above the heads of the others; but for the most part they stood rooted firmly to one spot—now bowing their heads almost to their feet— now flinging themselves so violently back, that we, standing behind, could see their faces foreshortened upside down; and this with such incredible rapidity, that their long hair had scarcely time either to rise or fall, but remained as if suspended in mid-air. Still the frenzy mounted; still the pace quickened. Some shrieked—some groaned—some, unable to support themselves any longer, were held up in their places by the bystanders. All were mad for the time being. Our own heads seemed to be going round at last; and more than one of the ladies present looked longingly towards the door. It was, in truth, a horrible sight, and needed only darkness and torchlight to be quite diabolical.

At length, just as the fury was at its height and the very building seemed to be rocking to and fro above our heads, one poor wretch staggered out of the circle and fell writhing and shrieking close against our feet. At the same moment, the leader clapped his hands; the performers, panting and exhausted, dropped into a sitting posture; and the first zikr, as it is called, came abruptly to an end. Some few, however, could not stop immediately, but kept on swaying and muttering to themselves; while the one in the fit, having ceased to shriek, lay out stiff and straight, apparently in a state of coma.

There was a murmur of relief and a simultaneous rising among the spectators. It was announced that another zikr, with a reinforcement of fresh Dervishes, would soon begin; but the Europeans had had enough of it, and few remained for the second performance.

Going out, we paused beside the poor fellow on the floor, and asked if nothing could be done for him.

"He is struck by Mahommed," said gravely an Egyptian official who was standing by.

At that moment, the leader came over; knelt down beside him; touched him lightly on the head and breast; and whispered something in his ear. The man was then quite rigid, and white as death. We waited, however, and after a few more minutes saw him struggle back into a dazed, half-conscious state, when he was helped to his feet and led away by his friends.

The courtyard as we came out was full of Dervishes sitting on cane benches in the shade, and sipping coffee. The green leaves rustled overhead, with glimpses of intensely blue sky between; and brilliant patches of sunshine flickered down upon groups of wild-looking, half-savage figures in parti-coloured garments. It was one of those ready-made subjects that the sketcher passes by with a sigh, but which live in his memory for ever.

From hence, being within a few minutes' drive of Old Cairo, we went on as far as the Mosque of Amr —an uninteresting ruin standing alone among the rubbish-mounds of the first Mohammedan capital of Egypt. It is constructed on the plan of a single quadrangle 255 feet square, surrounded by a covered colonnade one range of pillars in depth on the west (which is the side of the entrance); four on the north; three on the south; and six on the east, which is the place of prayer, and contains three holy niches and the pulpit. The columns, 245 in number, have been brought from earlier Roman and Byzantine buildings. They are of various marbles and have all kinds of capitals. Some being originally too short, have been stilted on disproportionately high bases; and in one instance the necessary height has been obtained by adding a second capital on the top of the first. We observed one column of that rare black and white speckled marble of which there is a specimen in the pulpit of St. Mark's in Venice; and one of the holy niches contains some fragments of Byzantine mosaics. But the whole building seems to have been put together in a barbarous way, and would appear to owe its present state of dilapidation more to bad workmanship than to time. Many of the pillars, especially on the western side, are fallen and broken; the octagonal fountain in the centre is a roofless ruin; and the little minaret at the S. E. corner is no longer safe.

Apart, however, from its poverty of design and detail, the Mosque of Amr is interesting as a point of departure in the history of Saracenic architecture. It was built by Amr Ebn el-As, the Arab conqueror of Egypt, in the twenty-first year of the Hegira (A.D. 642), just ten years after the death of Mahomet; and it is the earliest Saracenic edifice in Egypt. We were glad, therefore, to have seen it for this reason, if for no other. But it is a barren, dreary place; and the glare reflected from all sides of the quadrangle was so in-

tense that we were thankful to get away again into
the narrow streets beside the river.

Here we presently fell in with a wedding procession consisting of a crowd of men, a band, and some
three or four hired carriages full of veiled women, one
of whom was pointed out as the bride. The bridegroom walked in the midst of the men, who seemed
to be teasing him, drumming round him, and opposing
his progress; while, high above the laughter, the shouting, the jingle of tambourines and the thrumming of
darabookahs, was heard the shrill squeal of some in-
strument that sounded exactly like a bagpipe.

It was a brilliant afternoon, and we ended our
day's work, I remember, with a drive on the Shoobra
road and a glance at the gardens of the Khedive's
summer palace. The Shoobra road is the Champs
Elysées of Cairo, and is thronged every day from four ·
to half-past six. Here little sheds of road-side cafés
alternate with smart modern villas; ragged Fellahs on
jaded donkeys trot side by side with elegant attachés
on high-stepping Arabians; while tourists in hired carriages, Jew bankers in unexceptionable phaetons, veiled
hareems in London-built broughams, Italian shop-
keepers in preposterously fashionable toilettes, grave
Sheykhs on magnificent Cairo asses, officers in frogged
and braided frocks, and English girls in tall hats and
close-fitting habits followed by the inevitable little
solemn-looking English groom, pass and repass, pre-
cede and follow each other, in one changing, restless,
heterogeneous stream, the like of which is to be seen
in no other capital in the world. The sons of the
Khedive drive here daily, always in separate carriages
and preceded by four Saïses, and four guards. They

are of all ages and sizes, from the Prince Héritier, a pale, gentlemanly-looking young man of four or five and twenty, down to one tiny, imperious atom of about six, who is dressed like a little man, and is constantly leaning out of his carriage-window and shrilly abusing his coachman.

Apart, however, from those who frequent it, the Shoobra road is a really fine drive; broad; level; raised some six or eight feet above the cultivated plain; closely planted on both sides with acacias and sycamore fig-trees; and reaching straight away for four miles out of Cairo, counting from the Railway terminus to the Summer palace. The carriage-way is about as wide as the road across Hyde Park that connects Bayswater with Kensington; and towards the Shoobra end, it runs close beside the Nile. Many of the sycamores are of great size and quite patriarchal girth. Their branches meet overhead nearly all the way, weaving a delicious shade and making a cool green tunnel of the long perspective.

We did not stay long in the Khedive's gardens, for it was already getting late when we reached the gates; but we went far enough to see that they were tolerably well kept, not over formal, and laid out with a view to masses of foliage, shady paths, and spaces of turf inlaid with flower-beds, after the style of the famous Sarntheim and Moser gardens at Botzen in the Tyrol. Here are Sont trees (*Acacia Nilotica*) of unusual size, powdered all over with little feathery tufts of yellow blossom; orange and lemon trees in abundance; heaps of little green limes; bananas bearing heavy pendent bunches of ripe fruit; winding thickets of pomegranates, oleanders, and salvias; and great beds, and banks, and

trellised walks of roses.   Among these, however, I observed none of the rarer varieties.   As for the Pointset-
tia, it grows in Egypt to a height of twenty feet, and
bears blossoms of such size and colour as we in England can form no idea of.   We saw large trees of it
both here and at Alexandria that seemed as if bending beneath a mantle of crimson stars, some of which
cannot have measured less than twenty-two inches in
diameter.

A large Italian fountain in a rococo style is the
great sight of the place.   We caught a glimpse of it
through the trees, and surprised the gardener who was
showing us over by declining to inspect it more nearly.
He could not understand why we preferred to give
our time to the shrubs and flower-beds.

Driving back presently towards Cairo with a big
handful of roses apiece, we saw the sun going down in
an aureole of fleecy pink and golden clouds, the Nile
flowing by like a stream of liquid light, and a little
fleet of sailing boats going up to Boulak before a puff
of north wind that had sprung up as the sun neared
the horizon.   That puff of north wind, those gliding
sails, had a keen interest for us now, and touched us
nearly; because—I have delayed this momentous revela-
tion till the last moment—because we were to start to-
morrow!

And this is why I have been able, in the midst of
so much that was new and bewildering, to remember
quite circumstantially the dates, and all the events
connected with these last two days.   They were to be
our last two days in Cairo; and to-morrow morning,
Saturday, the 13th of December, we were to go on
board a certain dahabeeyah now lying off the iron

bridge at Boulák, therein to begin that strange aquatic life to which we had been looking forward with so many hopes and fears, and towards which we had been steering through so many preliminary difficulties.

But the difficulties were all over now, and everything was settled; though not in the way we had at first intended. For, in place of a small boat, we had secured one of the largest on the river; and instead of going alone, we had decided to throw in our lot with that of three other travellers. One of these three was already known to the Writer. The other two, friends of the first, were on their way out from Europe, and not expected in Cairo for another week. We knew nothing of them but their names.

Meanwhile L. and the Writer, assuming sole possession of the dahabeeyah, were about to start ten days in advance; it being their intention to push on as far as Rhoda (the ultimate point then reached by the Nile railway), and there to await the arrival of the rest of the party. Now Rhoda (more correctly Roda) is just one hundred and eighty miles S. of Cairo; and we calculated upon seeing the Sakkarah pyramids, the Toora quarries, the tombs of Beni Hassan, and the famous grotto of the Colossus on the Sledge, before our fellow-travellers should be due.

"It depends on the wind, you know," said our Dragoman, with a lugubrious smile.

We knew that it depended on the wind; but what then? In Eygpt, the wind is supposed always to blow from the north at this time of the year, and we had ten good days at our disposal. The observation was clearly irrelevant.

CHAPTER III.

Cairo to Bedreshayn.

A RAPID raid into some of the nearest shops, for things remembered at the last moment—a breathless gathering up of innumerable parcels—a few hurried farewells on the steps of the hotel—and away we rattle as fast as a pair of rawboned greys can carry us. For this morning, every moment is of value. We are already late; we expect visitors to luncheon on board at midday; and we are to weigh anchor at two P.M. Hence our anxiety to reach Boulak before the bridge is opened, so that we may drive across to the western bank against which our dahabeeyah lies moored. Hence also our mortification when we arrive just in time to see the bridge swing apart and the first tall mast glide through.

Presently, however, when those on the lookout have observed our signals of distress, a smart-looking *sandal*, or jolly-boat, decked with gay rugs and cushions, manned by five smiling Arabs, and flying a bright little new Union Jack, comes swiftly threading her way in and out among the lumbering barges now crowding through the bridge. In a few more minutes, we are afloat. For this is our sandal, and these are five of our crew; and of the three dahabeeyahs moored over yonder in the shade of the palms, the biggest by far, and the trimmest, is our own dear, memorable "Philæ."

Close behind the "Philæ" lies the "Bagstones," a neat little dahabeeyah in the occupation of two English ladies who chanced to cross with us in the Simla from

Brindisi, and of whom we have seen so much ever since that we regard them by this time as quite old friends in a strange land. The other, lying off a few yards ahead, carries the tricolor, and is chartered by a party of French gentlemen. All three are to sail to-day.

And now we are on board, and have shaken hands with the captain, and are as busy as bees; for there are cabins to put in order, flowers to arrange, and a hundred little things to be seen to before the guests arrive. It is wonderful, however, what a few books and roses, an open piano, and a sketch or two, will do. In a few minutes the comfortless hired look has vanished, and long enough before the first comers are announced, the Philæ wears an aspect as cosy and home-like as if she had been occupied for a month.

As for the luncheon, it certainly surprised the givers of the entertainment quite as much as it must have surprised their guests. Being, no doubt, a pre-arranged display of professional pride on the part of dragoman and cook, it was more like an excessive Christmas dinner than a modest mid-day meal. We sat through it unflinchingly, however, for about an hour and three quarters, when a startling discharge of fire-arms sent us all running upon deck, and created a wholesome diversion in our favour. It was the French boat signalling her departure, shaking out her big sail, and going off triumphantly.

I fear that we of the Bagstones and Philæ—being mere mortals and Englishwomen—could not help feeling just a little spiteful when we found the tricolor had started first; but then it was a consolation to know that the Frenchmen were going only to Assouan. Such is the *esprit du Nil.* The people in dahabeeyahs despise Cook's tourists; those who are bound for the Second Cataract look down with lofty compassion upon those whose ambition extends only to the first; and travellers who engage their boat by the month hold their heads a trifle higher than those who contract for the trip. We, who were going as far as we liked and for as long as we liked, could afford to be magnanimous. So we forgave the Frenchmen, went down again to the saloon, and had coffee and music.

It was nearly three o'clock when our Cairo visitors wished us "bon voyage" and good-bye. Then the ladies of the Bagstones, who, with their nephew, had been of the party, went back to their own boat; and both captains prepared to sail at a given signal. For the Bagstones had entered into a solemn convention to start with us, moor with us, and keep with us, if practicable, all the way up the river. It is pleasant now to remember how this sociable compact, instead of falling through as such compacts are wont to do, was quite literally carried out as far as Aboo Simbel; that is to say, during a period of seven weeks' hard going, and for a distance of upwards of eight hundred miles.

And now at last all is ready. The awning that has all day roofed in the upper deck is taken down; the captain stands at the head of the steps; the steersman is at the helm; the dragoman has loaded his musket. Are the Bagstones ready? We wave a handkerchief of inquiry—the signal is answered—the mooring ropes are loosened—the sailors pole · the boat off from the bank —bang go the guns, six from the Philæ, and six from the Bagstones, and away we go, our huge sail filling as it takes the wind!

Happy are the Nile travellers who start thus with a fair breeze on a brilliant afternoon. The good boat cleaves her way swiftly and steadily. Water-side palaces and gardens glide by, and are left behind. The domes and minarets of Cairo drop quickly out of sight. The mosque of the citadel, and the ruined fort that looks down upon it from the mountain ridge above, diminish in the distance. The Pyramids stand up sharp and clear.

We sit on the high upper deck, which is furnished with lounge-chairs, tables, and foreign rugs, like a drawing-room in the open air; and there enjoy the prospect at our ease. The valley is wide here, and the banks are flat, showing a steep verge of crumbling alluvial mud next the river. Long belts of palm groves; tracts of young corn only an inch or two above the surface; and clusters of mud huts relieved now and then by a little whitewashed cupola or a stumpy minaret, succeed each other on both sides of the river; while the horizon is bounded to right and left by long ranges of yellow limestone mountains, in the folds of which sleep inexpressibly tender shadows of pale violet and blue.

Thus the miles glide away, and by and by we approach Toora—a large, new-looking mud village, and the first of any extent that we have yet seen. Some of the houses are whitewashed; a few have glass windows, and many seem to have been left unfinished. A space of white, stony, glaring plain, separates the village from the quarried mountains beyond, the flanks of which show all gashed and hewn away. One great cliff seems to have been cut sheer off for a distance of perhaps half-a-mile. Where the cuttings are fresh, the limestone comes out dazzling white, and long slopes of débris heaped against the foot of the cliffs glisten like snow-drifts in the sun. Yet the outer surface of the mountains is orange-tawny, like the Pyramids. As for the piles of rough-hewn blocks that lie ranged along the bank ready for transport, they look more as if they were cut out of salt than stone. Here lies moored a whole fleet of cargo boats, laden and lading; and along the tramway that extends from the river-side to the quarries, we see long trains of mule-carts coming and going.

For all the new buildings in Cairo, the Khedive's palaces, the public offices, the smart modern villas, the glaring new streets, the theatres, and foot-pavements, and cafés, all come from here—just as the Pyramids did, more than six thousand years ago. There are hieroglyphed tablets and sculptured grottoes to be seen in the most ancient part of the quarries, if one were inclined to stop for them at this early stage of the journey; and Champollion tells of two magnificent outlines done in red ink upon the living rock by some master-hand of Pharaonic times, the cutting of which was never even begun. A substantial new barrack and an esplanade planted with sycamore figs bring the straggling village to an end.

And now, as the afternoon wanes, we draw near to a dense, wide-spreading forest of stately date-palms on the western bank, knowing that beyond them, though unseen, lie the mounds of Memphis and all the wonders of Sakkarah. Then the sun goes down behind the Libyan hills; and the palms stand out black and bronzed against a golden sky; and the Pyramids, left far behind, look grey and ghostly in the distance.

Presently, when it is quite dusk and the stars are out, we moor for the night at Bedreshayn, which is the nearest point for visiting Sakkarah. There is a railway station here, and a considerable village, both lying back about half-a-mile from the river; and the distance from Cairo, which is reckoned at fifteen miles by the line, is probably about eighteen by water.

Such was our first day on the Nile. And perhaps, before going farther on our way, I ought to describe the Philæ, and introduce Reïs Hassan and his crew.

A Dahabeeyah, at the first glance, is more like a civic, or an Oxford University barge, than anything in the shape of a boat with which we in England are familiar. It is shallow and flat-bottomed, and is adapted for either sailing or rowing. It carries two masts; a big one near the prow, and a smaller one at the stern. The cabins are on deck, and occupy the after-part of the vessel; and the roof of the cabins forms the raised deck, or open-air drawing-room, already mentioned. This upper deck is reached from the lower deck by two little flights of steps, and is the exclusive territory of the passengers. The lower deck is the territory of the crew. A Dahabeeyah is, in fact, not very unlike the Noah's Ark of our childhood, with this difference—the habitable part, instead of occupying the middle of the vessel, is all at one end, top-heavy and many-windowed; while the fore-deck is not more than six feet above the level of the water. The hold, however, is under the lower deck, so serving to counterbalance the weight at the other end. Not to multiply comparisons unnecessarily, I may say that a large Dahabeeyah reminds one of old

pictures of the Bucentaur; especially when the men are
at their oars.

The kitchen—which is a mere shed like a Dutch
oven in shape, and contains only a charcoal stove and
a row of stewpans—stands between the big mast and
the prow, removed as far as possible from the passengers'
cabins. In this position the cook is protected from a
favourable wind by his shed; but in the case of a contrary wind he is screened by an awning. How, under
even the most favourable circumstances, these men can
serve up the elaborate dinners that are the pride of a
Nile cook's heart, is sufficiently wonderful; but how
they achieve the same results when wind-storms and
sand-storms are blowing, and every breath is laden
with the fine grit of the desert, is little short of miraculous.

Thus far all Dahabeeyahs are alike. The cabin
arrangements differ, however, according to the size of
the boat; and it must be remembered that in describing the Philæ, I describe a Dahabeeyah of the largest
build—her total length from stem to stern being just
one hundred feet, and the width of her upper deck at
the broadest part little short of twenty.

Our floor being on a somewhat lower level than the
men's deck, we went down three steps to the entrance
door, on each side of which was an external cupboard,
one serving as a store-room and the other as a pantry.
This door led into a passage, out of which opened four
sleeping-cabins; two on each side. These cabins
measured about eight feet in length by four and a half
in width, and contained a bed, a chair, a fixed washing-
stand, a looking-glass against the wall, a shelf, a row
of hooks, and under each bed two large drawers for

clothes. At the end of this little passage another door opened into the dining saloon—a spacious, cheerful room some twenty feet long, situated in the widest part of the boat, and lighted by four windows on each side, and a skylight. The panelled walls and ceiling were painted in white picked out with gold; a cushioned divan covered with a smart woollen reps ran along each side; and a gay Brussels carpet adorned the floor. The dining-table stood in the centre of the room; and there was ample space beside for a piano, two little book-cases, and several chairs. The window-curtains and portières were of the same reps as the divan, the pre-vailing colours being scarlet and orange. Add a couple of mirrors in gilt frames; a vase of flowers on the table (for we were rarely without flowers of some sort, even in Nubia, where our daily bouquet had to be made with a few bean blossoms and castor-oil berries); plenty of books; the gentlemen's guns and sticks in one corner; and the hats of all the party hanging in the spaces between the windows; and it will be easy to realise the homely, habitable look of our general sitting-room.

Another door and passage opening from the upper end of the saloon led to three more sleeping-rooms, two of which were single and one double; a bath-room; a tiny back staircase leading to the upper deck; and the stern cabin saloon. This last, following the form of the stern, was semicircular, lighted by eight windows, and surrounded by a divan. Under this, as under the saloon divans and all the beds, there ran a row of deep drawers, which, being fairly divided, held our clothes, wine and books. The entire length of the Dahabeeyah being exactly one hundred feet, I take the cabin part

to have occupied about fifty-six or fifty-seven feet (that
is to say, about six or seven feet over the exact half),
and the lower deck to have measured the remaining
forty-three feet.   But these dimensions, being given
from memory, are approximate.

For the crew there was no sleeping accommodation
whatever, unless they chose to creep into the hold
among the luggage and packing cases.   But this they
never did.   They just rolled themselves up at night,
heads and all, in rough brown blankets, and lay about
the lower deck like dogs.

The Reïs, or captain, the steersman and twelve
sailors, the dragoman, head cook, assistant cook, two
waiters, and the boy who cooked for the crew, completed our equipment.   Reïs Hassan—short, stern-look-
ing, authoritative—was a Cairo Arab.   The Dragoman,
Elias Talhamy, was a Syrian of Beyrout.   The two
waiters, Michael and Habeeb, and the head cook, a
wizened old *cordon bleu* named Hassan Bedawee, were
also Syrians.   The steersman and five of the sailors
were from Thebes; four belonged to a place near Philæ;
one came from a village opposite Kom Ombos; one
from Cairo, and two were Nubians from Assouan.   They
were of all shades, from yellowish bronze to a hue not
far removed from black; and though, at the first mention of it, nothing more incongruous can well be
imagined than a sailor in petticoats and a turban, yet
these men in their loose blue gowns, bare feet, and
white muslin turbans, looked not only picturesque, but
dressed exactly as they should be.   They were, for the
most part, fine young men, slender but powerful, square
in the shoulders, like the ancient Egyptian statues, with

the same slight legs and long flat feet. More docile, active, good-tempered, friendly fellows never pulled an oar. Simple and trustful as children, frugal as anchorites, they worked cheerfully from sunrise to sunset, sometimes towing the Dahabeeyah on a rope all day long, like barge-horses; sometimes punting for hours, which is the hardest work of all; yet always singing at their task, always smiling when spoken to, and made as happy as princes with a handful of coarse Egyptian tobacco, or a bundle of fresh sugar-canes bought for a few pence by the river-side. We soon came to know them all by name—Mehemet Ali, Salame, Khaleefeh, Riskalli, Hassan, Moosa, and so on; and as none of us ever went on shore without one or two of them to act as guards and attendants, and as the poor fellows were constantly getting bruised hands or feet, and coming to the upper deck to be doctored, a feeling of genuine friendliness was speedily established between us.

The ordinary pay of a Nile sailor is two pounds a month, with an additional allowance of about three and sixpence a month for flour. Bread is their staple food, and they make it themselves at certain places along the river where there are large public ovens for the purpose. This bread, which is cut up in slices and dried in the sun, is as brown as gingerbread and as hard as biscuit. They eat it soaked in hot water, flavoured with oil, pepper, and salt, and stirred in with boiled lentils till the whole becomes of the colour, flavour, and consistence of thick pea-soup. Except on grand occasions, such as Christmas Day, or the anniversary of the Flight of the Prophet, when the passengers treat them to a sheep, this mess of bread and lentils, with a little coffee twice a day, and now and

5*

then a handful of dates, constitutes their only food throughout the journey.

The Nile season is the harvest-time of the sailors. When the warm weather sets in and the travellers migrate with the swallows, these poor fellows disperse in all directions; some to seek a living as porters in Cairo; others to their homes in Middle and Upper Egypt where, for about fourpence a day they take hire as labourers, or work at Shadoof* irrigation till the Nile again overspreads the land. The Shadoof work is hard, and a man has to keep on at it for nine hours out of every twenty-four; but he prefers it, for the most part, to employment in the government sugar-factories, where the wages average after the same rate but are paid in bread, which, being doled out by unscrupulous inferiors, is too often of light weight and bad quality. The sailors who succeed in getting a berth on board a cargo-boat for the summer are the most fortunate.

Our captain, pilot and crew, were all Mahommedans. The cook and his assistant were Syrian Mahommedans. The dragoman and waiters were Christians of the Syrian Latin church. Only one out of the fifteen natives could write or read; and that one was a sailor named Egendi, who acted as a sort of second mate. He used sometimes to write letters for the others, holding a scrap of tumbled paper across the palm of his left hand, and scrawling upon it in rude Arabic characters with a reed-pen of his own making. This Egendi, though perhaps the least interesting of the crew, was a man of many accomplishments—an excellent comic actor, a bit of a shoemaker,

* *Shadoof*: See page 106.

and a first-rate barber. More than once, when we happened to be stationed far from any village, he shaved his messmates all round, and turned them out with heads as smooth as billiard balls.

There are, of course, good and bad Mahommedans, as there are good and bad churchmen of every denomination; and we had both sorts on board. Some of the men were very devout, never failing to perform their ablutions and say their prayers at sunrise and sunset. Others never dreamed of doing so. Some would not touch wine—had never tasted it in their lives, and would have suffered any extremity rather than break the law of their Prophet. Others had a nice taste in clarets, and a delicate appreciation of the respective merits of rum or whiskey punch. It is, however, only fair to add that we never gave them these things except on special occasions; as on Christmas Day, or when they had been wading in the river, or in some other way undergoing extra fatigue in our service. Nor do I believe there was a man on board who would have spent a para of his scanty earnings on any drink stronger than coffee. Coffee and tobacco are, indeed, the only luxuries in which the Egyptian peasant indulges; and our poor fellows were never more grateful than when we distributed among them a few pounds of cheap native tobacco. This abominable mixture, which sells in the Bazaars at sixpence the pound, is raised from inferior seed in a soil wholly devoid of potash, and therefore chemically unsuited to the plant. Also it is systematically spoiled in the growing. Instead of being nipped off when green and dried in the shade, the leaves are allowed to wither on the stalk before they are gathered. The result is a kind of rank hay without strength or flavour, which is smoked by only the very poorest class, and carefully avoided by all who can afford to buy Turkish or Syrian tobacco.

Twice a day, after their mid-day and evening meals, our sailors were wont to sit in a circle and solemnly smoke a certain big pipe of the kind known as a hubble-bubble. The hubble-bubble (which was of most primitive make and consisted of a cocoa-nut and two reeds) was common property; and, being filled by the captain, went round from hand to hand, from mouth to mouth, while it lasted.

They smoked cigarettes at other times, and seldom went on shore without a tobacco-pouch and a tiny book of cigarette-papers. Fancy a bare-legged Arab making cigarettes! No Frenchman, however, could twist them up more deftly, or smoke them with a better grace.

A Nile sailor's service expires with the season, so that he is generally a landsman for about half the year; but the captain's appointment is permanent. He is expected to live in Cairo, and is responsible for his Dahabeeyah during the summer months, while it lies up at Boulak. Reïs Hassan had a wife and a comfortable little home on the outskirts of Old Cairo, and was looked upon as a well-to-do personage among his fellows. He received four pounds a month all the year round from the owner of the Philæ—a magnificent, broad-shouldered Arab of about six foot nine, with a delightful smile, the manners of a gentleman, and the rapacity of a Shylock.

Our men treated us to a concert that first night, as we lay moored under the bank near Bedreshayn.

Being told that it was customary to provide musical instruments,. we had given them leave to buy a Tar and Darabookah before starting. The tar, or tambourine, was pretty enough, being made of rosewood inlaid with mother-of-pearl; but a more barbarous affair than the darabookah was surely never constructed. This primitive drum is about a foot and a half in length, funnel-shaped, moulded of sun-dried clay, and covered over at the top with strained parchment. It is held under the left arm and played like a tom-tom with the fingers of the right hand; and it weighs about four pounds. We would willingly have added a double pipe or a cocoa-nut fiddle* to the strength of the band, but none of our men could play them. The tar and darabookah, however, answered the purpose well enough, and were perhaps better suited to their strange singing than more tuneful instruments.

We had just finished dinner when they began. First came a prolonged wail that swelled, and sank, and swelled again, and at last died away. This was the principal singer leading off with the keynote. The next followed suit on the third of the key; and finally all united in one long, shrill descending cry, like a yawn, or a howl, or a combination of both. This, twice repeated, preluded their performance and worked them up, apparently, to the necessary pitch of musical enthusiasm. The primo tenore then led off in a quavering roulade, at the end of which he slid into a melancholy chant to which the rest sang chorus. At the close of each verse they yawned and howled again; while the singer, carried away by his emotions, broke

* *Arabic—Kemengeh.*

out every now and then into a repetition of the same
amazing and utterly indescribable vocal wriggle with
which he had begun. Whenever he did this, the rest
held their breath in respectful admiration, and uttered
an approving "Ah!"—which is here the customary expression of applause.

We thought their music horrible that first night, I
remember; though we ended, as I believe most travellers do, by liking it. We, however, paid them the
compliment of going upon deck and listening to their
performance. As a night-scene, nothing could be more
picturesque than this group of turbaned Arabs sitting
in a circle, crosslegged, with a lantern in the midst of
them. The singer quavered; the musicians thrummed;
the rest softly clapped their hands to time, and waited
their turn to chime in with the chorus. Meanwhile the
lantern lit up their swarthy faces and their glittering
teeth. The great mast towered up into the darkness. The river gleamed below. The stars shone
overhead. We felt we were indeed strangers in a
strange land.

CHAPTER IV.

Sakkarah and Memphis.

HAVING arrived at Bedreshayn after dark and there
moored for the night, we were roused early next morning by the furious squabbling and chattering of some
fifty or sixty men and boys who, with a score or two
of little rough-coated, depressed-looking donkeys, were
assembled on the high bank above. Seen thus against
the sky, their tattered garments fluttering in the wind,
their brown arms and legs in frantic movement, they

looked like a troop of mad monkeys let loose. Every moment the uproar grew shriller. Every moment more men, more boys, more donkeys, appeared upon the scene. It was as if some new Cadmus had been sowing boys and donkeys broadcast, and they had all come up at once for our benefit.

Then it appeared that Talhamy, knowing how eight donkeys would be wanted for our united forces, had sent up to the village for twenty-five, intending, with perhaps more wisdom than justice, to select the best and dismiss the others. The result was overwhelming. Misled by the magnitude of the order and concluding that Cook's party had arrived, every man, boy, and donkey in Bedreshayn and the neighbouring village of Mitrahenny had turned out in hot haste and rushed down to the river; so that by the time breakfast was over, there were steeds enough in readiness for all the English in Cairo. I pass over the tumult that ensued when our party at last mounted the eight likeliest beasts and rode away, leaving the indignant multitude to disperse at leisure.

And now our way lies over a dusty flat, across the railway line, past the long straggling village, and through the famous plantations known as the Palms of Memphis. There is a crowd of patient-looking Fellaheen at the little whitewashed station, waiting for the train; and the usual rabble of clamorous water, bread, and fruit sellers. Bedreshayn, though a collection of mere mud hovels, looks pretty, nestling in the midst of stately date-palms. Square pigeon-towers, embedded round the top with layers of wide-mouthed pots, and stuck with rows of leafless acacia-boughs like ragged banner-poles, stand up at intervals among the huts. The

pigeons go in and out of the pots, or sit preening
their feathers on the branches. The dogs dash out
and bark madly at us, as we go by. The little brown
children pursue us with cries of "Backsheesh!" The
potter, laying out rows of soft, grey, freshly-moulded
clay bowls and goollahs* to bake in the sun, stops
open-mouthed, and stares as if he had never seen a
European till this moment. His young wife snatches
up her baby and pulls her veil more closely over her
face, fearing the evil eye.

The village being left behind, we ride on through
one long palm grove after another; now skirting the
borders of a large sheet of tranquil back-water; now
catching a glimpse of the far-off pyramids of Geezeh;
now passing between the huge irregular mounds of
crumbled clay that mark the site of Memphis. Next
beyond these we come out upon a high embanked
road some twenty feet above the plain, which here
spreads out like a wide lake and spends its last dark-
brown alluvial wave against the yellow rocks that define
the edge of the desert. High on this barren plateau,
seen for the first time in one unbroken panoramic line,
there stands a solemn company of pyramids; those of
Sakkarah straight before us, those of Dashoor to the
left, those of Abooseer to the right, and the great
Pyramids of Geezeh always in the remotest distance.

It might be thought there would be some monotony
in such a scene, and but little beauty. On the contrary, however, there is beauty of a most subtle and
exquisite kind—transcendent beauty of colour, and at-

---

* The goollah, or kulleh, is a porous water-jar of sun-dried Nile mud.
These jars are made of all sizes and in a variety of remarkably graceful forms,
and cost from about one farthing to twopence apiece.

mosphere, and sentiment; and no monotony either in
the landscape or in the forms of the pyramids. One
of these which we are now approaching is built in a
succession of platforms gradually decreasing towards
the top. Another down yonder at Dashoor curves outward at the angles, half dome, half pyramid, like the
roof of the Palais de Justice in Paris. No two are
of precisely the same size, or built at precisely the
same angle; and each cluster differs somehow in the
grouping.

Then again the colouring!—colouring not to be
matched with any pigments yet invented. The Libyan
rocks, like rusty gold—the paler hue of the driven
sand-slopes—the warm maize of the nearer Pyramids
which, seen from this distance, takes a tender tint of
rose, like the red bloom on an apricot—the delicate
tone of these objects against the sky — the infinite
gradation of that sky, soft and pearly towards the
horizon, blue and burning towards the zenith—the
opalescent shadows, pale blue, and violet, and greenish-
grey, that nestle in the hollows of the rock and the
curves of the sand-drifts—all this is beautiful in a way
impossible to describe, and alas! impossible to copy.
Nor does the lake-like plain with its palm-groves and
corn-flats form too tame a foreground. It is exactly
what is wanted to relieve that glowing distance.

And now, as we follow the zigzags of the road, the
new pyramids grow gradually larger; the sun mounts
higher; the heat increases. We meet a train of camels,
buffaloes, shaggy brown sheep, men, women, and children of all ages. The camels are laden with bedding,
rugs, mats, and crates of poultry, and carry, besides, two women with babies and one very old man.

The younger men drive the tired beasts. The rest
follow. The dust rises after them in a cloud. It is
evidently the migration of a family of three, if not four,
generations. One cannot help being struck by the
patriarchal simplicity of the incident. Just thus, with
flocks and herds, and all his clan, went Abraham into
the land of Canaan close upon four thousand years
agó; and one at least of these Sakkarah pyramids was
even then the oldest building in the world.

It is a touching and picturesque procession—much
more picturesque than ours, and much more numerous;
notwithstanding that our united forces, including donkey-
boys, porters, and miscellaneous hangers-on, number
nearer thirty than twenty persons. For there are the
M. B.'s and their nephew, and L. and the Writer, and
L.'s maid, and Talhamy, all on donkeys; and then
there are the owners of the donkeys, also on donkeys;
and then every donkey has a boy; and every boy has
a donkey; and every donkey-boy's donkey has an inferior boy in attendance. Our style of dress, too,
however convenient, is not exactly in harmony with
the surrounding scenery; and one cannot but feel, as
these draped and dusty pilgrims pass us on the road,
that we cut a sorry figure with our hideous palm-leaf
hats, green veils, and white umbrellas.

But the most amazing and incongruous figure in
our whole procession is unquestionably George. Now
George is an English north-country groom whom the
M. B.'s have brought out from the wilds of Lancashire,
partly because he is a good shot and may be useful
to "Master Alfred" after birds and crocodiles; and
partly from a well-founded belief in his general abilities.
And George, who is a fellow of infinite jest and infinite

resource, takes to Eastern life as a duckling to the water. He picks up Arabic as if it were his mother tongue. He skins birds like a practised taxidermist. He can even wash and iron on occasion. He is, in short, groom, footman, housemaid, laundry-maid, stroke oar, game-keeper, and general factotum all in one. And besides all this, he is gifted with a comic gravity of countenance that no surprises and no disasters can upset for a moment. To see this worthy anachronism cantering along in his groom's coat and gaiters, livery-buttons, spotted neckcloth, tall hat and all the rest of it; his long legs dangling within an inch of the ground on either side of the most diminutive of donkeys; his double-barrelled fowling-piece under his arm, and that imperturbable look in his face, one would have sworn that he and Egypt were friends of old, and that he had been brought up on pyramids from his earliest childhood.

It is a long and shelterless ride from the palms to the desert; but we come to the end of it at last, mounting just such another sand-slope as that which leads up from the Geezeh road to the foot of the Great Pyramid. The edge of the plateau here rises abruptly from the plain in one long range of low per-pendicular cliffs pierced with dark mouths of rock-cut sepulchres; while the sand-slope by which we are climbing pours down through a breach in the rock, as an Alpine snow-drift flows through a mountain gap from the ice-level above.

And now, having dismounted through compassion for our unfortunate little donkeys, the first thing we observe is the curious mixture of débris underfoot. At Geezeh one treads only sand and pebbles; but here at

Sakkarah the whole plateau is thickly strewn with scraps of broken pottery, limestone, marble, and alabaster; flakes of green and blue glaze; bleached bones; shreds of yellow linen; and lumps of some odd-looking dark brown substance, like dried-up sponge. Presently some one picks up a little noseless head of the common blue ware used for funereal statuettes, and immediately we all fall to work, grubbing for treasure—a pure waste of precious time; for though the sand is full of débris, it has been sifted so often and so carefully by the Arabs that it no longer contains anything worth looking for. Meanwhile one finds a fragment of iridescent glass—another a morsel of shattered vase—a third an opaque bead of some kind of yellow paste. Then, with a shock that the present Writer, at all events, will not soon forget, we suddenly discover that these scattered bones are human—that those linen shreds are shreds of cerement cloths—that yonder odd-looking brown lumps are rent fragments of what once was living flesh! And now for the first time we realise that every inch of this ground on which we are standing, and all these hillocks and hollows and pits in the sand, are violated graves.

"Ce n'est que le premier pas qui coûte." We soon became quite hardened to such sights, and learned to rummage among dusty sepulchres with no more compunction than would have befitted a gang of professional body-snatchers. These are experiences upon which one looks back afterwards with wonder, and something like remorse; but so infectious is the universal callousness, and so overmastering is the passion for relic-hunting, that I do not doubt we should again do the same things under the same circumstances.

Most Egyptian travellers, if questioned, would have to make a similar confession. Shocked at first, they denounce with horror the whole system of sepulchral excavation, legal as well as predatory; acquiring, however, a taste for scarabs and mummy-gods, they soon begin to buy with eagerness the spoils of the dead; finally they forget all their former scruples, and ask no better fortune than to discover and confiscate a tomb for themselves.

Notwithstanding that I had first seen the Pyramids of Geezeh, the size of the Sakkarah group—especially of the Pyramid in stages—took me by surprise. They are all smaller than the Pyramids of Cheops and Chephren, and would no doubt look sufficiently insignificant if seen with them in close juxtaposition; but taken by themselves they are quite vast enough for grandeur. As for the Pyramid in platforms (which is the largest at Sakkarah, and next largest to the Pyramid of Chephren) its position is so fine, its architectural style so exceptional, its age so immense, that one altogether loses sight of these questions of relative magnitude. If Egyptologists are right in ascribing the royal title hieroglyphed on the inner door of this pyramid to Ouenephes, the fourth king of the First Dynasty, then it is the only extant monument of that earliest period, and consequently the most ancient building in the world. It had been standing from five to seven hundred years when King Cheops began his Great Pyramid at Geezeh. It was over two thousand years old when Abraham was born. It is now about six thousand eight hundred years old according to Manetho and Mariette, or about four thousand eight hundred, according to the computation of Bunsen. One's im-

agination recoils upon the brink of such a gulf of
time.

The door of this pyramid was carried off, with other
precious spoils, by Lepsius, and is now in the museum
at Berlin.   The evidence that identifies the inscription
is tolerably direct.   According to Manetho, an Egyptian
historian who wrote in Greek and lived in the reign of
Ptolemy Philadelphus, King Ouenephes built for himself a pyramid at a place called Ko-komeh.   Now a
tablet of late discovered in the Serapeum by M. Mariette
gives the name of Ka-kem to the necropolis of Sakkarah; and as the pyramid in stages is not only the
largest on this platform, but also the only one in which
a royal cartouche has been found, the conclusion seems
obvious.

When a building has already lasted five or six thousand years in a climate where mosses and lichens, and
all those natural signs of age to which we are accustomed in Europe are unknown, it is not to be supposed
that a few centuries more or less can tell upon its outward appearance; yet to my thinking the pyramid of
Ouenephes looks older than those of Geezeh.   If this
be only fancy, it gives one, at all events, the impression
of belonging structurally to a ruder architectural period.
The idea of a monument composed of diminishing platforms is in its nature more primitive than that of a
smooth four-sided pyramid; and though, as Dr. Lepsius
suggests, the smooth pyramids may all have been carried up in stages and filled in afterwards, the filling-in
seems to be a later idea, and belongs apparently to a
later period.   We remarked that the masonry on one
side—I think on the side facing eastwards—was in

a much more perfect condition than on either of the others.

Wilkinson describes the interior as "a hollow dome supported here and there by wooden rafters." The sepulchral chamber was lined with blue porcelain tiles, one of which may be seen in the British Museum. We should have liked to go inside, but this is no longer possible, the entrance being blocked by a recent fall of masonry.

Making up now for lost time, we rode on as far as the house built in 1850 for the accommodation of M. Mariette during the excavation of the Serapeum—a labour that extended over a period of more than four years.

The Serapeum, it need hardly be said, is the famous and long-lost sepulchral temple of the sacred bulls. These bulls (honoured by the Egyptians as successive incarnations of Osiris) inhabited the temple of Apis at Memphis while they lived, and, being mummied after death, were buried in catacombs prepared for them in the desert. M. Mariette, now Conservator of Antiquities to the Khedive with the title of Bey, was then travelling in the interests of the French Government. In his own simple and interesting account of this great discovery, he affirms that he was indebted for it to a certain passage in Strabo, which describes the Temple of Serapis as being situate in a district where the sand was so drifted by the wind that the approach to it was in danger of being overwhelmed; while the sphinxes on either side of the great avenue were already more or less buried, some having only their heads above the surface. "If Strabo had not written this passage," says M. Mariette, "it is probable that the Serapeum would still be lost under the sands of the necropolis of Sakkarah.   One day, however, (in 1850) being attracted to Sakkarah by my Egyptological studies, I perceived the head of a sphinx showing above the surface.   It evidently occupied its original position.   Close by lay a libation-table on which was engraved a hieroglyphic inscription to Apis-Osiris.   Then that passage in Strabo came to my memory, and I knew that beneath my feet lay the avenue leading to the long and vainly sought Serapeum.   Without saying a word to any one, I got some workmen together and we began excavating.   The beginning was difficult; but soon the lions, the peacocks, the Greek statues of the Dromos, the inscribed tablets of the Temple of Nectanebo * rose up from the sands.   Thus was the Serapeum discovered."

The house — a slight, one-storied building on a space of rocky platform—looks down upon a sandy hollow which now presents much the same appearance that it must have presented when M. Mariette was first reminded of the fortunate passage in Strabo.   One or two heads of sphinxes peep up here and there in a ghastly way above the sand, and mark the line of the great avenue.   The upper half of a boy riding on a peacock, apparently of rude execution, is also visible. The rest is already as completely overwhelmed as if it had never been uncovered.   One can scarcely believe that only twenty-four years ago, the whole place was entirely cleared at so vast an expenditure of time and labour.   The work, as I have already mentioned, took

---

* Nectanebo I. and Nectanebo II. were the last native Pharaohs of ancient Egypt, and flourished between B.C. 378 and B.C. 340. An earlier Temple must have preceded the Serapeum built by Nectanebo I.

four years to complete. This avenue alóne was six hundred feet in length and bordered by an army of sphinxes, one hundred and forty-one of which were found *in situ*. As the excavation neared the end of the avenue, the causeway, which followed a gradual descent between massive walls, lay seventy feet below the surface. The labour was immense, and the difficulties were innumerable. The ground had to be contested inch by inch. "In certain places," says M. Mariette, "the sand was fluid, so to speak, and baffled us like water continually driven back and seeking to regain its level."

If, however, the toil was great, so also was the reward. A main avenue terminated by a semicircular platform, round which stood statues of famous Greek philosophers and poets; a second avenue at right angles to the first; the remains of the great Temple of the Serapeum; three smaller temples; and three distinct groups of Apis catacombs, were brought to light. A descending passage opening from a chamber in the great Temple led to the catacombs—vast labyrinths of vaults and passages hewn out of the solid rock on which the Temples were built. These three groups of excavations represent three epochs of Egyptian history. The first and most ancient series consists of isolated vaults dating from the XVIIIth to the XXth dynasty; that is to say from about B.C. 1703 to B.C. 1288. The second group, which dates from the reign of Sheshonk I. (XXIInd dynasty, B.C. 980) to that of Tirhaka, the last king of the XXVth dynasty, is more systematically planned, and consists of one long tunnel bordered on each side by a row of funereal chambers. The third belongs to the Greek period, beginning with Psam-

6*

metichus I. (XXVIth dynasty, B.C. 665) and ending
with the latest Ptolemies. Of these, the first are again
choked with sand; the second are considered unsafe;
and the third only is accessible to travellers.

After a short but toilsome walk and some delay
outside a prison-like door at the bottom of a steep
descent, we were admitted by the guardian—a gaunt
old Arab with a lantern in his hand. It was not an
inviting looking place within. The outer daylight fell
upon a rough step or two, beyond which all was dark.
We went in. A hot, heavy atmosphere met us on the
threshold; the door fell to with a dull clang, the echoes
of which went wandering away as if into the central
recesses of the earth; the Arab chattered and gesticu-
lated. He was telling us that we were now in the
great vestibule, and that it measured ever so many feet
in this and that direction; but we could see nothing—
neither the vaulted roof overhead, nor the walls on any
side, nor even the ground beneath our feet. It was
like the darkness of infinite space.

A lighted candle was then given to each person,
and the Arab led the way. He went dreadfully fast,
and it seemed at every step as if one were on the
brink of some frightful chasm. Gradually, however,
our eyes became accustomed to the gloom, and we
found that we had passed out of the vestibule into the
first great corridor. All was vague, mysterious, shadowy.
A dim perspective loomed out of the darkness. The
lights twinkled and flitted, like wandering sparks of
stars. The Arab held his lantern to the walls here
and there, and showed us some votive tablets inscribed
with hieroglyphed records of pious visits paid by devout
Egyptians to the sacred tombs. Of these they found

five hundred when the catacombs were first opened;
but M. Mariette sent them nearly all to the Louvre.

A few steps farther, and we came to the tombs—a
succession of great vaulted chambers hewn out at irregular distances along both sides of the central corridor, and sunk some six or eight feet below the surface. In the middle of each chamber stood an enormous
sarcophagus of polished granite. The Arab, flitting on
ahead like a black ghost, paused a moment before
each cavernous opening, flashed the light of his lantern
on the sarcophagus, and sped away again, leaving us
to follow as we could.

So we went on, going every moment deeper into
the solid rock, and farther from the open air and the
sunshine. Thinking it would be cold underground, we
had brought warm wraps in plenty; but the heat, on
the contrary, was intense, and the atmosphere stifling.
We had not calculated on the dryness of the place, nor
had we remembered that ordinary mines and tunnels
are cold because they are damp. But here for in-
calculable ages—for thousands of years probably before the Nile had even cut its path through the rocks
of Silsilis—a cloudless African sun had been pouring
its daily floods of light and heat upon the dewless
desert overhead. The place might well be unendurable.
It was like a great oven stored with the slowly accumulated heat of cycles so remote and so many that
the earliest periods of Egyptian history seem, when
compared with them, to belong to yesterday.

Having gone on thus for a distance of nearly two
hundred yards, we came to a chamber containing the
first hieroglyphed sarcophagus we had yet seen; all the
rest being polished, but plain. Here the Arab paused;

and finding access provided by means of a flight of
wooden steps, we went down into the chamber, walked
round the sarcophagus, peeped inside by the help of a
ladder, and examined the hieroglyphs with which it is
covered.   Enormous as they look from above, one can
form no idea of the bulk of these huge monolithic
masses except from the level on which they stand.
This sarcophagus, which dates from the reign of Amasis,
of the XXVIth dynasty, measured fourteen feet in length
by eleven in height, and consisted of a single block of
highly-wrought black granite.   Four persons might sit
down in it round a small card-table, and play a rubber
comfortably.

From this point the corridor branches off for another two hundred yards or so, leading always to more
chambers and more sarcophagi, of which last there are
altogether twenty-four. Three only are inscribed; none
measure less than from thirteen to fourteen feet in
length; and all are empty.   The lids in every instance
have been pushed back a little way, and some are
fractured; but the spoilers have been unable wholly to
remove them. According to M. Mariette, the place was
pillaged by the early Christians, who, besides carrying
off whatever they could find in the way of gold and
jewels, seem to have destroyed the mummies of the
bulls, and razed the great Temple nearly to the ground.
Fortunately, however, they either overlooked, or left as
worthless, some hundreds of exquisite bronzes and the
five hundred votive tablets before mentioned, which, as
they record not only the name and rank of the visitor,
but also, with few exceptions, the name and year of
the reigning Pharaoh, afford invaluable historical data,
and are likely to do more than any previously discovered

documents towards clearing up disputed points of Egyptian chronology.

It is a curious fact that one out of the three inscribed sarcophagi should bear the oval of Cambyses —that Cambyses of whom it is related that, having desired the priest of Memphis to bring before him the God Apis, he drew his dagger in a transport of rage and contempt, and stabbed the animal in the thigh. According to Plutarch, he slew the beast and cast out its body to the dogs; according to Herodotus, "Apis lay some time pining in the temple, but at last died of his wound, and the priests buried him secretly;" but according to one of these precious Serapeum tablets, the wounded bull did not die till the fourth year of the reign of Darius. So wonderfully does modern discovery correct and illustrate tradition.

And now comes the sequel to this ancient story in the shape of an anecdote related by M. About, who tells how M. Mariette, being recalled suddenly to Paris some months after the opening of the Serapeum, found himself without the means of carrying away all his newly-excavated antiquities, and so buried fourteen cases in the desert, there to await his return. One of these cases contained the only Apis mummy that had escaped discovery by the early Christians, and this mummy was that of the identical Apis stabbed by Cambyses. That the creature had actually survived his wound was proved by the condition of one of the thigh-bones, which showed unmistakable signs of both injury and healing.

Nor does the story end here. M. Mariette being gone, and having taken with him all that was most portable among his treasures, there came to Memphis one whom M. About indicates as "a young and august

stranger" travelling in Egypt for his pleasure.   The
Arabs, tempted perhaps by a princely backsheesh, revealed the secret of the hidden cases; whereupon
the Archduke swept off the whole fourteen, despatched
them to Alexandria, and immediately shipped them for
Trieste, there to decorate a certain beautiful château,
where they doubtless may be seen to this day. "Quant
au coupable," says M. About, who professes to have
had the story direct from M. Mariette, "il a fini si
tragiquement dans un autre hemisphère que, tout bien
pesé, je renonce à publier son nom." But through so
transparent a disguise it is not difficult to identify the
unfortunate hero of this curious anecdote.

The sarcophagus in which the Apis was found
remains in the vaults of the Serapeum; but we did not
see it.   Having come more than two hundred yards
already, and being by this time well-nigh suffocated,
we did not care to put two hundred more between
ourselves and the light of day.   So we turned back at
the half distance—having, however, first burned a pan
of magnesian powder, which flared up wildly for a few
seconds; lit the huge gallery and all its cavernous
recesses and the wondering faces of the Arabs; and
then went out with a plunge, leaving the darkness
denser than before.

From hence, across a farther space of sand, we
went in all the blaze of noon to the tomb of one Ti, a
priest and commoner of the Fifth Dynasty, who married
with a lady named Nofre-hotepes, the granddaughter
of a Pharaoh, and here built himself a magnificent
tomb in the desert.

Of the façade of this tomb, which must originally
have looked like a little temple, only two large pillars

remain. Next comes a square courtyard surrounded by a roofless colonnade, from one corner of which a covered passage leads to two chambers. In the centre of the courtyard yawns an open pit some twenty-five feet in depth, with a shattered sarcophagus just visible in the gloom of the vault below. All here is limestone —walls, pillars, pavements, even the excavated débris with which the pit had been filled in when the vault was closed for ever. The quality of this limestone is close and fine like marble, and so white that, although the walls and columns of the courtyard are covered with sculptures of most exquisite execution and of the greatest interest, the reflected light is so intolerable, that we find it impossible to examine them with the interest they deserve. In the passage, however, where there is shade, and in the large chamber, where it is so dark that we can see only by the help of lighted candles, we find a succession of bas-reliefs so numerous and so closely packed that it would take half a day to see them properly. Ranged in horizontal parallel lines about a foot and a half in depth, these extraordinary pictures, row above row, cover every inch of wall-space from floor to ceiling. The relief is singularly low. I should doubt if it anywhere exceeds a quarter of an inch. The surface, which is covered with a thin film of very fine cement, has a quality and polish like ivory. The figures measure an average height of about twelve inches; and all are coloured.

Here, as in an open book, we have the biography of Ti. His whole life, his pleasures, his business, his domestic relations, are brought before us with just that faithful simplicity that makes the charm of Montaigne and Pepys. Here are no strange funereal gods, no

emblems that it would require the profound knowledge of a Birch or a Brugsch to decipher. A child
might read the pictured chronicles that illuminate these
walls, and take as keen a pleasure in them as the wisest
archæologist.

Ti was a wealthy man, and his wealth was of the
agricultural sort. He owned flocks and herds and
vassals in plenty. He kept many kinds of birds and
beasts — geese, ducks, pigeons, cranes, oxen, goats,
donkeys, antelopes, and gazelles. He was fond of
fishing and fowling, and used sometimes to go after
crocodiles and hippopotami, which came down as low
as Memphis in his time. He was a kind husband too,
and a good father, and loved to share his pleasures
with his family. Here we see him sitting in state with
his wife and children, while professional singers and
dancers perform before them. Yonder they walk out
together and look on while the farm-servants are at
work, and watch the coming in of the boats that bring
home the produce of Ti's more distant lands. Here
the geese are being driven home; the cows are crossing
a ford; the oxen are ploughing; the sower is scattering
his seed; the reaper plies his sickle; the oxen tread
the grain; the corn is stored away in the granary.
There are evidently no independent tradesfolk in these
early days of the world. Ti has his own artificers on
his own estate, and all his goods and chattels are home-
made. Here the carpenters are fashioning new furniture for the house; the shipwrights are busy on new
boats; the potters mould pots; the metal-workers smelt
ingots of red gold. It is plain to see that Ti lived
like a king within his own boundaries. He makes an
imposing figure, too, in all these scenes, and, being

represented about eight times as large as his servants, sits and stands a giant among pigmies. His wife (we must not forget that she was of the blood royal) is as big as himself; and the children are depicted about half the size of their parents. Curiously enough, Egyptian art never outgrew this early naïveté. The great man remained a big man to the last days of the Ptolemies, and the fellah was always a dwarf.

Apart from these and one or two other mannerisms, nothing can be more natural than the drawing, or more spirited than the action, of all these men and animals. The most difficult and transitory movements are expressed with masterly certitude. The donkey kicks up his heels and brays—the crocodile plunges—the wild duck rises on the wing; and the fleeting action is caught in each instance with a truthfulness that no Landseer could distance. The forms, which have none of the conventional stiffness of later Egyptian work, are modelled roundly and boldly, yet finished with exquisite precision and delicacy. The colouring, however, is purely decorative; and being laid on in single tints, with no attempt at gradation or shading, conceals rather than enhances the beauty of the sculptures. These, indeed, are best seen where the colour is entirely rubbed off. The tints are yet quite brilliant in parts of the larger chamber; but in the passage and courtyard, which have been excavated only a few years and are with difficulty kept clear from day to day, there is not a vestige of colour left. This is the work of the sand—that patient labourer whose office it is not only to preserve but to destroy. The sand secretes the work of the sculptor, but effaces the work of the painter. In sheltered places where it accumulates

passively like a snow-drift, it brings away only the
surface-detail, leaving the under colours rubbed and
dim. But nothing, as I had occasion constantly to
remark in the course of the journey, removes colour
so effectually as sand that is exposed to the shifting
action of the wind.

This tomb, as we have seen, consists of a portico,
a courtyard, two chambers, and a sepulchral vault; but
it also contains a secret passage of the kind that M.
Mariette calls a serdab. These serdabs, which are
constructed in the thickness of the walls and have no
entrances, seem to be peculiar to tombs of the Ancient
Empire (i. e. the period of the Pyramid Kings); and
they contain statues of the deceased of all sizes, in
wood, limestone, and granite. Twenty statues of Ti
were found immured in the serdab of his tomb, all
broken save one—a spirited figure in limestone, standing about seven feet high, and now in the museum at
Boulak. This statue (No. 24 in the large vestibule)
represents a fine young man in a white tunic, and is
evidently a portrait. The features are regular; the expression is good-natured; the whole tournure of the
head is more Greek than Egyptian. The flesh is
painted of a yellowish brick tint, and the figure stands
in the usual hieratic attitude, with the left leg advanced,
the hands clenched, and the arms straightened close
to the sides. One seems to know Ti so well after seeing the wonderful pictures in his tomb, that this charming statue interests one like the portrait of a familiar
friend.

How pleasant it was, after being suffocated in the
Serapeum and broiled in the tomb of Ti, to return to
M. Mariette's little deserted house, and eat our luncheon

on the cool stone terrace that looks northward over the
desert! Some wooden tables and benches are hospitably
left here, for the accommodation of travellers, and fresh
water in ice-cold goollahs is provided by the old Arab-
guardian. The yards and offices at the back are full
of broken statues and fragments of inscriptions in red
and black granite. Two sphinxes from the famous
avenue adorn the terrace, and look down upon their
half-buried companions in the sand-hollow below. The
yellow desert, barren and undulating, with a line of
purple peaks on the horizon, reaches away into the far
distance. To the right, under a jutting ridge of rocky
plateau not two hundred yards from the house, yawns
an open-mouthed black-looking cavern shored up with
heavy beams and approached by a slope of débris.
This is the forced entrance to the earlier vaults of the
Serapeum, in one of which was found a mummy described by M. Mariette as that of an Apis, but pro-
nounced by Brugsch to be the body of Prince Kha-em-uas,
governor of Memphis and the favourite son of Rameses
the Great.

This remarkable mummy that looked as much like
a bull as a man, was found covered with jewels and
gold chains and precious amulets engraved with the
name of Kha-em-uas, and had on its face a golden
mask; all which treasures are now to be seen in the
Louvre. If it was the mummy of an Apis, then the
jewels with which it was adorned were probably the
offering of the prince at that time ruling in Memphis.
If, on the contrary, it was the mummy of the prince,
then, in order to be buried in a place of peculiar
sanctity, he probably usurped one of the vaults prepared
for the god. The question is a curious one, and re-

mains unsolved to this day; but it could no doubt be settled at a glance by Professor Owen.

Far more startling, however, than the discovery of either Apis or jewels, was the sight seen by M. Mariette on first entering that long-closed sepulchral chamber. The mine being sprung and the opening cleared, he went in alone; and there, on the thin layer of sand that covered the floor, he found the footprints of the workmen who, 3700 * years before, had laid that shapeless mummy in its tomb and closed the doors upon it, as they believed, for ever.

And now—for the afternoon is already waning fast —the donkeys are brought round, and it is time to move on. We have the site of Memphis and the famous prostrate colossus yet to see, and the long road lies all before us. So back we ride across the desolate sands; and with a last, long, wistful glance at the Pyramid in platforms, go down from the territory of the dead into the land of the living.

There is a wonderful fascination about this pyramid. One is never weary of looking at it—of repeating to one's-self that it is indeed the oldest building on the face of the whole earth. The king who erected it came to the throne, according to Manetho, about eighty years after the death of Menes, the founder of the Egyptian monarchy. All we have of him is his pyramid; all we know of him is his name. And these belong, as it were, to the infancy of the human race. In dealing with Egyptian dates one is apt to think lightly of periods that count only by centuries; but it is a habit of mind that leads to error, and should be combated. The present writer found it useful to be constantly

* The date is M. Mariette's.

comparing relative chronological eras. For instance, in realising the immense antiquity of the Sakkarah pyramid, it is some help to remember that from the time when it was built by King Ouenephes to the time when the King Cheops erected the great Pyramid of Geezeh, there probably lies a space of years equivalent to that which, in the history of England, extends from the date of the Conquest to the accession of George the Second. * And yet Cheops himself—the Khufu of the monuments—is but a shadowy figure hovering, as it seems to us, upon the threshold of Egyptian history.

And now the desert is left behind, and we are nearing the palms that lead to Memphis. We have of course been dipping into Herodotus—every one takes Herodotus up the Nile—and our heads are full of the ancient glories of this famous city. We know that Menes turned the course of the river in order to build it on this very spot; and that all the most illustrious Pharaohs adorned it with temples, palaces, pylons, and precious sculptures. We had read of the great Temple of Ptah that Rameses the Great enriched with colossi of himself; and of the sanctuary where Apis lived in state, taking his exercise in a pillared courtyard where every column was a statue; and of the artificial lake, and the sacred groves, and the obelisks, and all the

---

* There was no worship of Apis in the days of King Ouenephes, nor, indeed, until the reign of Kaiechos, more than one hundred and twenty years after his time. But at some subsequent period or other of the Ancient Empire, his pyramid was appropriated by the priests of Memphis for the mummies of the Sacred Bulls. This, of course, was done ages before any of the known Apis-catacombs were excavated. There are doubtless many more of these catacombs yet undiscovered, nothing prior to the XVIIIth Dynasty having yet been found.

wonders of a city that even in its later days was one
of the most populous in Egypt.

Thinking over these things by the way, we agree
that it is well to have left Memphis till the last. We
shall appreciate it the better for having first seen that
other city on the edge of the desert to which, for nearly
six thousand years, all Memphis was quietly migrating,
generation after generation. We know now how poor
folk laboured and how great gentlemen amused themselves in those early days when there were hundreds
of Tis with town-houses at Memphis and villas by the
Nile. From the Serapeum, too, buried and ruined as
it is, one cannot but come away with a profound impression of the splendour and power of a religion that
could command for its myths such faith, such homage,
and such public works.

And now we are once more in the midst of the
palm-woods, threading our way among the same mounds
that we passed in the morning. Presently those in
front strike away from the beaten road across a grassy
flat to the right; and the next moment we are all
gathered round the brink of a muddy pool in the
midst of which lies a shapeless block of blackened
and corroded limestone. This, it seems, is the famous
prostrate colossus of Rameses the Great, which belongs
to the British government, but which the British government is too economical to remove. So here it lies,
face downward; drowned once a year by the Nile;
visible only when the pools left by the inundation have
evaporated, and all the muddy hollows are dried up.
It is one of two which stood at the entrance to the
great Temple of Ptah; and by those who have gone
down into the hollow and seen it from below in the

dry season, it is reported of as a noble and very beautiful specimen of the best period of Egyptian art.

Where, however, is the companion colossus? Where is the Temple itself? Where are the pylons, and the obelisks, and the avenues of sphinxes? Where, in short, is Memphis?

The dragoman shrugs his shoulders and points to the barren mounds among the palms.

They look like gigantic dust-heaps, and stand from thirty to forty feet above the plain. Nothing grows upon them, save here and there a tuft of stunted palm; and their substance seems to consist chiefly of crumbled brick, broken potsherds, and fragments of limestone. Some few traces of brick foundations and an occasional block or two of shaped stone are to be seen in places low down against the foot of one or two of the mounds; but one looks in vain for any sign that might indicate the outline of a boundary wall, or the position of a great public building.

And is this all?

No — not quite all. There are some mud-huts yonder, in among the trees; and in front of one of these we find a number of sculptured fragments — battered sphinxes, torses without legs, sitting figures without heads — in green, black, and red granite. Ranged in an irregular semicircle on the sward, they seem to sit in forlorn conclave, half solemn, half ludicrous, with the goats browsing round, and the little Arab children hiding behind them.

Near this, in another pool lies another colossus — not the fellow to that which we saw first, but a smaller one, also face downwards, of red granite.

And this is all that remains of Memphis, eldest

cities:—a few huge rubbish-heaps, a dozen or so of broken statues, and a name! One looks round, and tries in vain to realise the lost splendours of the place. Where is the Memphis that King Menes came from Thinis to found — the Memphis of Ouenephes, and Cheops, and Chephren, and all the early kings who built their pyramid-tombs in the adjacent desert? Where is the Memphis of Herodotus, of Strabo, of Abd-el-Latif? Where are those stately ruins that even in the middle ages extended over a space estimated at "half a day's journey in every direction"? One can hardly believe that a great city ever flourished on this spot, or understand how it should have been effaced so utterly. Yet here it stood—here where the grass is green, and the palms are growing, and the Arabs build their hovels on the verge of the inundation. The great colossus marks the site of the main entrance to the Temple of Ptah. It lies where it fell, and no man has moved it. That tranquil sheet of palm-fringed back-water, beyond which we see the village of Mitra-henny and catch a distant glimpse of the pyramids of Geezeh, occupies the basin of a vast artificial lake excavated by Menes. The very name of Memphis survives in the dialect of the Fellâh, who calls the place of the mounds Tel Monf*—just as Sakkarah fossilises the name of Sokari, one of the special denominations of the Memphite Osiris.

No capital in the world dates so far back as this, or kept its place in history so long. Founded four thousand years before our era, it beheld the rise and

---

* *Tel:* Arabic for mound. Many of these mounds preserve the ancient names of the cities they entomb; as Tel Bast (Bubastis); Kóm Ombo (Ombos); etc. etc. *Tel* and *Kóm* are synonymous terms.

fall of thirty-one dynasties; it survived the rule of the Persian, the Greek, and the Roman; it was, even in its decadence, second only to Alexandria in population and extent; and it continued to be inhabited up to the time of the Arab invasion. It then became the quarry from which Fostat (Old Cairo) was built; and as the new city rose on the Eastern bank, the people of Memphis quickly abandoned their ancient capital to desolation and decay.

Still a vast field of ruins remained. Abd-el-Latif, writing at the commencement of the thirteenth century, speaks with enthusiasm of the colossal statues and lions, the enormous pedestals, the archways formed of only three stones, the bas-reliefs and other wonders that were yet to be seen upon the spot. Marco Polo, if his wandering tastes had led him to the Nile, might have found some of the palaces and temples of Memphis still standing; and Sandys, who in A.D. 1610 went at least as far south of Cairo as Kafr el Iyat, says that "up the River for twenty miles space there was nothing but ruines." Since then, however, the very "ruines" have vanished; the palms have had time to grow; and modern Cairo has doubtless absorbed all the building material that remained from the middle ages.

Everything we know about the early history of Memphis comes from Herodotus; and it is satisfactory to find that in this, as in other instances, modern science is constantly testifying to the accuracy of his facts, even when they are most remote and least credible. That Menes six or seven thousand years ago should have turned the course of the Nile to create a site for his new city seems only a little more improbable than that Lake Mœris should have been dug by another

574732   7*

Pharaoh of the Ancient Empire (Amenemhat III.) to receive and store the superfluous waters of the inundations. Both undertakings appear too vast for the power and knowledge of even the pyramid builders. Yet Linant Bey has not long since discovered the dyke of Menes at Kosheysh, where there is a great bend in the river, and the dyke of Mœris in the central plateau of the Fyoom. These things are the romance of archæology. They bring us as it were face to face with persons and events appertaining to a past so infinitely remote that they seem to belong to another world than ours, and to other conditions of being.

Memphis is a place to read about, and think about, and remember; but it is a disappointing place to see. To miss it, however, would be to miss the first link in the whole chain of monumental history that unites the Egypt of antiquity with the world of to-day. Those melancholy mounds and that heron-haunted lake must be seen, if only that they may take their due place in the picture-gallery of one's memory.

It had been a long day's work, but it came to an end at last; and as we trotted our donkeys back towards the river, a gorgeous sunset was crimsoning the palms and pigeon-towers of Bedreshayn. Everything seemed now to be at rest. A buffalo, contemplatively chewing the cud, lay close against the path and looked at us without moving. The children and pigeons were gone to bed. The pots had baked in the sun and been taken in long since. A tiny column of smoke went up here and there from amid the clustered huts; but there was scarcely a moving creature to be seen. Presently we passed a tall, beautiful Fellah woman standing grandly by the wayside, with her veil thrown

back and falling in long folds to her feet. She smiled,
put out her hand, and murmured "Backsheesh!" Her
fingers were covered with rings, and her arms with
silver bracelets. She begged because to beg is honour-
able, and customary, and a matter of inveterate habit;
but she evidently neither expected nor needed the
backsheesh she condescended to ask for.

A few moments more and the sunset has faded,
the village is left behind, the last half-mile of plain is
trotted over. And now—hungry, thirsty, dusty, worn
out with new knowledge, new impressions, new ideas
—we are once more at home and at rest.

CHAPTER V.
Bedreshayn to Minieh.

It is the rule of the Nile to hurry up the river as
fast as possible, leaving the ruins to be seen as the
boat comes back with the current; but this, like many
another canon, is by no means of universal application.
The traveller who starts late in the season has, indeed,
no other course open to him. He must press on with
speed to the end of his journey, if he would get back
again at low Nile without being irretrievably stuck on
a sand-bank till the next inundation floats him off
again. But for those who desire not only to see the
monuments, but to follow, however superficially, the
course of Egyptian history as it is handed down through
Egyptian art, it is above all things necessary to start
early and to see many things by the way.

For the history of ancient Egypt goes against the
stream. The earliest monuments lie between Cairo
and Siout, while the last temples to the old gods are

chiefly found in Nubia. Those travellers, therefore,
who hurry blindly forward with or without a wind,
now sailing, now tracking, now punting, passing this
place by night, and that by day, and never resting till
they have gained the farthest point of their journey,
begin at the wrong end and see all their sights in precisely inverse order. Memphis and Sakkarah and the
tombs of Beni Hassan should undoubtedly be visited
on the way up. So should El Kab, and Tel el Amarna,
and the oldest parts of Karnak and Luxor. It is not
necessary to delay long at any of these places. They
may be seen cursorily on the way up, and be more
carefully studied on the way down; but they should
be seen as they come, no matter at what trifling cost
of present delay, and despite any amount of ignorant
opposition. For in this way only is it possible to trace
the progression and retrogression of the arts from the
Pyramid-builders to the Cæsars; or to understand at
the time and on the spot, in what order that vast and
august procession of dynasties swept across the stage
of history.

For ourselves, as will presently be seen, it happened that we could carry only a part of this programme into effect; but that part, happily, was the
most important. We never ceased to congratulate ourselves on having made acquaintance with the Pyramids
of Geezeh and Sakkarah before seeing the tombs of
the kings at Thebes; and I feel that it is impossible
to over-estimate the advantage of studying the sculptures of the tomb of Ti before one's taste is brought
into contact with the debased style of Denderah and
Esneh. We began the Great Book, in short, as it always should be begun—at its first page; thereby ac-

quiring just that necessary insight without which many an after-chapter must have lost more than half its interest.

If I seem to insist upon this point, it is because things contrary to custom need a certain amount of insistance, and are sure to be met by opposition. No dragoman, for example, could be made to understand the importance of historical sequence in a matter of this kind; especially in the case of a contract trip. To him, Cheops, Rameses, and the Ptolemies are one. As for the monuments, they are all ancient Egyptian, and one is just as odd and unintelligible as another. He cannot quite understand why travellers come so far and spend so much money to look at them; but sets it down to a habit of harmless curiosity—by which he profits.

The truth is, however, that the mere sightseeing of the Nile demands some little reading and organising, if only to be enjoyed. We cannot all be profoundly learned; but we can at least do our best to understand what we see—to get rid of obstacles—to put the right thing in the right place. For the land of Egypt is, as I have said, a Great Book—not very easy reading, perhaps, under any circumstances; but at all events quite difficult enough already without the added puzzlement of being read backwards.

And now our next point along the river, as well as our next link in the chain of early monuments, was Beni Hassan, with its famous rock-cut tombs of the XIIth Dynasty; and Beni Hassan was still more than a hundred and forty-five miles distant. We ought to have gone on again directly—to have weighed anchor and made a few miles that very evening on returning

to the boats; but we insisted on a second day in the
same place. This, too, with the favourable wind still
blowing. It was against all rule and precedent. The
captain shook his head, the dragoman remonstrated, in
vain.

"You will come to learn the value of a wind, when
you have been longer on the Nile," said the latter,
with that air of melancholy resignation which he always
assumed when not allowed to have his own way. He
was an indolent good-tempered man, spoke English
fairly well, and was perfectly manageable; but that air
of resignation came to be aggravating in time.

The M. B.'s being of the same mind, however, we
had our second day, and spent it at Memphis. We
ought to have crossed over to Toora, and have seen
the great quarries from which the casing-stones of the
Pyramids came, and all the finer limestone with which
the Temples and Palaces of Memphis were built. But
the whole mountain-side seemed as if glowing at a
white heat on the opposite side of the river, and we
said we would put off Toora till our return. So we
went our own way; and Alfred shot pigeons; and the
writer sketched Mitrahenny, and the palms; and the
sacred lake of Menes; and the rest grubbed among
the mounds for treasure, finding many curious fragments of glass and pottery, and part of an engraved
bronze Apis; and we had a green, tranquil, lovely day,
barren of incident, but very pleasant to remember.

The good wind continued to blow all that night;
but fell at sunrise, precisely when we were about to
start. The river now stretched away before us, smooth
as glass, and there was nothing for it, said Reïs
Hassan, but tracking. We had heard of tracking often

enough since coming to Egypt; but without having any definite idea of the process. Coming on deck, however, before breakfast, we found nine of our poor fellows harnessed to a rope like barge-horses, towing the huge boat against the current. Seven of the M. B.'s crew, similarly harnessed, followed at a few yards' distance. The two ropes met and crossed and dipped into the water together. Already our last night's mooring-place was out of sight; and the Pyramid of Ouenephes stood up amid its lesser brethren on the edge of the desert, as if bidding us good-bye. But the sight of the trackers jarred, somehow, with the placid beauty of the picture. We got used to it, as one gets used to everything, in time; but it looked like slaves' work, and shocked our English notions disagreeably.

That morning, still tracking, we pass the Pyramids of Dashoor. A dilapidated brick Pyramid standing in the midst of them, looks like an aiguille of black rock thrusting itself up through the limestone bed of the desert. Palms line the bank and intercept the view; but we catch flitting glimpses here and there, looking out especially for that dome-like Pyramid that we observed the other day from Sakkarah. Seen in the full sunlight, it looks larger and whiter, and more than ever like the roof of the old Palais de Justice far away in Paris.

Thus the morning passes. We sit on deck writing letters; reading; watching the sunny river-side pictures that glide by at a foot's pace and are so long in sight. Palm-groves, sand-banks, patches of fuzzy-headed Doora, and fields of some yellow-flowering herb, succeed each other. A boy plods along the bank, leading

a camel. They go slowly; but they soon leave us behind. A native boat meets us, floating down side-wise
with the current. A girl comes to the water's edge
with a great empty jar on her head, and waits to fill it
till the trackers have gone by. The pigeon-towers of
a mud village peep above a clump of lebbich trees, a
quarter of a mile inland. Here a solitary brown man,
with only a felt skull-cap on his head and a slip of
scanty tunic fastened about his loins, works a shadoof,*
stooping and rising, stooping and rising, with the
regularity of a pendulum. It is the same machine
that we shall see by and by depicted in the tombs at
Thebes; and the man is so evidently an ancient
Egyptian, that we find ourselves wondering how he
escaped being mummified four or five thousand years
ago.

By and by a little breeze springs up. The men
drop the rope and jump on board—the big sail is set
—the breeze freshens—and away we go again, as mer-

---

* The Shadoof has been so well described by the Rev. F. B. Zincke, that
I cannot do better than quote him verbatim:—"Mechanically, the Shadoof is
an application of the lever. In no machine which the wit of man, aided by the
accumulation of science, has since invented, is the result produced so great in
proportion to the degree of power employed. The lever of the Shadoof is a
long stout pole poised on a prop. The pole is at right angles to the river. A
large lump of clay from the spot is appended to the inland end. To the river
end is suspended a goat-skin bucket. This is the whole apparatus. The man
who is working it stands on the edge of the river. Before him is a hole full of
water fed from the passing stream. When working the machine, he takes hold
of the cord by which the empty bucket is suspended, and bending down, by
the mere weight of his shoulders dips it in the water. His effort to rise gives
the bucket full of water an upward cant, which, with the aid of the equipoising
lump of clay at the other end of the pole, lifts it to a trough into which, as it
tilts on one side, it empties its contents. What he has done has raised the
water six or seven feet above the level of the river. But if the river has subsided twelve or fourteen feet, it will require another Shadoof to be worked in
the trough into which the water of the first has been brought. If the river has
sunk still more, a third will be required before it can be lifted to the top of the
bank, so as to enable it to flow off to the fields that require irrigation."—*Egypt
of the Pharaohs and the Khedive*, p. 445 *et seq.*

rily as the day we left Cairo. Towards sunset we see a strange object, like a giant obelisk broken off half-way, standing up on the Western bank against an orange-gold sky. This is the yet unopened Pyramid of Maydoom, commonly called the False Pyramid. It looks quite near the bank; but this is an effect of powerful light and shadow, for it lies back at least four miles from the river. That night, having sailed on till past nine o'clock, we moor about a mile from Benisooef, and learn with some surprise that a man must be despatched to the governor of the town, for guards. Not that anything ever happened to anybody at Benisooef, says Talhamy; but that the place is sup-posed not to have a first-rate reputation. If we have guards, we at all events make the governor respon-sible for our safety and the safety of our possessions. So the guards are sent for; and being posted on the bank, snore loudly all night long, just outside our windows.

Meanwhile the wind shifts round to the South, and next morning it blows full in our faces. The men, however, track up to Benisooef to a point where the buildings come down to the water's edge and the towing-path ceases; and there we lay-to for awhile among a fleet of filthy native boats, close to the landing-place.

The approach to Benisooef is rather pretty. The Khedive has an Italian-looking villa here, which peeps up white and dazzling from the midst of a thickly-wooded park. The town lies back a little from the river. A few coffee-houses and a kind of promenade face the landing-place; and a mosque built to the verge of the bank stands out picturesquely against the bend of the river.

And now it is our object to turn that corner, so as to get into a better position for starting when the wind drops. The current here runs deep and strong, so that we have both wind and water dead against us. Half our men clamber round the corner like cats, carrying the rope with them; the rest keep the Dahabeeyah off the bank with punting poles. The rope strains—a pole breaks—we struggle forward a few feet, and can get no farther. Then the men rest a bit; try again; and are again defeated. So the fight goes on. The promenade and the windows of the mosque become gradually crowded with lookers-on. Some three or four cloaked and bearded men have chairs brought, and sit gravely smoking their chibouques on the bank above, enjoying the entertainment. Meanwhile the water-carriers come and go, filling their goat-skins at the landing-place; donkeys and camels are brought down to drink; girls in dark blue gowns and coarse black veils come with huge water-jars laid sidewise upon their heads, and, having filled and replaced them upright, walk away with stately steps, as if each ponderous vessel were a crown.

So the day passes. Driven back again and again, but still resolute, our sailors, by dint of sheer doggedness, get us round the bad corner at last. The 'Bagstones' follows suit a little later; and we both moor about a quarter of a mile above the town. Then follows a night of adventures. Again our guards sleep profoundly; but the bad characters of Benisooef are very wide awake. One gentleman, actuated no doubt by the friendliest motives, pays a midnight visit to the

'Bagstones'; but being detected, chased, and fired at, escapes by jumping overboard. Our turn comes about two hours later, when the writer, happening to be awake, hears a man swim softly round the Philæ. To strike a light and frighten everybody into sudden activity is the work of a moment. The whole boat is instantly in an uproar. Lanterns are lighted on deck; a patrol of sailors is set; Talhamy loads his gun; and the thief slips away in the dark, like a fish.

The guards, of course, slept sweetly through it all. Honest fellows! They were paid a shilling a night to do it, and they had nothing on their minds.

Having lodged a formal complaint next morning against the inhabitants of the town, we received a visit from a sallow personage clad in a long black robe and a voluminous white turban. This was the Chief of the Guards. He smoked a great many pipes; drank numerous cups of coffee; listened to all we had to say; looked wise; and finally suggested that the number of our guards should be doubled.

I ventured to object that if they slept unanimously, forty would not be of much more use than four. Whereupon he rose; drew himself to his full height; touched his beard; and said with a magnificent melodramatic air:—

"If they sleep, they shall be bastinadoed till they die!"

And now our good luck seemed to have deserted us. For three days and nights the adverse wind continued to blow with such force that the men could not even track against it. Moored under that dreary bank, we saw our ten days' start melting away, and could only make the best of our misfortunes. Happily the

long island close by, and the banks on both sides of
the river were populous with sand-grouse; so Alfred
went out daily with his faithful George and his un-
erring gun, and brought home game in abundance;
while we took long walks, sketched boats and camels,
and chaffered with native women for silver torques and
bracelets. These torques (in Arabic *Tôk*) are tubular
but massive, penannular, about as thick as one's little
finger, and finished with a hook at one end and a
twisted loop at the other. The girls would sometimes
put their veils aside and make a show of bargaining;
but more frequently, after standing for a moment with
great wondering black velvety eyes staring shyly into
ours, they would take fright like a troop of startled
deer, and vanish with shrill cries, half of laughter, half
of terror.

At Benisooef we encountered our first sand-storm.
It came down the river about noon, showing like a
yellow fog on the horizon, and rolling rapidly before
the wind. It tore the river into angry waves, and blotted
out the landscape as it came. The distant hills disappeared first; then the palms beyond the island; then
the boats close by. Another second, and the air was full
of sand. The whole surface of the plain seemed in
motion. The banks rippled. The yellow dust poured
down through every rift and cleft in hundreds of tiny
cataracts. But it was a sight not to be looked upon
with impunity. Hair, eyes, mouth, ears, were instantly
filled, and we were driven to take refuge in the saloon.
Here, although every window and door had been shut
before the storm came, the sand found its way in
clouds. Books, papers, carpets were covered with it;
and it settled again as fast as it was cleared away.

This lasted just one hour, and was followed by a burst of heavy rain; after which the sky cleared and we had a lovely afternoon. From this time forth we saw no more rain in Egypt.

At length, on the morning of the fourth day after our first appearance at Benisooef and the seventh since leaving Cairo, the wind veered round again to the north, and we once more got under way. It was delightful to see the big sail again towering up overhead, and to hear the swish of the water under the cabin windows; but we were still one hundred and nine miles from Rhoda, and we knew that nothing but an extraordinary run of luck could possibly get us there by the twenty-third of the month, with time to see Beni-Hassan on the way. Meanwhile, however, we make fair progress, mooring at sunset when the wind falls, about three miles north of Bibbeh. Next day, by help of the same light breeze which again springs up a little after dawn, we go at a good pace between flat banks fringed here and there with palms, and studded with villages more or less picturesque. There is not much to see, and yet one never wants for amusement. Now we pass an island of sand-bank covered with snow-white paddy-birds, which rise tumultuously at our approach. Next comes Bibbeh perched high along the edge of the precipitous bank, its odd-looking Coptic Convent roofed all over with little mud domes, like clustered earth-bubbles. By and by we pass a deserted sugar-factory with shattered windows and a huge, gaunt, blackened chimney, worthy of Birmingham or Sheffield. And now we catch a glimpse of the railway, and hear the last scream of a departing engine. At night we moor within sight of the factory chimneys and hydraulic tubes of Magagha, and next day get on nearly to Golosaneh, which is the last station-town before Minieh.

It is now only too clear that we must give up all thought of pushing on to Beni-Hassan before the rest of the party come on board. We have reached the evening of our ninth day; we are still forty-eight miles from Rhoda; and another adverse wind might again delay us indefinitely on the way. All risks taken into account, we decide to put off our meeting till the twenty-fourth and transfer the appointment to Minieh; thus giving ourselves time to track all the way in case of need. So an Arabic telegram is concocted, and our fleetest runner sent off with it to Golosaneh before the office closes for the night.

The breeze, however, does not fail, but comes back next morning with the dawn. Having passed Golosaneh, we come to a wide reach in the river, at which point we are honoured by a visit from a Moslem Santon of peculiar sanctity, named "Holy Sheykh Cotton." Now Holy Sheykh Cotton, who is a well-fed, healthy-looking young man of about thirty, makes his first appearance swimming, with his garments twisted into a huge turban on the top of his head, and only his chin above water. Having made his toilet in the small boat, he presents himself on deck, and receives an enthusiastic welcome. Reïs Hassan hugs him—the pilot kisses him—the sailors come up one by one, bringing little tributes of tobacco and piastres, which he accepts with the air of a Pope receiving Peter's Pence. All dripping as he is, and smiling like an affable Triton, he next proceeds to touch the tiller, the ropes, and the ends of the yards, "in order," says Talhamy, "to make them holy;" and then, with some kind of final charm or muttered incantation, plunges into the river again, and swims off to repeat the same performance on board the Bagstones.

From this moment the prosperity of our voyage is assured. The captain goes about with a smile on his stern face, and the crew look as happy as if we had given them a guinea. For nothing can go wrong with a Dahabeeyah that has been "made holy" by Holy Sheykh Cotton. We are certain now to have favourable winds—to pass the Cataract without accident—to come back in health and safety, as we set out. But what, it may be asked, has Holy Sheykh Cotton done to make his blessing so efficacious? He gets money in plenty; he fasts no oftener than other Mahommedans; he has two wives; he never does a stroke of work; and he looks the picture of sleek prosperity. Yet he is a saint of the first water; and when he dies, miracles will be performed at his tomb, and his eldest son will succeed him in the business.

We had the pleasure of becoming acquainted with a good many saints in the course of our Eastern travels; but I do not know that we ever found they had done anything to merit the position. One very horrible old man named Sheykh Saleem has, it is true, been sitting on a dirt heap near Farshoot, unclothed, unwashed, unshaven, for the last half-century or more, never even lifting his hand to his mouth to feed himself; but Sheykh Cotton had gone to no such pious lengths, and was not even dirty.

We are by this time drawing towards a range of yellow cliffs that have long been visible on the horizon, and which figure in the maps as Gebel et Tayr. The Arabian desert has been closing up to the Eastern bank for some time past, and now rolls on in undulating drifts to the water's edge. Yellow boulders crop out here and there above the mounded sand, which looks as if it might cover many a forgotten Temple. Presently the clay bank is gone, and a low barrier of limestone rock, black and shiny next the water-line, has taken its place. And now, a long way ahead, where the river bends and the level cliffs lead on into the far distance, a little brown speck is pointed out as the Convent of the Pulley. Perched on the brink of the precipice, it looks no bigger than an ant-heap. We had heard much of the fine view to be seen from the platform on which this Convent is built, and it had originally entered into our programme as a place to be visited on the way. But Minieh has to be gained now at all costs; so this project is abandoned with a sigh.

And now the rocky barrier rises higher, quarried here and there in dazzling gaps of snow-white cuttings. And now the Convent shows clearer; and the cliffs become loftier; and the bend in the river is reached; and a long perspective of flat-topped precipice stretches away into the dim distance.

It is a day of saints and swimmers. As the Dahabeeyah approaches, a brown poll is seen bobbing up and down in the water a few hundred yards ahead. Then one, two, three bronze figures dash down a steep ravine below the Convent walls, and plunge into the river—a shrill chorus of voices, growing momentarily more audible, is borne upon the wind—and in a few minutes the boat is beset by a shoal of mendicant monks vociferating with all their might "*Ana Christian ya Howadji!—Ana Christian ya Howadji!*" (I am a Christian, Oh traveller!) As these are only Coptic monks and not Moslem santons, the sailors, half in rough play, half in earnest, drive them off with punting poles; and only one shivering, streaming object, wrapped in a borrowed blanket, is allowed to come on board. He is a fine shapely man aged about forty, with splendid eyes and teeth, a well-formed head, a skin the colour of a copper beech-leaf, and a face expressive of such ignorance, timidity, and half-savage watchfulness as makes one's heart ache.

And this is a Copt; a descendant of the true Egyptian stock; one of those whose remote ancestors exchanged the worship of the old gods for Christianity under the rule of Theodosius some fifteen hundred years ago, and whose blood is supposed to be purer of Mahommedan intermixture than any in Egypt. Remembering these things, it is impossible to look at him without a feeling of profound interest. It may be only fancy, yet I think I see in him a different type to that of the Arab—a something, however slight, that recalls the sculptured figures in the tomb of Ti.

But while we are thinking about his magnificent pedigree, our poor Copt's teeth are chattering piteously. So we give him a shilling or two for the sake of all that he represents in the history of the world; and with these and the donation of an empty bottle he swims away contented, crying again and again:—"*Ketther-kháyrak Sittát! Ketther-kháyrak keteer!* (Thank you, ladies! thank you much!)

And now the Convent with its clustered domes is passed and left behind. The rock here is of the same rich tawny hue as at Toora, and the horizontal strata of which it is composed have evidently been deposited by water. That the Nile must at some remote time have flowed here at an immensely higher level seems also probable; for the whole face of the range is honey-combed and water-worn for miles in succession. Seeing how these fantastic forms—arched, and clustered, and pendent—resemble the recessed ornamentation of Saracenic buildings, I could not help wondering whether some early Arabian architect might not once upon a time have taken a hint from some such rocks as these.

Thus the day wanes, and the level cliffs keep with us all the way—now breaking into little lateral valleys and *culs-de-sac* in which nestle clusters of tiny huts and green patches of lupin; now plunging sheer down into the river; now receding inland, and leaving space for a belt of cultivated soil and a fringe of feathery palms. By and by comes the sunset, when every cast shadow in the recesses of the cliffs turns to pure violet; and the face of the rock glows with a ruddier gold; and the palms on the western bank stand up in solid bronze against a crimson horizon. Then the sun dips, and instantly the whole range of cliffs turns to a dead, greenish grey, while the sky above and behind them is as suddenly suffused with pink. When this effect has lasted for something like eight minutes, a vast arch of deep blue shade, about as large in diameter as a rainbow, creeps slowly up the eastern horizon, and remains distinctly visible so long as the pink flush against which it is defined yet lingers in the sky. Finally the flush fades out; the blue becomes uniform; the stars begin to show; and only a broad glow in the west marks which way the sun went down. About a quarter of an hour later comes the after-glow, when for a few minutes the sky is filled with a soft, magical light, and the twilight gloom lies warm upon the landscape. When this goes, it is night; but still one long beam of light streams up in the track of the sun, and remains visible for more than two hours after the darkness has closed in.

Such is the sunset we see this evening as we approach Minieh; and such is the sunset we are destined to see with scarcely a shade of difference at the same hour and under precisely the same conditions for many a month to come. It is very beautiful, very tranquil, full of wonderful light and most subtle gradations of tone, and attended by certain phenomena of which I shall have more to say presently; but it lacks the variety and gorgeousness of our northern skies. Nor, given the dry atmosphere of Egypt, can it be otherwise. Those who go up the Nile expecting, as I did, to see magnificent Turneresque pageants of purple, and flame-colour, and gold, will be disappointed as I was. For your Turneresque pageant cannot be achieved without such accessories of cloud and vapour as in Nubia are wholly unknown, and in Egypt are of the rarest occurrence. Once, and only once, in the course of an unusually protracted sojourn on the river, had we the good fortune to witness a grand display of the kind; and then we had been nearly three months in the Dahabeeyah.

Meanwhile, however, we never weary of these stainless skies, but find in them, evening after evening, fresh depths of beauty and repose. As for that strange transfer of colour from the mountains to the sky, we had repeatedly observed it while travelling in the Dolomites the year before, and had always found it take place, as now, at the moment of the sun's first disappearance. But what of this mighty after-shadow,

climbing half the heavens and bringing night with it?
Can it be the rising Shadow of the World projected
on the one horizon as the sun sinks on the other? I
leave the problem for wiser travellers to solve. We
had not science enough amongst us to account for it.

That same evening, just as the twilight came on,
we saw another wonder—the new moon on the first
night of her first quarter; a perfect orb, dusky, distinct,
and outlined all round with a thread of light no thicker
than a hair. Nothing could be more brilliant than
this tiny rim of flashing silver; while every detail of
the softly-glowing globe within its compass was clearly
visible. Tycho with its vast crater showed like a vol-
cano on a raised map; and near the edge of the
moon's surface, where the light and shadow met, keen
sparkles of mountain-summits catching the light and
relieved against the dusk, were to be seen by the
naked eye. Two or three evenings later, however,
when the silver ring was changed to a broad crescent,
the unilluminated part was as it were extinguished,
and could no longer be discerned even by help of a
glass.

The wind having failed as usual at sunset, the crew
set to work with a will and punted the rest of the way,
so bringing us to Minieh about nine that night. Next
morning we found ourselves moored close under the
Khedive's summer palace—so close that one could
have tossed a pebble against the lattice windows of his
Highness's hareem. A fat gate-keeper sat outside in
the sun, smoking his morning chibouque and gossip-
ing with the passers by. A narrow promenade scantily
planted with sycamore figs ran between the palace and
the river. A steamer or two, and a crowd of native

boats, lay moored under the bank; and yonder, at the
farther end of the promenade, a minaret and a cluster
of whitewashed houses showed which way one must
turn in going to the town.

It chanced to be market-day; so we saw Minieh
under its best aspect, than which nothing could well
be more squalid, dreary, and depressing. It was like a
town dropped unexpectedly into the midst of a ploughed
field; the streets being mere trodden lanes of mud and
dust, and the houses a succession of windowless prisons
with their backs to the thoroughfare. The Bazaar,
which consists of two or three lanes a little wider than
the rest, is roofed over here and there with rotting
palm-rafters and bits of tattered matting; while the
market is held in a space of waste ground outside the
town. The former with its little cupboard-like shops,
in which the merchants sit cross-legged like shabby
old idols in shabby old shrines—the ill-furnished shelves
—the familiar Manchester goods—the gaudy native
stuffs—the old red saddles and faded rugs hanging up
for sale—the smart Greek stores where Bass's ale, claret,
curaçoa, Cyprus, Vermouth, cheese, pickles, sardines,
Worcester sauce, blacking, biscuits, preserved meats,
candles, cigars, matches, sugar, salt, stationery, fireworks, jams, and patent medicines can all be bought
at one fell swoop—the native cook's shop exhaling
savoury perfumes of Kebabs and lentil soup, and presided over by an Abyssinian Soyer blacker than the
blackest historical personage ever was painted—the
surging, elbowing, clamorous crowd—the donkeys, the
camels, the street-cries, the chatter, the dust, the flies,
the fleas, and the dogs, all put us in mind of the poorer
quarters of Cairo. In the market, it is even worse.

Here are hundreds of country folk sitting on the ground
behind their baskets of fruits and vegetables. Some
have eggs, butter, and buffalo-cream for sale; while
others sell sugar-canes, limes, cabbages, tobacco, barley,
dried lentils, split beans, maize, wheat and doorah.
The women go to and fro with bouquets of live poultry.
The chickens scream; the sellers rave; the buyers bargain at the tops of their voices; the dust flies in
clouds; the sun pours down floods of light and heat;
you can scarcely hear yourself speak; and the crowd
is as dense as that other crowd which at this very
moment, on this very Christmas Eve, is circulating
among the alleys of Leadenhall Market.

The things were very cheap. A hundred eggs cost
about fourteen-pence in English money; chickens sold
for fivepence each; pigeons from twopence to twopence-
halfpenny; and fine live geese for two shillings a head.
The turkeys, however, which were large and excellent,
were priced as high as three-and-sixpence; being about
half as much as one pays in Middle and Upper Egypt
for a lamb. A good sheep may be bought for sixteen shillings or a pound. The M.B.'s, who had no
dragoman and did their own marketing, were very
busy here, laying in stores of fresh provision, bargaining fluently in Arabic, and escorted by a body-guard
of sailors.

A solitary Dôm palm, the northernmost of its race
and the first specimen one meets with on the Nile,
grows in a garden adjoining this market-place; but we
could scarcely see it for the blinding dust. Now a
Dôm palm is just the sort of tree that De Wint should
have painted—odd, angular, with long forked stems,
each of which terminates in a shock-headed crown of

stiff finger-like fronds shading heavy clusters of big, shiny nuts about the size of Jerusalem artichokes. It is, I suppose, the only nut in the world of which one throws away the kernel and eats the shell; but the kernel is as hard as marble, while the shell is fibrous, and tastes like stale gingerbread. The Dôm palm must bifurcate, for bifurcation is the law of its being; but I could never discover whether there was any fixed limit to the number of stems into which it might subdivide. At the same time, I do not remember to have seen any with less than two heads or more than six.

Coming back through the town, we were accosted by a withered one-eyed hag like a reanimated mummy, who offered to tell our fortunes. Before her lay a dirty rag of handkerchief full of shells, pebbles, and chips of broken glass and pottery. Squatting toad-like under a sunny bit of wall, the lower part of her face closely veiled, her skinny arms covered with blue and green glass bracelets and her fingers with misshapen silver rings, she hung over these treasures; shook, mixed, and interrogated them with all the fervour of divination; and delivered a string of the prophecies usually forthcoming on these occasions.

"You have a friend far away, and your friend is thinking of you. There is good fortune in store for you; and money coming to you; and pleasant news on the way. You will soon receive letters in which there will be something to vex you, but more to make you glad. Within thirty days you will unexpectedly meet one whom you dearly love," etc. etc. etc.

It was just the old familiar story retold in Arabic, without even such variations as might have been ex-

pected from the lips of an old Fellaha born and bred
in a provincial town of Middle Egypt.

It may be that ophthalmia especially prevailed in
this part of the country, or that being brought unexpectedly into the midst of a large crowd, one observed
the people more narrowly, but I certainly never saw
so many one-eyed human beings as that morning at
Minieh. There must have been present in the streets
and market-place from ten to twelve thousand native
of all ages, and I believe it is no exaggeration to say
that at least every twentieth person, down to little tod-
dling children of three and four years of age, was blind
of an eye. Not being a particularly well-favoured race,
this defect added the last touch of repulsiveness to
faces already sullen, ignorant, and unfriendly. A more
unprepossessing population I would never wish to see
—the men half stealthy, half insolent; the women bold
and fierce; the children filthy, sickly, stunted, and
stolid. Nothing in provincial Egypt is so painful to
witness as the neglected condition of very young children. Those belonging to even the better class are
for the most part shabbily clothed and of more than
doubtful cleanliness; while the offspring of the very
poor are simply encrusted with dirt and sores, and
swarming with vermin. It is at first hard to believe
that the parents of these unfortunate babies err, not
from cruelty, but through sheer ignorance and super-
stition. Yet so it is; and the time when these people
can be brought to comprehend the most elementary
principles of sanitary reform is yet far distant. To wash
young children is injurious to health; therefore the
mothers suffer them to fall into a state of personal un-
cleanliness that is alone enough to engender disease.

To brush away the flies that beset their eyes is impious; hence ophthalmia and various kinds of blindness. I have seen infants lying in their mothers' arms with six or eight flies in each eye. I have seen the little helpless hands put down reprovingly, if they approached the seat of annoyance. I have seen children of four and five years old with the surface of one or both eyes eaten away; and others with a large fleshy lump growing out where the pupil had been destroyed. Taking these things into account, the wonder is, after all, not that three children should die in Egypt out of every five—not that each twentieth person in certain districts should be blind, or partially blind; but that so many as forty per cent of the whole infant population should actually live to grow up, and that ninety-five per cent should enjoy the blessing of sight. For my own part, I had not been many weeks on the Nile before I began systematically to avoid going about the native towns whenever it was practicable to do so. That I may so have lost an opportunity of now and then seeing more of the street-life of the people is very probable; but such outside glimpses are of little real value, and I at all events escaped the sight of much poverty, sickness, and squalor. The condition of the inhabitants is not worse, perhaps, in an Egyptian Beled* than in many an Irish village; but the condition of the children is so distressing that one would willingly go any number of miles out of the way rather than witness their suffering, without the power to alleviate it.**

---

* *Beled*—Village.
** Miss Whately, whose evidence on this subject is peculiarly valuable, states that the majority of native children die off at, or under, two years of age (*Among the Huts*, p. 29); while M. About, who enjoyed unusual opportunities of inquiring into facts connected with the population and resources of the

If the population in and about Minieh are personally unattractive, their appearance at all events matches their reputation, which is as bad as that of their neighbours. Of the manners and customs of Benisouef we had already some experience; while public opinion charges Minieh, Rhoda, and most of the towns and villages north of Siout, with the like marauding propensities. As for the villages at the foot of Beni Hassan, they have been mere dens of thieves for many generations; and though razed to the ground some years ago by way of punishment, are now rebuilt, and in as bad odour as ever. It is necessary, therefore, in all this part of the river, not only to hire guards at night, but, when the boat is moored, to keep a sharp look-out against thieves by day. In Upper Egypt it is very different. There the natives are good-looking, good-natured, gentle, and kindly; and though clever enough at manufacturing and selling modern antiquities, are not otherwise dishonest.

That same evening—(it was Christmas eve)—nearly two hours earlier than their train was supposed to be due, the rest of our party arrived at Minieh.

CHAPTER VI.

Minieh to Siout.

IT is Christmas Day. The M.B's are coming to dinner; the cooks are up to their eyes in entrées; the crew are treated to a sheep in honour of the occasion;

country, says that the nation loses three children out of every five. "L'ignorance publique, l'oubli des premiers éléments d'hygiène, la mauvaise alimentation, l'absence presque totale des soins médicaux, tarissent la nation dans sa source. Un peuple qui perd régulièrement trois enfants sur cinq ne saurait croître sans miracle."—*Le Fellah*, p. 165.

the new-comers are unpacking; and we are all gradually
settling down into our respective places. Now the new-
comers consist of four persons:—a Painter, a Happy
Couple, and a maid. The Painter has already been up
the Nile three times, and brings a fund of experience
into the council. He knows all about sandbanks, and
winds, and mooring-places; is acquainted with most of
the native governors and consuls along the river; and
is great on the subject of what to eat, drink, and avoid.
The stern-cabin is given to him for a studio, and
contains frames, canvases, drawing-paper and easels
enough to start a provincial school of art. He is going
to paint a big picture at Aboo-Simbel. The Happy
Couple, it is unnecessary to say, are on their wedding
tour. In point of fact, they have not yet been married
a month. The bridegroom is what the world chooses
to call an idle man; that is to say, he has scholarship,
delicate health, and leisure. The bride, for convenience,
shall be called the Little Lady. Of people who are
struggling through that helpless phase of human life
called the honeymoon, it is not fair to say more than
that they are both young enough to make the situation
interesting.

Meanwhile the deck must be cleared of the new
luggage that has come on board, and the day passes in
a confusion of unpacking, arranging, and putting away.
Such running to and fro as there is down below; such
turning-out of boxes, and knocking-up of temporary
shelves; such talking, and laughing, and hammering!
Nor is the bustle confined to downstairs. Talhamy and
the waiters are just as busy above, adorning the upper
deck with palm-branches and hanging the boat all round
with rows of coloured lanterns. One can hardly believe,

however, that it is Christmas Day—that there are fires blazing at home in every room; that the church-field, perhaps, is white with snow; and that the familiar bells are ringing merrily across the frosty air. Here at midday it is already too hot on deck without the awning, and when we moor towards sunset near a riverside village in a grove of palms, the cooler air of evening is delicious.

There is novelty in even such a commonplace matter as dining out, on the Nile. You go and return in your felucca, as if it was a carriage; and your entertainers summon you by firing a dinner-gun instead of sounding a gong. Wise people who respect the feelings of their cooks fire a dressing-gun as well; for watches soon differ in a hopeless way for want of the church-clock to set them by, and it is always possible that host and guest may be half an hour or so apart in their reckoning.

The customary guns having therefore been fired, and the party assembled, we sat down to one of cook Bedawee's prodigious banquets. Not, however, till the plum-pudding, blazing demoniacally, appeared upon the scene, did any of us succeed in believing that it was really Christmas Day.

Nothing could be prettier or gayer than the spectacle that awaited us when we rose from table. A hundred and fifty coloured lanterns outlined the boat from end to end, sparkled up the masts, and cast broken reflections in the moving current. The upper-deck, hung with flags and partly closed in with awnings, looked like a bower of palms. The stars and the crescent moon shone overhead. Dim outlines of trees and headlands, and a vague perspective of gleaming river, were visible in the distance; while a light gleamed now and then in the direction of the village, or a dusky figure flitted along the bank.

Meanwhile there was a sound of revelry by night; for our sailors had invited the Bagstones' crew to unlimited coffee and tobacco, and had quite a large party on the lower deck. They drummed, they sang, they danced, they dressed up, improvised a comic scene, and kept their audience in a roar. Reïs Hassan did the honours. George, Talhamy, and the maids sat apart at the second table and sipped their coffee genteelly. We looked on and applauded. At ten o'clock a pan of magnesium powder was burned, and our Fantasia ended, like a pantomime in a blaze of glory.

In Egypt, by the way, any entertainment that is enlivened by music, dancing, or fireworks, is called a Fantasia.

And now, sometimes sailing, sometimes tracking, sometimes punting, we go on day by day, making what speed we can. Things do not, of course, always fall out exactly as one would have them. The wind too often fails when we most need it, and gets up when there is something to be seen on shore. Thus, after a whole morning of tracking, we reach Beni Hassan at the moment when a good breeze has suddenly filled our sails for the first time in forty-eight hours; and so, yielding to counsels which we afterwards deplored, we pass on with many a longing look at the terraced doorways pierced along the cliffs. At Rhoda, in the same way, we touch only for a few minutes to post and inquire for letters, and put off till our return the inland excursion to Dayr el Nakhl, where is to be seen

the famous painting of the Colossus on the Sledge.
But sights deferred are fated sometimes to remain unseen, as we found by and by to our exceeding loss
and regret.

Meanwhile the skies are always cloudless; the days
warm; the evenings exquisite. We of course live very
much in the open air. When there is no wind, we land
and take long walks by the river-side. When on board,
we sketch, write letters, read Champollion, Bunsen, and
Sir Gardener Wilkinson, and work hard at Egyptian
dynasties. The sparrows and water-wagtails perch
familiarly on the awnings and hop about the deck;
the cocks and hens chatter, the geese cackle, the
turkeys gobble in their coops close by; and our sacrificial sheep, leading a solitary life in the felucca, comes
baa-ing in the rear. Sometimes we have as many as
a hundred chickens on board (to say nothing of pigeons
and rabbits) and two or even three sheep in the felucca.
The poultry-yard is railed off, however, at the extreme
end of the stern, so that the creatures are well away
from the drawing-room; and when we moor at a suitable
place, they are let out for a few hours to peck about
the banks and enjoy their liberty. L. and the Little
Lady feed these hapless prisoners with breakfast-
scraps every morning, to the profound amusement of
the steersman, who, unable to conceive any other
motive, imagines they are fatting them for table.

Such is our Noah's Ark life—pleasant, peaceful and
patriarchal. Even on days when there is little to see
and nothing to do, it is never dull. Trifling incidents
which have for us the excitement of novelty are continually occurring. Other Dahabeeyahs, their flags and
occupants, are a constant source of interest. Meeting

at mooring-places for the night, we now and then exchange visits. Passing each other by day, we dip ensigns, fire salutes, and punctiliously observe the laws of maritime etiquette. Sometimes a Cook's Excursion-steamer hurries by, crowded with tourists; or a government tug towing three or four great barges closely packed with wretched-looking, half-naked fellaheen bound for forced labour on some new railway or canal. Occasionally we pass a Dahabeeyah sticking fast upon a sandbank; and sometimes we stick on one ourselves. Then the men fly to their punting poles, or jump into the river like water-dogs, and, grunting in melancholy cadence, shove the boat off with their shoulders.

The birds, too, are new, and we are always looking out for them. Perhaps we see a top-heavy pelican balancing his huge yellow bill over the edge of the stream, and fishing for his dinner—or a flight of wild geese trailing across the sky towards sunset—or a select society of vultures perched all in a row upon a ledge of rock, and solemn as the bench of bishops. Then there are the herons who stand on one leg and doze in the sun; the strutting hoopoes with their legendary top-knots; the blue and green bee-eaters hovering over the uncut doora. The pied kingfisher, black and white like a magpie, sits fearlessly under the bank and never stirs, though the tow-rope swings close above his head and the Dahabeeyah glides within a few feet of the shore. The paddy-birds whiten the sandbanks by hundreds, and rise in a cloud at our approach. The sacred hawk, circling overhead, utters the same sweet, piercing, melancholy note that the Pharaohs listened to of old.

The scenery, meanwhile, is for the most part of the

ordinary Nile pattern; and for many a mile we see the
same things over and over again:—the level bank
shelving down steeply to the river; the strip of cultivated soil, green with maize or tawny with doora;
the frequent mud-village and palm-grove; the deserted
sugar-factory with its ungainly chimney and shattered
windows; the water-wheel slowly revolving with its
necklace of pots; the shadoof worked by two brown
athletes; the file of laden camels; the desert, all sand-
hills and sand-plains, with its background of mountains;
the long reach, and the gleaming sail ahead. Sometimes, however, as at Kom Ahmar, we skirt the ancient
brick mounds of some forgotten city, with fragments of
arched foundations, and even of walls and doorways,
reaching down to the water's edge; or, sailing close
under ranges of huge perpendicular cliffs, as at Gebel
Aboofayda, startle the cormorants from their haunts,
and peer as we pass into the dim recesses of many a
rock-cut tomb excavated just above the level of the inundation.

This Gebel Aboofayda has a bad name for sudden
winds; especially at the beginning and end of the range,
where the Nile bends abruptly and the valley opens out
at right angles to the river. It is fine to see Reïs
Hassan, as we approach one of the worst of these bad
bits—a point where two steep ravines divided by a
bold headland command the passage like a pair of grim
cannon, and rake it with blasts from the North-Eastern
desert. Here the current, flowing deep and strong, is
met by the wind and runs high in crested waves. Our
little Captain, kicking off his shoes, himself springs up
the rigging and there stands silent and watchful. The
sailors, ready to shift our mainsail at the word of com-

mand, cling some to the Shoghool* and some to the
end of the yard; the boat tears on before the wind;
the great bluff looms up darker and nearer. Then
comes a breathless moment. Then a sharp, sudden
word from the little man in the main rigging; a yell
and a whoop from the sailors; a slow, heavy lurch of
the flapping sail; and the corner is turned in safety.

The cliffs here are very fine; much loftier and less
uniform than at Gebel-et-Tayr; rent into strange forms,
as of sphinxes, cheesewrings, towers, and bastions;
honeycombed with long ranges of rock-cut tombs; and
undermined by water-washed caverns in which lurk a
few lingering crocodiles. If at Gebel-et-Tayr the rock
is worn into semblances of Arabesque ornamentation,
here it looks as if inscribed all over with mysterious
records in characters not unlike the Hebrew. Records
they are, too, of pre-historic days—chronicles of his
own deeds carved by the great God Nile himself, the
Hapimu of ancient time—but the language in which
they are written has never been spoken by man.

As for the rock-cut tombs of Gebel Aboofayda, they
must number many hundreds. For nearly twelve miles
the range runs parallel to the river, and throughout that
distance the face of the cliffs is pierced with innumerable doorways. Some are small and square, twenty or
thirty together, like rows of portholes. Others are
isolated. Some are cut so high up that they must have
been approached from above; others again come close
upon the level of the river. Some of the doorways are
faced to represent jambs and architraves; some, excavated laterally, appear to consist of a series of chambers, and are lit from without by small windows cut in

* *Arabic* Shoghool: a rope by which the mainsail is regulated.

9*

the rock. One is approached by a flight of rough steps
leading up from the water's edge; and another, hewn
high in the face of the cliff, just within the mouth of
a little ravine, shows a simple but imposing façade
supported by four detached pillars. No modern travellers seem to visit these tombs; while those of the .
old school, as Wilkinson, Champollion, etc., dismiss
them with a few observations. Yet, with the single
exception of the mountains behind Thebes, there is
not, I believe, any one spot in Egypt which contains
such a multitude of sepulchral excavations. Many
look, indeed, as if they might belong to the same interesting and early epoch as those of Beni Hassan.

I may here mention that about half-way, or rather
less than half-way, along the whole length of the range,
I observed two large hieroglyphed steles incised upon
the face of a projecting mass of boldly rounded cliff at
a height of perhaps a hundred and fifty feet above the
river. These steles, apparently royal ovals, and sculptured as usual side by side, may have measured from
twelve to fifteen feet in height; but in the absence of
any near object by which to scale them, I could form
but a rough guess as to their actual dimensions. The
boat was just then going so fast, that to sketch or take
notes of the hieroglyphs was impossible. Before I
could adjust my glass they were already in the rear;
and by the time I had called the rest of the party
together, they were no longer distinguishable.

Coming back several months later, I looked for
them again, but without success; for the intense midday sun was then pouring full upon the rocks, to the
absolute obliteration of everything like shallow detail.
While watching vainly, however, for the steles, I was

compensated by the unexpected sight of a colossal bas-relief high up on the northward face of a cliff standing, so to say, at the corner of one of those little recesses or *culs-de-sac* which here and there break the uniformity of the range. The sculptural relief of this large subject was apparently very low; but owing to the angle at which it met the light, one figure, which could not have measured less than eighteen or twenty feet in height, was distinctly visible. I immediately drew L.'s attention to the spot; and she not only discerned the figure without the help of a glass, but believed like myself that she could see traces of a second.

As neither the steles nor the bas-relief would seem to have been observed by previous travellers, I may add for the guidance of others that the round and tower-like rock upon which the former are sculptured lies about a mile to the southward of the Sheykh's tomb and palm-tree (a strikingly picturesque bit which no one can fail to notice), and a little beyond some very large excavations near the water's edge; while the bas-relief is to be found a short distance below the Coptic convent and cemetery.

Having for nearly twelve miles skirted the base of Gebel Aboofayda—by far the finest panoramic stretch of rock scenery on this side of the second cataract—the Nile takes an abrupt bend to the eastward, and thence flows through many miles of cultivated flat. On coming to this sudden elbow, the wind which had hitherto been carrying us along at a pace but little inferior to that of a steamer, now struck us full on the beam, and drove the boat to shore with such violence that all the steersman could do was just to run the Philæ's nose into the bank, and steer clear of some ten or twelve native cangias that had been driven in before us. The Bagstones rushed in next; and presently a large iron-built Dahabeeyah, having come gallantly along under the cliffs with all sail set, was seen to make a vain struggle at the fatal corner, and then plunge headlong at the bank, like King Agib's ship upon the Loadstone Mountain.

Imprisoned here all the afternoon, we exchanged visits of condolence with our neighbours in misfortune; had our ears nearly cut to pieces by the driving sand; and failed signally in the endeavour to take a walk on shore. Still the fury of the storm went on increasing. The wind howled; the river raced in turbid waves; the sand drove in clouds; and the face of the sky was darkened as if by a London fog. Meanwhile one boat after another was hurled to shore, and before nightfall we numbered a fleet of some twenty odd craft, native and foreign.

It took the united strength of both crews all next day to warp the Philæ and Bagstones across the river by means of a rope and an anchor; an expedient that deserves special mention, not for its amazing novelty or ingenuity, but because our men declared it to be impracticable. Their fathers, they said, had never done it. Their fathers' fathers had never done it. Therefore it was impossible. Being impossible, why should they attempt it?

They did attempt it, however, and much to their astonishment, they succeeded.

It was, I think, towards the afternoon of this second day, when strolling by the margin of the river, that we first made the acquaintance of that renowned insect, the Egyptian beetle. He was a very fine specimen of his race; nearly half-an-inch long in the back; as black and shiny as a scarab cut in jet; and busily engaged in the preparation of a large rissole of mud, which he presently began laboriously propelling up the bank. We stood and watched him for some time, half in admiration, half in pity. His rissole was at least four times bigger than himself, and to roll it up that steep incline to a point beyond the level of next summer's inundation was a labour of Hercules for so small a creature. One longed to play the part of the Dèus ex machina, and carry it up the bank for him; but that would have been a dénouement beyond his power of appreciation.

We all know the old story of how this beetle lays its eggs by the river's brink; encloses them in a ball of moist clay; rolls the ball to a safe place on the edge of the desert; buries it in the sand; and when his time comes, dies content, having provided for the safety of his successors. Hence his mythic fame; hence all the quaint symbolism that by degrees attached itself to his little person, and ended by investing him with a special sacredness which has often been mistaken for actual worship. Standing by thus, watching the movements of the creature, its untiring energy, its extraordinary muscular strength, its business-like devotion to the matter in hand, one sees how subtle a lesson the old Egyptian moralists had presented before them for contemplation, and with how fine a combination of wisdom and poetry they regarded this little black scarab not only as an emblem of the creative and preserving power, but of the immortality of the soul. As a type, no insect has ever had so much greatness thrust upon him. He became a hieroglyph, and stood for a word signifying both To Be and To Transform. His portrait was multiplied a million-fold; sculptured over the portals of temples; fitted to the shoulders of a God; engraved on gems; moulded in pottery; painted on sarcophagi and the walls of tombs; worn by the living and buried with the dead.

Every traveller on the Nile brings away a handful of the smaller scarabs, genuine or otherwise. One may not particularly care to possess them; yet one cannot help buying them, if only because other people do so, or to get rid of a troublesome dealer, or to give to friends at home. I doubt, however, if even the most enthusiastic scarab-fanciers really feel in all its force the symbolism attaching to these little gems, or appreciate the exquisite naturalness of their execution, till they have seen the living beetle at its work.

In Nubia, where the strip of cultivable land is generally but a few feet in breadth, the scarab's task is comparatively light, and the breed multiplies freely. But in Egypt he has often a wide plain to traverse with his burden, and is therefore scarce in proportion to the difficulty with which he maintains the struggle for existence. The scarab race in Egypt would seem indeed to have diminished very considerably since the days of the Pharaohs, and the time is not perhaps far distant when the naturalist will look in vain for specimens on this side of the first cataract. As far as my own experience goes, I can only say that I saw scores of these beetles during the Nubian part of the journey; but that to the best of my recollection this was the only occasion upon which I observed one in Egypt.

The Nile makes four or five more great bends be-

tween Gebel Aboofayda and Siout; passing Manfaloot
by the way, which town lies some distance back from
the shore. All things taken into consideration—the
fitful wind that came and went continually; the tremendous zigzags of the river; the dead calm that befel
us when only eight miles from Siout; and the long day
of tracking that followed, with the town in sight the
whole way—we thought ourselves fortunate to get in
by the evening of the third day after the storm. These
last eight miles are, however, for open, placid beauty,
as lovely in their way as anything north of Thebes.
The valley is here very wide and fertile; the town,
with its multitudinous minarets, appears first on one
side and then on the other, according to the windings
of the river; the distant pinky mountains look almost
as transparent as the air or the sunshine; while the
banks unfold an endless succession of charming little
subjects, every one of which looks as if it asked to be
sketched as we pass. A shadoof and a clump of palms
—a triad of shaggy black buffaloes, up to their shoulders
in the river and dozing as they stand—a wide-spreading sycamore-fig, in the shade of which lie a man and
camel asleep—a fallen palm uprooted by the last inundation, with its fibrous roots yet clinging to the bank
and its crest in the water—a group of Sheykhs' tombs
with glistening white cupolas relieved against a background of dark foliage—an old disused water-wheel
lying up sidewise against the bank like a huge teetotum,
and garlanded with wild tendrils of a gourd—such are
a few out of many bits by the way, which, if they offer
nothing very new, at all events present the old material
under fresh aspects, and in combination with a distance
of such ethereal light and shade, and such opalescent

tenderness of tone, that it looks more like an air-drawn
mirage than a piece of the world we live in.

Like a mirage, too, that fairy town of Siout seemed
always to hover at the same unattainable distance, and
after hours of tracking to be no nearer than at first.
Sometimes, indeed, following the long reaches of the
river, we appeared to be leaving it behind; and although,
as I have said, we had eight miles of hard work to get
to it, I doubt whether it was ever more than three
miles distant as the bird flies. It was late in the
afternoon, however, when we turned the last corner;
and the sun was already setting when the boat reached
the village of Hamra, which is the mooring-place for
Siout—Siout itself, with clustered cupolas and arrowy
minarets, lying back in the plain, at the foot of a great
mountain pierced with tombs.

Now it was in the bond that our crew were to be
allowed twenty-four hours for making and baking bread
at Siout, Esneh, and Assouan. No sooner, therefore,
was the Dahabeeyah moored than Reïs Hassan and the
steersman started away at full speed on two little
donkeys, to buy flour; while Mehemet Ali, one of our
most active and intelligent sailors, rushed off to hire
the oven. For here, as at Esneh and Assouan, there
are large flour-stores and public bakehouses for the
use of sailors on the river, who make and bake their
bread in large lots; cut it into slices; dry it in the
sun; and preserve it in the form of rusks for months
together. Thus prepared, it takes the place of ship-
biscuit; and is so far superior to ship-biscuit that it
neither moulds nor breeds the maggot, but remains
good and wholesome to the last crumb.

Siout, frequently written Asyoot, is the capital of

Middle Egypt, and has the best bazaars of any town up the Nile. Its red and black pottery is famous throughout the country; and its pipe-bowls (supposed to be the best in the East), being largely exported to Cairo, find their way not only to all parts of the Levant, but to every Algerine and Japanese shop in London and Paris. No lover of peasant pottery will yet have forgotten the Egyptian stalls in the Ceramic Gallery of the International Exhibition of 1871. All those quaint red vases and lustrous black tazzas, all those exquisite little coffee services, those crocodile paper-weights, those barrel-shaped and bird-shaped bottles, came from Siout. There is a whole street of such pottery here in the town. Your Dahabeeyah is scarcely made fast before a dealer comes on board and ranges his brittle wares along the deck. Others display their goods upon the bank. But the best things are only to be had in the Bazaars; and not even in Cairo is it possible to find Siout ware so choice in colour, form, and design as that which the two or three best dealers bring out, wrapped in soft paper, when a European customer appears in the market.

Besides the street of pottery, there is a street of red shoes; another of native and foreign stuffs; and the usual run of saddlers' shops, kebab-stalls, and Greek stores for the sale of everything in heaven or earth from third-rate cognac to patent wax vestas. The houses are of plastered mud or sun-dried bricks, as at Minieh. The thoroughfares are dusty, narrow, unpaved and crowded, as at Minieh. The people are one-eyed, dirty, and unfragrant, as at Minieh. The children's eyes are full of flies and their heads are covered with sores, as at Minieh. In short, it is Minieh over again

on a larger scale; differing only in respect of its inhabitants, who, instead of being sullen, thievish, and
unfriendly, are too familiar to be pleasant, and the
most unappeasable beggars out of Ireland. So our
mirage turns to sordid reality, and Siout, which from
afar off looked like the capital of Dreamland, resolves
itself into a big mud town as ugly and ordinary as its
fellows. Even the minarets, so elegant from a distance,
betray for the most part but rough masonry and clumsy
ornamentation when closely looked into.

A lofty embanked road planted with fine sycamore-
figs leads from Hamra to Siout; and another embanked
road leads from Siout to the mountain of tombs. Of
the ancient Egyptian city no vestige remains, the
modern town being built upon the mounds of the
earlier settlement; but the City of the Dead—so much
of it, at least, as was excavated in the living rock—
survives, as at Memphis, to commemorate the departed
splendour of the place.

We took donkeys to the edge of the desert, and
went up to the sepulchres on foot. The mountain,
which looked a delicate salmon pink when seen from
afar, now showed bleached and arid and streaked with
ochreous yellow. Layer above layer, in beds of strongly
marked stratification, it towered overhead; tier above
tier, the tombs yawned, open-mouthed, along the face
of the precipice. I picked up a fragment of the rock,
and found it light, porous, and full of little cells, like
pumice. The slopes were strewn with such stones, as
well as with fragments of mummy, shreds of mummy-
cloth, and human bones all whitening and withering in
the sun.

The first tomb we came to was the so-called Stab

Antar—a magnificent but cruelly mutilated excavation, consisting of a grand entrance, a vaulted corridor, a great hall, two side-chambers and a sanctuary. The ceiling of the corridor, now smoke-blackened and defaced, has been richly decorated with intricate patterns in light green, white, and buff, upon a ground of dark bluish-green stucco. The wall to the right on entering is covered with a long hieroglyphed inscription. In the sanctuary, vague traces of seated figures, male and female, with lotus blossoms in their hands, are dimly visible. Two colossal warriors incised in outline upon the levelled rock — the one very perfect, the other hacked almost out of recognition—stand on each side of the huge portal. A circular hole in the threshold marks the spot where the great door once worked upon its pivot; and a deep pit, now partially filled in with rubbish, leads from the centre of the hall to some long-rifled vault deep down in the heart of the mountain. Wilful destruction has been at work on every side. The wall-sculptures are chipped and defaced—the massive pillars that once supported the superincumbent rock have been quarried away—the interior is heaped high with débris. Enough is left, however, to attest the antique stateliness of the tomb; and the hieroglyphed inscription remains almost intact to tell its age and history.

This inscription (erroneously entered in Murray's Guide as uncopied, but interpreted by Brugsch, who published extracts from it as far back as 1862,) shows the excavation to have been made for one Hepoukefa, governor of the Lycopolite Nome, and, according to Ampère's reading, Priest of the Upper Nile, under a Pharaoh of the XIIIth Dynasty. It is also famous

among scientific students for certain passages which
contain important information regarding the intercalary
days of the Egyptian kalendar.* We observed that
these hieroglyphs, as well as the full-length figures on
the jambs of the doorway, appeared to have been
incised, filled in with stucco, and then coloured. The
stucco had for the most part fallen out, though enough
remained to show the singular style of the work; of
which I do not remember to have seen any other
example.**

From this tomb to the next we crept by way of a
passage tunnelled in the mountain, and emerged into
a spacious, quadrangular grotto, even more dilapidated
than the first. It had been originally supported by
square pillars left standing in the substance of the
rock; but, like the pillars in the tomb of Hepoukefa,
they had been hewn away in the middle and looked
like stalactite columns in process of formation. For
the rest, two half-filled pits, a broken sarcophagus, and
a few painted hieroglyphs upon a space of stuccoed
wall, were all that remained.

One would have liked to see the sepulchre in
which Ampère, the brilliant and eager disciple of
Champollion, deciphered the ancient name of Siout;
but since he does not specify the cartouche by which
it could be identified, one might wander about the
mountain for a week without being able to find it.
Having first described the Stabl Antar, he says:—"In
another grotto I found twice over the name of the
city written in hieroglyphic characters, Çi-ou-t. This

* See *Recueil des Monuments Egyptiens*, Brugsch. Part I. Planche XI.
Published 1862.
** I am told that the hieroglyphs on the base of the Maydoum Pyramid are
treated in this way.

name forms part of an inscription which also contains an ancient royal cartouche; so proving that the present name of the city dates back to Pharaonic times."*

Here, then, we trace a double process of preservation. This town, which in the ancient Egyptian was written Ssout, became Lycopolis under the Greeks; continued to be called Lycopolis throughout the period of Roman rule in Egypt; reverted to its old historic name under the Copts of the middle ages, who wrote it Siôout; and survives in the Asyoot of the Arab fellah. Nor is this by any means a solitary instance, Khemmis in the same way became Panopolis, reverted to the Coptic Chmin, and to this day as Ekhmeem perpetuates the legend of its first foundation. As with these fragments of the old tongue, so with the race. Subdued again and again by invading hordes; inter mixed for centuries together with Phœnician, Persian, Greek, Roman, and Arab blood, it fuses these heterogeneous elements in one common mould, reverts persistently to the early type, and remains Egyptian to the last. So strange is the tyranny of natural forces. The sun and soil of Egypt demand one special breed of men, and will tolerate no other. Foreign residents cannot rear children in the country. In the Isthmus of Suez, which is considered the healthiest part of Egypt, an alien population of twenty thousand persons failed in the course of ten years to rear one infant born upon the soil. Children of an alien father and an Egyptian mother will die off in the same way in

* *Voyage en Egypte et en Nubie*, by J. J. Ampère. The cartouche may perhaps be that of *Rakameri*, mentioned by Brugsch: Histoire d'Egypte, chap. vi. First Edition.

early infancy, unless brought up in the simple native fashion. And it is affirmed of the descendants of mixed marriages that after the third generation the foreign blood seems to be eliminated, while the traits of the race are restored in their original purity.

These are but a few instances of the startling conservatism of Egypt—a conservatism that interested me particularly, and to which I shall frequently have occasion to return.

Each Nome, or county, of ancient Egypt had its sacred animal; and Siout was called Lycopolis by the Greeks* because the wolf (now almost extinct in the land) was there held in the same kind of reverence as the cat at Bubastis, the crocodile at Ombos, and the lion at Leontopolis. Mummy-wolves are, or used to be, found in the smaller tombs about the mountain, as well as mummy-jackals; Anubis, the jackal-headed god, being the presiding deity of the district. A mummied jackal from this place, curiously wrapped in striped bandages, is to be seen in the First Egyptian Room at the British Museum.

But the view from the mountain above Siout is finer than its tombs and more ancient than its mummies. Seen from within the great doorway of the second grotto, it looks like a framed picture. For the foreground, we have a dazzling slope of limestone débris; in the middle distance, a wide plain clothed with the delicious tender green of very young corn; farther away yet, the cupolas and minarets of Siout rising from the midst of a belt of palm-groves; beyond these again, the molten gold of the great river glittering

---

* The Greeks translated the sacred names of Egyptian places; the Copts adopted the civil names.

away, coil after coil, into the far distance; and all
along the horizon, the everlasting boundary of the
desert. Large pools of placid water left by the last
inundation lie here and there, like lakes amid the
green. A group of brown men are wading yonder
with their nets. A funeral comes along the embanked
road—the bier carried at a rapid pace on men's
shoulders, and covered with a red shawl; the women
taking up handfuls of dust and scattering it upon their
heads as they walk. We can see the dust flying, and
hear the shrill wail of the mourners borne upon the
breathless air. The cemetery towards which they are
going lies round to the left, at the foot of the mountain—
a wilderness of little white cupolas with here and there
a tree. Broad spaces of shade sleep under the spreading sycamores by the road-side; a hawk circles overhead; and Siout, bathed in the splendour of the morning sun, looks as fairy-like as ever.

Lepsius is reported to have said that the view from
this hill-side was the finest in Egypt. But Egypt is a
long country, and questions of precedence are delicate
matters to deal with. It is, however, a very beautiful
view; though most travellers who know the scenery
about Thebes and the approach to Assouan would
hesitate, I should fancy, to give the preference to a
landscape from which the nearer mountains are excluded by the position of the spectator.

The tombs here, as in many other parts of Egypt,
are said to have been largely appropriated by early
Christian anchorites during the reigns of the later
Roman Emperors; and to these recluses may perhaps
be ascribed the legend that makes Lycopolis the abode
of Joseph and Mary during the years of their sojourn

in Egypt. It is, of course, but a legend, and wholly improbable. If the Holy Family ever journeyed into Egypt at all, which certain Biblical critics now hold to be doubtful, they probably rested from their wanderings at some town not very far from the Eastern border —as Rameses, or Pithom, or Bubastis. Siout would, at all events, lie at least 250 miles to the southward of any point to which they might reasonably be supposed to have penetrated.

Still, one would like to believe a story that laid the scene of Our Lord's childhood in the midst of this beautiful and glowing Egyptian pastoral. With what a profound and touching interest it would invest the place! With what different eyes we should look down upon a landscape which must have been dear and familiar to Him in all its details, and which, from the nature of the ground, must have remained almost unchanged from His day to ours! The mountain with its tombs, the green corn-flats, the Nile and the desert, looked then as they look now. It is only the Moslem minarets that are new. It is only the pylons and sanctuaries of the ancient worship that have passed away.

CHAPTER VII.

Siout to Denderah.

WE started from Siout with a couple of tons of new brown bread on board, which, being cut into slices and laid to dry in the sun, was speedily converted into rusks and stored away in two huge lockers on the upper deck. The sparrows and water-wagtails had a good time while the drying went on; but no one seemed to grudge the toll they levied.

We often had a "big" wind now; though it seldom began to blow before ten or eleven A.M., and generally fell at sunset. Now and then, when it chanced to keep up, and the river was known to be free from shallows, we went on sailing through the night; but this seldom happened, and when it did happen, made sleep impossible—so that nothing but the certainty of doing a great many miles between bed-time and breakfast could induce us to put up with it.

We had now been long enough afloat to find out that we had almost always one man on the sick list, and were therefore habitually short of a hand for the navigation of the boat. There never were such fellows for knocking themselves to pieces as our sailors. They were always bruising their feet, wounding their hands, getting sunstrokes, and whitlows, and sprains, and disabling themselves in some way. L., with her little medicine chest and her roll of lint and bandages, soon had a small but steady practice, and might have been seen about the lower deck most mornings after breakfast, repairing these damaged Alis and Hassans. It was well for them that we carried "an experienced surgeon," for they were entirely helpless and despondent when hurt, and ignorant of the commonest remedies. Nor is this helplessness confined to natives of the sailor and fellah class. The provincial proprietors and officials are to the full as ignorant, not only of the uses of such simple things as poultices or wet compresses, but of the most elementary laws of health. Doctors there are none south of Cairo; and such is the general mistrust of state-medicine, that when, as in

10*

the case of any widely-spread epidemic, a medical officer is sent up the river by order of the government, half the people are said to conceal their sick, while the other half reject the remedies prescribed for them. Their trust in the skill of the passing European is, on the other hand, unbounded. Appeals for advice and medicine were constantly being made to us by both rich and poor; and there was something very pathetic in the simple faith with which they accepted any little help we were able to give them. Meanwhile L.'s medical reputation, being confirmed by a few simple cures, rose high among the crew. They called her the Hakeem Sitt (the Doctor-Lady); obeyed her directions and swallowed her medicines as reverently as if she were the College of Surgeons personified; and showed their gratitude in all kind of pretty, childlike ways—singing her favourite Arab song as they ran beside her donkey — searching for sculptured fragments whenever there were ruins to be visited—and constantly bringing her little gifts of pebbles and wild flowers.

Above Siout, the picturesqueness of the river is confined for the most part to the Eastern bank. We have almost always a near range of mountains on the Arabian side, and a more distant chain on the Libyan horizon. Gebel Sheykh el Raáineh succeeds to Gebel Aboofayda, and is followed in close succession by the cliffs of Gow, of Gebel Sheykh el Hereedee, of Gebel Ayserat and Gebel Tookh—all alike ridged in strongly-marked beds of level limestone strata; flat-topped and even, like lines of giant ramparts; and more or less pierced with orifices which we know to be tombs, but which look like loopholes from a distance.

Flying before the wind with both sails set, we see the rapid panorama unfold itself day after day, mile after mile, hour after hour. Villages, palm-groves, rock-cut sepulchres, flit past and are left behind. To-day we enter the region of the Dôm palm. To-morrow we pass the map-drawn limit of the crocodile. The cliffs advance, recede, open away into desolate-looking valleys, and show faint traces of paths leading to excavated tombs on distant heights. The headland that looked shadowy in the distance a couple of hours ago, is reached and passed. The cargo-boat on which we have been gaining all the morning is outstripped and dwindling in the rear. Now we pass a bold bluff sheltering a sheykh's tomb and a solitary Dôm palm— now an ancient quarry from which the stone has been cut in smooth masses, leaving great halls, and corridors, and stages, in the mountain side. At Gow,* the scene of an insurrection headed by a crazy Dervish some ten years ago, we see, in place of a large and populous village, only a tract of fertile corn-ground, a few ruined huts, and a group of decapitated palms. We are now skirting Gebel Sheykh Hereedee; here bordered by a rich margin of cultivated flat; yonder

---

* According to the account given in her Letters by Lady Duff Gordon, the Dervish, who had acquired a reputation for unusual sanctity by repeating the name of Allah 3000 times every night for three years, believed that he had by these means rendered himself invulnerable; and so, proclaiming himself the appointed Slayer of Antichrist, stirred up a revolt among the villages bordering Gebel Sheykh Hereedee; instigated an attack on an English dahabeeyah, and brought down upon himself and all that country-side the swift and summary vengeance of the government. Steamers with troops commanded by Fadl Pasha were despatched up the river: rebels were shot; villages sacked; crops and cattle confiscated. The women and children of the place were then distributed among the neighbouring hamlets; and Gow, which was as large a village as Luxor, ceased to exist. The Dervish's fate remained uncertain. He was shot, according to some; and by others it was said that he had escaped into the desert under the protection of a tribe of Bedouins.

leaving space for scarce a strip of roadway between
the precipice and the river. Then comes Raáineh, a
large village of square mud towers, lofty and battle-
mented, with string-courses of pots for the pigeons—
and later on, Girgeh, once the capital town of Middle
Egypt, where we put in for half-an-hour to post and
inquire for letters. Here the Nile is fast eating away
the bank and carrying the town by storm. A ruined
mosque with pointed arches, roofless cloisters, and a
leaning column that must surely have come to the
ground by this time, stands just above the landing-
place. A hundred years ago it lay a quarter of a mile
from the river; ten years ago it was yet perfect; after
a few more inundations, it will be swept away. Till
that time comes, however, it helps to make Girgeh one
of the most picturesque towns in Egypt.

At Farshoot we see the sugar-works in active
operation—smoke pouring from the tall chimneys;
steam issuing from the traps in the basement; cargo-
boats unlading fresh sugar-cane against the bank;
heavily-burdened Arabs transporting it to the factory;
bullock-trucks laden with cane-leaf for firing. A little
higher up, at Sahil Bajoora on the opposite side of the
river, we find the bank strewn for full a quarter of a
mile with sugar-cane *en masse.* Hundreds of camels
are either arriving laden with it, or going back for
more—dozens of cargo-boats are drawn up to receive
it—swarms of brown Fellaheen are stacking it on board
for unshipment again at Farshoot. The camels snort
and growl; the men shout; the overseers in blue-
fringed robes and white turbans, stalk to and fro, and
keep the work going. The mountains here recede so
far as to be almost out of sight, and a plain rich in

sugar-cane and date-palms widens out between them and the river.

And now the banks are lovely with an unwonted wealth of verdure. The young corn clothes the plain like a carpet; while the yellow-tasselled mimosa, the feathery tamarisk, the dôm and date palm, and the spreading sycamore-fig, border the towing-path like garden trees beside a garden walk.

Farther on still, when all this greenery is left behind and the banks have again become flat and bare, we see to our exceeding surprise what seems to be a very large grizzled ape perched on the top of a dust-heap on the western bank. The creature is evidently quite tame, and sits on its haunches in just that chilly, melancholy posture that the Chimpanzee is wont to assume in his cage at the Zoological Gardens. Some six or eight Arabs, one of whom has dismounted from his camel for the purpose, are standing round and staring at him, much as the British public stands and stares at the specimen in the Regent's Park. Meanwhile a strange excitement breaks out among our crew. They crowd to the side; they shout; they gesticulate; the captain salaams; the steersman waves his hand; all eyes are turned towards the shore.

"Do you see Sheykh Seleem?" cries Talhamy breathlessly, rushing up from below. "There he is! Look at him! That is Sheykh Seleem!"

And so we find out that it is not a monkey but a man—and not only a man, but a saint. Holiest of the holy, dirtiest of the dirty, white-pated, white-bearded, withered, bent, and knotted up, is the renowned Sheykh Seleem—he who, naked and unwashed, has sat on that same spot every day through summer heat and winter

cold for the last fifty years; never providing himself
with food or water; never even lifting his hand to his
mouth; depending on charity not only for his food but
for his feeding! He is not nice to look at, even by
this dim light and at this distance; but the sailors
think him quite beautiful, and call aloud to him for
his blessing as we go by.

"It is not by our own will that we sail past, O
father!" they cry. "Fain would we kiss thy hand; but
the wind blows and the mérkeb (boat) goes, and we
have no power to stay!"

But Sheykh Seleem neither lifts his head nor shows
any sign of hearing, and in a few minutes the mound
on which he sits is left behind in the gloaming.

At How, where the new town is partly built on
the mounds of the old (Diospolis Parva), we next
morning saw the natives transporting small boat-loads
of ancient brick-rubbish to the opposite side of the
river, for the purpose of manuring those fields from
which the early Doora crop had just been gathered in.
Thus, curiously enough, the mud left by some inundation of two or three thousand years ago comes at last
to the use from which it was then diverted, and is
found to be more fertilising than the new deposit. At
Kasr es Syad, a little farther on, we came to one of the
well-known "bad bits"—a place where the bed of the
river is full of sunken rocks, and sailing is impossible.
Here the men were half a day punting the dahabeeyah
over the dangerous part, while we grubbed among
the mounds of what was once the ancient city of
Chenoboscion. These remains, which cover a large
superficial area and consist entirely of crude brick
foundations, are very interesting and in good preserva-

tion. We traced the ground-plans of several houses; followed the passages by which they were separated; and observed many small arches which seemed built on too small a scale for doors or windows, but for which it was difficult to account in any other way. Brambles and weeds were growing in these deserted enclosures; while rubbish-heaps, excavated pits, and piles of broken pottery, divided the ruins and made the work of exploration difficult. We looked in vain for the dilapidated quay and sculptured blocks mentioned in Wilkinson's *General View of Egypt;* but if the foundation stones of the new sugar-factory close against the mooring-place could speak, they would no doubt explain the mystery. We saw nothing, indeed, to show that Chenoboscion had contained any stone structures whatever, save the broken shaft of one small granite column.

The village of Kasr es Syad consists of a cluster of mud huts and a sugar factory; but the factory was idle that day, and the village seemed half deserted. The view here is particularly fine. About a couple of miles to the southward, the mountains, in magnificent procession, come down again at right angles to the river, and thence reach away in long ranges of precipitous headlands. The plain, terminating abruptly against the foot of this gigantic barrier, opens back eastward to the remotest horizon—an undulating sea of glistening sand, bordered by a chaotic middle distance of mounded ruins. Nearest of all, a narrow foreground of cultivated soil, green with young crops and watered by frequent shadoofs, extends along the river-side to the foot of the mountains. A sheykh's tomb shaded by a single dôm palm is conspicuous

on the bank; while far away, planted amid the solitary sands, we see a large Coptic convent with many
cupolas; a cemetery full of Christian graves; and a
little oasis of date palms indicating the presence of a
spring.

The chief interest of this scene, however, centres
in the ruins; and these—looked upon from a little distance, blackened, desolate, half-buried, obscured every
now and then, when the wind swept over them, by
swirling clouds of dust—reminded us of the villages
we had seen not two years before, half-overwhelmed
and yet smoking, in the midst of a lava-torrent below
Vesuvius.

We now had the full moon again, making night
more beautiful than day. Sitting on deck for hours
after the sun had gone down, when the boat glided
gently on with half-filled sail and the force of the wind
was spent, we used to wonder if in all the world there
was another climate in which the effect of moonlight
was so magical. To say that every object far or near
was visible as distinctly as by day, yet more tenderly,
is to say nothing. It was not only form that was defined; it was not only light and shadow that were vivid
—it was colour that was present. Colour neither dead-
ened nor changed; but softened, glowing, spiritualised.
The amber sheen of the sand-island in the middle of
the river, the sober green of the palm-grove, the Little
Lady's turquoise-coloured hood, were clear to the sight
and relatively true in tone. The oranges showed through
the bars of the crate, like nuggets of pure gold. L.'s
crimson shawl glowed with a warmer dye than it ever
wore by day. The mountains were flushed as if in
the light of sunset. Of all the natural phenomena that

we beheld in the course of the journey, I remember none that surprised us more than this. We could scarcely believe at first that it was not some effect of afterglow, or some miraculous aurora of the East. But the sun had nothing to do with that flush upon the mountains. The glow was in the stone, and the moonlight but revealed the local colour.

For some days before they came in sight we had been eagerly looking for the Theban hills; and now, after a night of rapid sailing, we woke one morning to find the sun rising on the wrong side of the boat, the favourable wind dead against us, and a picturesque chain of broken peaks upon our starboard bow. By these signs we knew that we must have come to the great bend in the river between How and Keneh, and that these new mountains, so much more varied in form than those of Middle Egypt, must be the mountains behind Denderah. They seemed to lie upon the Eastern bank, but that was an illusion which the map disproved, and which lasted only till the great corner was fairly turned. To turn that corner, however, in the teeth of wind and current, was no easy task, and cost us two long days of hard tracking.

At a point about ten miles below Denderah, we saw some thousands of Fellaheen at work amid clouds of sand upon the embankments of a new canal. They swarmed over the mounds like ants, and the continuous murmur of their voices came to us across the river like the humming of innumerable bees. Others, following the path along the bank, were pouring towards the spot in an unbroken stream. The Nile must here be nearly half-a-mile in breadth; but the engineers in

European dress, and the overseers with long sticks in their hands, were plainly distinguishable by the help of a glass; while the tents in which these officials were camping out during the progress of the work gleamed white among the palms by the river-side. Such scenes must have been common enough in the old days when a conquering Pharaoh, returning from Libya or the land of Cush, set his captives to raise a dyke, or excavate a lake, or quarry a mountain. The Israelites, building the massive walls of Pithom and Rameses with bricks of their own making, must have presented exactly such a spectacle.

That we were witnessing a case of forced labour, could not be doubted. Those thousands yonder had most certainly been drafted off in gangs from hundreds of distant villages, and were but little better off, for the time being, than the captives of the ancient Empire. In all cases of forced labour under the present *régime*, however, it seems that the labourer is paid, though very insufficiently, for his unwilling toil; and that his captivity only lasts so long as the work for which he has been pressed remains in progress. In some cases the term of service is limited to three or four months, at the end of which time the men are supposed to be returned in barges towed by government steam-tugs. It too often happens, nevertheless, that the poor souls are left to get back how they can; and thus many a husband and father either perishes by the way, or is driven to take service in some village far from home. Meanwhile his wife and children, being scantily supported by the Sheykh el Beled, fall into a condition of semi-serfdom; and his little patch of ground, left untilled through seed-time and harvest, passes after the next inundation into the hands of a stranger.

But there is another side to this question of forced labour. Water must be had in Egypt, no matter at what cost. If the land is not sufficiently irrigated, the crops fail and the nation starves. Now the frequent construction of canals has from immemorial time been reckoned among the first duties of an Egyptian ruler; but it is a duty that cannot be performed without the willing or unwilling co-operation of several thousand workmen. Those who are best acquainted with the character and temper of the Fellah maintain the hopelessness of looking to him for voluntary labour of this description. Frugal, patient, easily contented as he is, no promise of wages, however high, would tempt him from his native village. What to him are the needs of a district six or seven hundred miles away? His own shadoof is enough for his own patch, and so long as he can raise his three little crops a year, neither he nor his family will starve. How, then, are these necessary public works to be carried out, unless by means of the *corvée?* M. About has put an ingenious summary of this "other-side" argument into the mouth of his ideal Fellah. "It is not the Emperor," says Ahmed to the Frenchman, "who causes the rain to descend upon your lands; it is the west wind—and the benefit thus conferred upon you exacts no penalty of manual labour. But in Egypt, where the rain from heaven falls scarcely three times in the year, it is the prince who supplies its place to us by distributing the waters of the Nile. This can only be done by the work of men's hands; and it is therefore to the interest of all that the hands of all should be at his disposal."

We regarded it, I think, as an especial piece of good fortune, when we found ourselves becalmed next day within three or four miles of Denderah. Abydos comes first in order according to the map; but then the Temples lie seven or eight miles from the river, and as we happened just thereabouts to be making some ten miles an hour, we put off the excursion till our return. Here, however, the ruins lay comparatively near at hand; and in such a position that we could approach them from below and rejoin our dahabeeyah a few miles higher up the river. So, leaving Reïs Hassan to track against the current, we landed at the first convenient point, and finding neither donkeys nor guides at hand, took an escort of three or four sailors, and set off on foot.

The way was long; the day was hot; and we had only the map to go by. Having climbed the steep bank and skirted an extensive palm-grove, we found ourselves in a country without paths or roads of any kind. The soil, squared off as usual like a gigantic chess-board, was traversed by hundreds of tiny water-channels, between which we had to steer our course as best we could. Presently the last belt of palms was passed—the plain, green with young corn and level as a lake, widened out to the foot of the mountains—and the Temple, islanded in that sea of rippling emerald, rose up before us upon its platform of blackened mounds.

It was still full two miles away; but it looked enormous—showing from this distance as a massive, low-browed, sharply-defined mass of dead-white masonry. The walls sloped in slightly towards the top; and the façade appeared to be supported on eight square piers,

with a large doorway in the centre. If sculptured ornament, or cornice, or pictured legend enriched those
walls, we were too far off to distinguish them. All
looked strangely naked and solemn—more like a tomb
than a temple.

Nor was the surrounding scene less deathlike in its
solitude. Not a tree, not a hut, not a living form,
broke the green monotony of the plain. Behind the
Temple, but divided from it by a farther space of
mounded ruins, rose the mountains—pinky, aerial, with
sheeny sand-drifts heaped in the hollows of their bare
buttresses, and spaces of soft blue shadow in their
misty chasms. Where the range receded, a long vista
of glittering desert opened to the Libyan horizon.

Then as we drew nearer, coming by and by to a
raised causeway which apparently connected the mounds
with some point down by the river, the details of the
Temple seemed gradually to emerge into distinctness.
We could now see the curve and under-shadow of the
cornice; and a small object in front of the façade that
had looked at first sight like a monolithic altar, resolved
itself into a massive gateway of the kind known as a
single pylon. Nearer still, among some low outlying
mounds, we came upon fragments of sculptured capitals
and mutilated statues half-buried in rank grass—upon
a series of stagnant nitre-tanks and deserted work-
shops—upon the telegraph-poles and wires that here
come striding along the edge of the desert and vanish
southward with messages for Nubia and the Soudan.

Egypt is the land of nitre. It is found wherever a
crude-brick mound is disturbed or an antique stone
structure demolished. The Nile mud is strongly im-
pregnated with it; and in Nubia we used to find it ly-

ing in thick talc-like flakes upon the surface of rocks
far above the present level of the inundation. These
tanks at Denderah had been sunk, we were told, when
the great Temple was excavated by Abbas Pasha more
than twenty years ago. The nitre then found was uti-
lised out of hand; washed and crystallised in the tanks;
and converted into gunpowder in the adjacent work-
shops. The telegraph wires are more recent intruders,
and the work of the Khedive; but one longed to put
them out of sight, and pull down the gunpowder sheds,
and fill up the tanks again with débris. For what had
the arts of modern warfare or the wonders of modern
science to do with Hathor, the Lady of Beauty and
the Western Shades, the Nurse of Horus, the Egyptian
Aphrodite, to whom yonder mountain of wrought stone
and all these wastes were sacred?

We were by this time near enough to see that the
square piers of the façade were neither square nor
piers, but huge round columns with human-headed
capitals; and that the walls, instead of being plain
and tomb-like, were covered with an infinite multitude
of sculptured figures. The pylon—rich with inscriptions and bas-reliefs, but disfigured by myriads of tiny
wasps' nests, like clustered mud-bubbles—now towered
high above our heads, and led to a walled avenue cut
direct through the mounds, and sloping downwards to
the main entrance of the Temple.

Not, however, till we stood immediately under those
ponderous columns, looking down upon the paved floor
below and up to the huge cornice that projected overhead like the crest of an impending wave, did we realise the immense proportions of the building. Lofty as
it looked from a distance, we now found that it was

only the interior that had been excavated, and that not more than two-thirds of its actual height were visible above the mounds. The level of the avenue was, indeed, at its lowest part full twenty feet above that of the first great hall; and we had still a steep temporary staircase to go down before reaching the original pavement.

The effect of the portico as one stands at the top of this staircase is of overwhelming majesty. Its breadth, its height, the massiveness of its parts, exceed in grandeur all that one has been anticipating throughout the long two miles of approach. The immense girth of the columns, the huge screens that connect them, the ponderous cornice jutting overhead, confuse the imagination, and in the absence of given measurements * appear, perhaps, even more enormous than they are. Looking up to the architrave, we see a sort of Egyptian Panathenaic procession of carven priests and warriors, some with standards and some with musical instruments. The winged globe, depicted upon a gigantic scale in the curve of the cornice, seems to hover above the central doorway. Hieroglyphs, emblems, strange forms of Kings and Gods, cover every foot of wall-space, frieze, and pillar. Nor does this wealth of surface-sculpture tend in any way to diminish the general effect of size. It would seem, on the contrary, as if complex decoration were in this instance the natural complement to simplicity of form. Every group, every inscription, appears to be necessary

---

* Sir G. Wilkinson states the total length of the Temple to be 93 paces, or 220 feet; and the width of the portico fifty paces. Murray gives no measurements: neither does Mariette Bey in his delightful little "Itineraire"; neither does Fergusson, nor Champollion, nor any other writer to whose works I have had access.

and in its place; an essential part of the building it helps to adorn. Most of these details are as perfect as on the day when the last workman went his way, and the architect saw his design completed. Time has neither marred the surface of the stone nor blunted the work of the chisel. Such injury as they have sustained is from the hand of man; and in no country has the hand of man achieved more and destroyed more than in Egypt. The Persians overthrew the masterpieces of the Pharaohs; the Copts mutilated the temples of the Ptolemies and Cæsars; the Arabs stripped the pyramids and carried Memphis away piecemeal. Here at Denderah we have an example of Græco-Egyptian work and early Christian fanaticism. Begun by the last of the Ptolemies * and bearing upon its latest ovals the name and style of Nero, the present building was still comparatively new when, in A.D. 379, the ancient religion was abolished under the edict of Theodosius. It was then the most gorgeous as well as the most recent of all those larger temples built during the prosperous foreign rule of the last seven hundred years. It stood, surrounded by groves of palm and acacia, within the precincts of the vast enclosure, the walls of which, 1000 feet in length, 35 feet in height, and 15 feet thick, are still traceable. A dromos, now buried under twenty feet of débris, led from the pylon to the portico. The pylon is there still, a partial ruin; and the Temple, with its roof, its staircases, and its secret treasure-crypts, is in all essential respects as perfect as on the day when its splendour was given

---

* The names of Augustus, Caligula, Tiberius, Domitian, Claudius, and Nero are found in the royal ovals; the oldest of all being those of Cleopatra and her son Ptolemy Cæsarion.

over to the spoilers. One can easily imagine how these spoilers sacked and ravaged all before them; how they desecrated the sacred places, and cast down the statues of the Goddess, and divided the treasures of the sanctuary. They did not, it is true, commit such wholesale destruction as the Persian invaders of nine hundred years before; but they were merciless iconoclasts, and hacked away the face of every figure within easy reach both inside and outside the building.

Among those that escaped, however, is the famous external bas-relief of Cleopatra on the back of the Temple. This curious sculpture is now banked up with rubbish for its better preservation, and can no longer be seen by travellers. It was, however, admirably photographed some two or three years ago by Signor Beati, and represents Cleopatra crowned with a headdress that combines the attributes of three goddesses; namely, the Vulture of Maut (the head of which is modelled in a masterly way), the horned disc of Hathor, and the throne of Isis. Her hair, falling in long masses below the headdress, is subdivided according to Egyptian fashion, into an infinite number of small plaits, each finished off with an ornamental tag. The women of Egypt and Nubia wear their hair so to this day, and unplait it, I am sorry to say, not oftener than once in every eight or ten weeks. The Nubian girls fasten each separate tail with a lump of Nile mud daubed over with yellow ochre; but Queen Cleopatra's silken tresses were probably tipped with gilded wax or gum.

It is difficult to know where decorative sculpture ends and portraiture begins in a work of this epoch. We cannot even be certain that a portrait was in-

tended; though the introduction of the royal oval in
which the name of Cleopatra (Klaupatra) is spelt with
its vowel sounds in full, would seem to point that way.
Mannerism apart, however, the face wants for neither
individuality nor beauty. The profile is almost faultless, and the chin and throat are lovely; while the whole
face, suggestive of cruelty, subtlety, and voluptuousness,
carries with it an undefinable impression not only of
portraiture, but of likeness.

It is not without something like a shock that one
first sees the unsightly havoc wrought upon the Hathor-
headed columns of the façade at Denderah. The
massive folds of the head-gear are there; the ears,
erect and pointed like those of a heifer, are there; but
of the benignant face of the Goddess not a feature
remains. Ampère, describing these columns in one of
his earliest letters from Egypt, speaks of them as being
still "brilliant with colours that time had had no power
to efface." Time, however, must have been unusually
busy during the thirty years that have gone by since
then; for though we presently found several instances
of painted bas-reliefs in the small inner chambers, I
do not remember to have observed any remains of
colour (save here and there a faint trace of yellow
ochre) on the external decorations.

Without, all was sunshine and splendour; within,
all was silence and mystery. A heavy, death-like smell,
as of long-imprisoned gases, met us on the threshold.
By the half-light that strayed in through the portico,
we could see vague outlines of a forest of giant
columns rising out of the gloom below and vanishing
into the gloom above. Beyond these again appeared
shadowy vistas of successive halls leading away into

depths of impenetrable darkness. It required no great courage to go down those stairs and explore those depths with a party of fellow-travellers; but it would have been a gruesome place to venture into alone.

Seen from within, the portico shows as a vast hall fifty feet in height and supported on twenty-four Hathor-headed columns. Six of these, being engaged in the screen, form part of the façade, and are the same upon which we have been looking from without. By degrees, as our eyes become used to the twilight, we see here and there a capital that still preserves the vague like-ness of a gigantic female face; while, dimly visible on every wall, pillar, and doorway, a multitude of fantastic forms—hawk-headed, ibis-headed, cow-headed, mitred, plumed, holding aloft strange emblems, seated on thrones, performing mysterious rites—seem to emerge from their places, like things of life. Looking up to the ceiling, now smoke-blackened and defaced, we discover elaborate paintings of scarabæi, winged globes, and zodiacal emblems divided by borders of intricate Greek patterns, the prevailing colours of which are verditer and chocolate. Bands of hieroglyphic inscrip-tions, of royal ovals, of Hathor heads, of mitred hawks, of lion-headed chimeras, of divinities and kings in bas-relief, cover the shafts of the great columns from top to bottom; and even here, every accessible human face, however small, has been laboriously mutilated.

Bewildered at first sight of these profuse and mys-terious decorations, we wander round and round; going on from the first hall to the second, from the second to the third; and plunging into deeper darkness at every step. We have been reading about these gods and emblems for weeks past—we have studied the plan of the Temple beforehand; yet now that we are actually here, our book-knowledge goes for nothing, and we feel as hopelessly ignorant as if we had been suddenly landed in a new world. Not till we have got over this first feeling of confusion—not till, resting awhile on the base of one of the columns, we re-read M. Mariette's exposition of the plan of the building and the character of the cerémonies intended to be performed within its walls, do we begin to realise the purport of the sculptures by which we are surrounded.

The ceremonial of Egyptian worship was essentially processional. Herein we have the central idea of every Temple, and the key to its construction. It was bound to contain store-chambers in which were kept vestments, instruments, divine emblems, and the like; laboratories for the preparations of perfumes and unguents; treasuries for the safe custody of holy vessels and precious offerings; chambers for the reception and purification of tribute in kind; halls for the assembling and marshalling of priests and functionaries; and, for processional purposes, corridors, staircases, courtyards, cloisters, and vast enclosures planted with avenues of trees and surrounded by walls which hedged in with inviolable secrecy the solemn rites of the priesthood.

In this plan, it will be seen, there is no provision made for anything in the form of public worship: but then an Egyptian Temple was not a place for public worship. It was, according to the learned and accurate definition of M. Mariette, a treasure-house; a sacristy; a royal oratory; a place of preparation, of consecration, of sacerdotal privacy. There, in costly shrines, dwelt the divine images. There they were robed and un-

robed; perfumed with incense; visited and worshipped
by the King. On certain great days of the kalendar,
as on the occasion of the festival of the new year, or
the panegyries of the local gods, these images were
brought out, paraded along the corridors of the temple,
carried round the roof, and borne with waving of banners, and chanting of hymns, and burning of incense,
through the sacred groves of the enclosure. To these
ceremonies none were admitted save those of royal or
priestly birth; while to the rest of the community, all
that took place within those massy walls was enveloped
in mystery. It may be questioned, indeed, whether
the great mass of the people had any kind of personal
religion. They were rigidly excluded from the temples
and their precincts, and they seem to have been
allowed no participation in the worship of the Gods.
If now and then, on high festival days, they caught a
far-off glimpse of moving figures and glittering ensigns
upon the summit of some isolated sanctuary, it was
all they ever beheld of the solemn services of their
church.

The Temple of Denderah consists of a portico; a
hall of entrance; a hall of assembly; a third hall, which
may be called the hall of the sacred boats; one small
ground-floor chapel; and upwards of twenty side-chambers of various sizes, most of which are totally dark.
Each one of these halls and chambers bears the sculptured record of its use. Hundreds of tableaux in bas-
relief, thousands of elaborate hieroglyphic inscriptions
cover every foot of available space on wall and ceiling
and soffit, on doorway and column, and on the lining-
slabs of passages and staircases. These precious texts
contain, amid much that is mystical and tedious, an

extraordinary wealth of indirect history. Here we find
programmes of ceremonial observances; numberless
legends of the Gods; chronologies of Kings with their
various titles; registers of weights and measures; cata-
logues of offerings; recipes for the preparation of oils
and essences; records of repairs and restorations done
to ·the Temple; geographical lists of cities and pro-
vinces; inventories of treasure, and the like. The hall
of assembly contains a kalendar of festivals, and sets
forth with studied precision the rites to be performed
on each recurring anniversary. On the ceiling of the
portico we find an astronomical zodiac; on the walls
of a small temple on the roof, the whole history of the
resurrection of Osiris, together with the order of prayer
for the twelve hours of the night, and a kalendar of
the festivals of Osiris in all the principal cities of
Upper and Lower Egypt. Fifty years ago, these inscriptions were the puzzle and despair of the learned;[*]
but since modern science has plucked out the heart
of their mystery, the whole Temple lies before us as
an open volume filled to overflowing with strange and
quaint and heterogeneous matter——a Talmud in sculptured stone.

Given such help as M. Mariette's little book affords,
one can trace out most of these curious things, and
identify the uses of every hall and chamber throughout
the building. We went to the sculptures as children
to a picture-book; and though we had not yet learned
to read, we made out the story well enough from the
illustrations.

---

[*] Some of the most interesting of these inscriptions are given in the learned
works of Brugsch and Duemichen, *Recueil de monuments Egyptiens* and
Geographische Inschriften, 1862-3-5-6.

The King, in his double character of Pharaoh and high priest, is always the hero. Wearing sometimes the truncated crown of Lower Egypt, sometimes the helmet-crown of Upper Egypt, and sometimes the pschent, which is a combination of both, he figures in every tableau and heads every procession. Beginning with the sculptures of the portico, we see him arrive, preceded by his five royal standards. He wears his long robe; his sandals are on his feet; he carries his staff in his hand. Two goddesses receive him at the door and conduct him into the presence of Thoth, the ibis-headed, and Horus, the hawk-headed, who pour upon him a double stream of the waters of life. Thus purified, he is crowned by the goddesses of Upper and Lower Egypt, and by them consigned to the local deities of Thebes and Heliopolis, who usher him into the supreme presence of Hathor. He then presents various offerings and recites certain prayers; whereupon the goddess promises him length of days, everlasting renown, and other good things. We next see him, always with the same smile and always in the same attitude, doing homage to Osiris, to Horus, and other divinities. He presents them with flowers, wine, bread, incense; while they in return promise him life, joy, abundant harvests, victory, and the love of his people. These pretty speeches, chefs d'œuvre of diplomatic style and models of elegant flattery, are repeated over and over again in scores of hieroglyphic groups. M. Mariette, however, sees in them something more than the language of the court grafted upon the language of the hierarchy; he detects the language of the schools, and discovers in the utterances here ascribed to the King and the Gods a reflection of that

contemporary worship of the Beautiful, the Good, and
the True, which characterised the teaching of the
Alexandrian Museum.*

Passing on from the portico to the Hall of Assembly, we enter a region of still dimmer twilight, beyond which all is dark. In the side-chambers, where
the heat is intense and the atmosphere stifling, we can
see only by the help of lighted candles. These rooms
are about twenty feet in length; separate like prison
cells; and perfectly dark. The sculptures that cover
their walls are, however, as numerous as those in the
outer halls, and indicate in each instance the purpose
for which the room was designed. Thus in the laboratories we find bas-reliefs of flasks and vases, and
figures carrying perfume-bottles of the familiar aryballos
form—in the tribute-chambers, offerings of lotus-lilies,
wheat-sheaves, maize, grapes, and pomegranates—in
the oratories of Isis, Osiris, and Pasht, representations
of these divinities enthroned, and receiving the homage
of the King—while in the treasury both King and
Queen appear laden with precious gifts of caskets,
necklaces, pectoral ornaments, sistrums, and the like.

---

* Hathor (or more correctly Hat-hor, *i.e.*, the abode of Horus), is not
merely the Aphrodite of ancient Egypt: she is the pupil of the eye of the Sun;
she is the goddess of that beneficent planet whose rising heralds the waters of
the inundation; she represents the eternal youth of nature, and is the direct
personification of the Beautiful. She is also Goddess of Truth. "I offer the
Truth to thee, O Goddess of Denderah!" says the King, in one of the inscriptions of the sanctuary of the Sistrum; "for truth is thy work, and thou thyself
art Truth." Lastly, her emblem is the Sistrum, and the sound of the Sistrum,
according to Plutarch, was supposed to terrify and expel Typhon (the evil
principle); just as in mediæval times the ringing of church-bells was supposed
to scare Beelzebub and his crew. From this point of view, the Sistrum becomes typical of the triumph of Good over Evil. M. Mariette, in his analysis
of the decorations and inscriptions of this temple, points out how the builders
were influenced by the prevailing philosophy of the age, and how they veiled
the Platonism of Alexandria beneath the symbolism of the ancient religion.
The Hat-hor of Denderah was in fact worshipped in a sense unknown to the
Egyptians of pre-Ptolemaic times.

It would seem that the image-breakers had no time to spare for these dark cells; for here the faces and figures are unmutilated, and in some places even the original colouring remains in excellent preservation. The complexion of the goddesses, for instance, is painted of a light buff; the King's skin is dark-red; that of Osiris, blue. Isis wears a rich robe of the well-known Indian pine-pattern; Pasht figures in a many-coloured garment curiously diapered; Osiris is clad in a red and green chain armour. The skirts of the goddesses are inconceivably scant; but they are rich in jewellery, and their headdresses, necklaces, and bracelets are full of minute and interesting detail. In one of the four oratories dedicated to Pasht, the King is depicted in the act of offering a pectoral ornament of so rich and elegant a design that had there been time and daylight to spare, the Writer would fain have copied it.

In the centre room at the extreme end of the Temple, exactly opposite the main entrance, lies the oratory of Hathor. This dark chamber into which no ray of daylight has ever penetrated contains the sacred niche, the Holy of Holies, in which was kept the great Golden Sistrum of the Goddess. The King alone was privileged to take out that mysterious emblem. Having done so, he enclosed it in a costly shrine, covered it with a thick veil, and placed it in one of the sacred boats of which we find elaborate representations sculptured on the walls of the hall in which they were kept. These boats, which were constructed of cedar-wood, gold, and silver, were intended to be hoisted on wrought poles, and so carried in procession on the shoulders of the priests. The niche is still there—a mere hole in the wall, some three feet square and about eight feet from the ground.

Thus, candle in hand, we make the circuit of these outer chambers. In each doorway, besides the place cut out for the bolt, we find a circular hole drilled above and a quadrant-shaped hollow below, where once upon a time the pivot of the door turned in its socket. The paved floors, torn up by treasure-seekers, are full of treacherous holes and blocks of broken stone. The ceilings are very lofty. In the corridors a dim twilight reigns; but all is pitch-dark beyond these gloomy thresholds. Hurrying along by the light of a few flaring candles, one cannot but feel oppressed by the strangeness and awfulness of the place. We speak with bated breath; and even our chattering Arabs for once are silent. The very air tastes as if it had been imprisoned here for centuries.

Finally, we take the staircase on the northern side of the Temple, in order to go up to the roof. Nothing that we have yet seen surprises and delights us so much, I think, as this staircase.

We have hitherto been tracing in their order all the preparations for a great religious ceremony. We have seen the King enter the Temple; undergo the symbolical purification; receive the twofold crown; and say his prayers to each divinity in turn. We have followed him into the laboratories, the oratories, and the holy of holies. All that he has yet done, however, is preliminary. The procession is yet to come, and here we have it. Here, sculptured on the walls of this dark staircase, the crowning ceremony of Egyptian worship is brought before our eyes in all its details. Here, one by one, we have the standard-bearers, the hierophants with the offerings, the priests, the whole long, wonderful procession, with the King marching at its head. Fresh and uninjured as if they had but just left the hand of the sculptor, these figures—each in his habit as he moved, each with his foot upon the step —mount with us as we mount, and go beside us all the way. Their attitudes are so natural, their forms so roundly cut, that one could almost fancy them in motion as the lights flicker by. Surely there must be some one weird night in the year when they step out from their places, and take up the next verse of their chanted hymn, and, to the sound of instruments long mute and songs long silent, pace the moonlit roof in ghostly order!

The sun is already down and the crimson light has faded, when at length we emerge upon that vast terrace. The roofing-stones are gigantic. Striding to and fro over some of the biggest, our Idle Man finds several that measure seven paces in length by four in breadth. In yonder distant corner, like a little stone lodge in a vast courtyard, stands a small temple supported on Hathor-headed columns; while at the Eastern end, forming a second and loftier stage, rises the roof of the portico.

Meanwhile the afterglow is fading. The mountains are yet clothed in an atmosphere of tender half-light; but mysterious shadows are fast creeping over the plain, and the mounds of the ancient city lie at our feet, confused and tumbled, like the waves of a dark sea. How high it is here—how lonely—how silent! Hark that thin plaintive cry! It is the wail of a night-wandering jackal. See how dark it is yonder, in the direction of the river! Quick, quick! We have lingered

too long. We must begone at once; for we are already
benighted.

We ought to have gone down by way of the opposite staircase (which is lined with sculptures of the
descending procession) and out through the Temple;
but there is no time to do anything but scramble down
by a breach in the wall at a point where the mounds
yet lie heaped against the south side of the building.
And now the dusk steals on so rapidly that before we
reach the bottom we can hardly see where to tread.
The huge side-wall of the portico seems to tower above
us to the very heavens. We catch a glimpse of two
colossal figures, one lion-headed and the other headless, sitting outside with their backs to the Temple.
Then, making with all speed for the open plain, we
clamber over scattered blocks and among shapeless
mounds. Presently night overtakes us. The mountains disappear; the Temple is blotted out; we have
only the faint starlight to guide us. We stumble on,
however, keeping all close together; firing a gun every
now and then, in the hope of being heard by those in
the boats; and as thoroughly and undeniably lost as
the Babes in the Wood.

At last, just as some are beginning to knock up
and all to despair, Talhamy fires his last cartridge.
An answering shot replies from near by; a wandering
light appears in the distance; and presently a whole
bevy of dancing lanterns and friendly brown faces
comes gleaming out from among a plantation of sugar-
canes, to welcome and guide us home. Dear, sturdy,
faithful little Reïs Hassan, honest Khaleefeh, laughing
Salame, gentle Mehemet Ali, and Moosa "black but
comely"—they were all there. What a shaking of

hands there was—what a gleaming of white teeth—
what a shower of mutually unintelligible congratula-
tions! For my own part, I may say with truth that I
was never much more rejoiced at a meeting in my
life.

CHAPTER VIII.
Thebes and Karnak.

COMING on deck the third morning after leaving
Denderah, we found the Dahabeeyah decorated with
palm-branches, our sailors in their holiday turbans,
and Reïs Hassan *en grande tenue;* that is to say in
shoes and stockings, which he only wore on very great
occasions.

"Naharik-said—good morning—Luxor!" said he,
all in one breath.

It was a hot, hazy morning, with dim ghosts of
mountains glowing through the mist, and a warm wind
blowing.

We ran to the side; looked out eagerly; but could
see nothing. Still the Captain smiled and nodded;
and the sailors ran hither and thither, sweeping and
garnishing; and Egendi, to whom his worst enemy
could not have imputed the charge of bashfulness,
said "Luxor—haroof*—all right!" every time he came
near us.

We had read and dreamed so much about Thebes,
and it had always seemed so far away, that but for
this delicate allusion to the promised sheep, we could
hardly have believed we were really drawing nigh unto
those famous shores. About ten, however, the mist

* *Arabic*, haroof—*English*, sheep.

was lifted away like a curtain, and we saw to the left
a rich plain studded with palm-groves; to the right a
broad margin of cultivated lands bounded by a bold
range of limestone mountains; and on the farthest
horizon another range, all grey and shadowy.

"Karnak — Goornah — Luxor!" says Reïs Hassan
triumphàntly, pointing in every direction at once.
Talhamy tries to show us Medinet Haboo and the
Memnonium. The Painter vows he can see the heads
of the sitting Colossi and the entrance to the Valley
of the Tombs of the Kings.

We, meanwhile, stare bewildered, incredulous; seeing none of these things; finding it difficult indeed, to
believe that any one else sees them. The river widens
away before us; the flats are green on either side; the
mountains are pierced with terraces of rock-cut tombs;
while far away inland, apparently on the verge of the
desert, we see here a clump of sycamores—yonder a
dark hillock—midway between both a confused heap
of something that may be either fallen rock or fallen
masonry; but nothing that looks like a Temple, nothing
to indicate that we are already within recognisable
distance of the grandest ruins in the world.

Presently, however, as the boat goes on, a massive,
windowless structure which looks (Heaven preserve us!)
just like a brand-new fort or prison, towers up above
the palm-groves to the left. This, we are told, is one
of the propylons of Karnak; while a few whitewashed
huts and a little crowd of masts now coming into
sight a mile or so higher up, mark the position of
Luxor. Then up capers Egendi with his never-failing
"Luxor—haroof—all right!" to fetch down the tar
and darrabooka. The captain claps his hands. A

circle is formed on the lower deck. The men, all
smiles, strike up their liveliest chorus, and so, with
barbaric music and well-filled sails, and flags flying,
and green boughs waving overhead, we make our
triumphal entry into Luxor.

The top of another pylon; the slender peak of an
obelisk; a colonnade of giant pillars half-buried in the
soil; the white houses of the English, American, and
Prussian Consuls, each with its flagstaff and ensign; a
steep slope of sandy shore; a background of mud walls
and pigeon-towers; a foreground of native boats and
gaily-painted Dahabeeyahs lying at anchor—such, as
we sweep by, is our first panoramic view of this
famous village. A group of turbaned officials sitting
in the shade of an arched doorway rise and salute us
as we pass. The assembled Dahabeeyahs dozing with
folded sails, like sea-birds asleep, are roused to
spasmodic activity. Flags are lowered; guns are fired;
all Luxor is startled from its midday siesta. Then,
before the smoke has had time to clear off, up comes
the Bagstones in gallant form; whereupon the Dahabeeyahs blaze away again as before.

And now there is a rush of donkeys and donkey-
boys, beggars, guides, and antiquity-dealers, to the
shore — the children screaming for backsheesh; the
dealers exhibiting strings of imitation scarabs; the
donkey-boys vociferating the names and praises of
their beasts; all alike regarding us as their lawful
prey.

"Hi, lady! Yankee-Doodle donkey; try Yankee-
Doodle!" cries one.

"Far-away Moses!" yells another. "Good donkey
—fast donkey—best donkey in Luxor!"

"This Prince of Wales's donkey!" shouts a third, hauling forward a decrepit little weak-kneed, moth-eaten looking animal, about as good to ride upon as a towel-horse. "First-rate donkey! splendid donkey! God save the Queen! Hurrah!"

But neither donkeys nor scarabs are of any importance in our eyes just now, compared with the letters we hope to find awaiting us on shore. No sooner, therefore, are the boats made fast than we are all off, some to the British Consulate and some to the Poste Restante, from both of which we return rich and happy.

Meanwhile we proposed to spend only twenty-four hours in Luxor. We were to ride round Karnak this first afternoon; to cross to Medinet Haboo and the Ramesseum* to-morrow morning; and to sail again as soon after midday as possible. We hoped thus to get a general idea of the topography of Thebes, and to carry away a superficial impression of the architectural style of the Pharaohs. It would be but a glimpse; yet that glimpse was essential. For Thebes represents the great central period of Egyptian art. The earlier styles lead up to that point; the later depart from it; and neither the earlier nor the later are intelligible without it. At the same time, however, travellers bound for the Second Cataract do well to put off everything like a detailed study of Thebes till the time of coming back. For the present, a rapid survey of the three principal groups of ruins is enough. It

---

* This famous building is supposed by some to be identical both with the Memnonium of Strabo and the Tomb of Osymandias as described by Diodorus Siculus. Champollion, however, following the sense of the hieroglyphed legends, in which it is styled "The House of Rameses" (the Second), has given to it the more appropriate name of the Ramesseum,

supplies the necessary link. It helps one to a right understanding of Edfou, of Philæ, of Aboo Simbel. In a word, it enables one to put things in their right places; and this, after all, is a mental process which every traveller must perform for himself.

Thebes, I need scarcely say, was built, like London, on both sides of the river. Its original extent must have been very great; but its public buildings, its quays, its hundred gates, and its thousands of private dwellings, are gone and have left no trace. The secular city, which was built of crude brick, has disappeared; while of the sacred edifices, five large groups of limestone ruins—three on the Western bank and two on the Eastern, together with the remains of several small temples and a vast multitude of tombs—are all that remain in permanent evidence of its ancient splendour. Luxor is a modern Arab village occupying the site of one of the oldest of these five ruins. It stands on the Eastern bank, close against the river, about two miles south of Karnak, and nearly opposite the famous sitting Colossi of the Western plain. On the opposite bank lie Goornah, the Ramesseum, and Medinet Haboo. The Temple of Goornah is almost *vis-à-vis* of Karnak. The Ramesseum faces about half-way between Karnak and Luxor. Medinet Haboo is placed farther to the South than any building on the Eastern side of the river. Behind these three Western groups, reaching far and wide along the edge of the Libyan range, lies the great Theban Necropolis; while farther back still, in the radiating valleys on the other side of the mountains, are found the Tombs of the Kings. The distance between Karnak and Luxor is a little less than two miles;

12*

while from Medinet Haboo to the Temple of Goornah
may be roughly guessed at something under four.
We have here, therefore, some indication of the extent, though not of the limits, of the ancient city.

Luxor is a large village inhabited by a mixed
population of Copts and Arabs, and doing a smart trade
in antiquities. The temple has here formed the nucleus
of the village, the older part of which has grown up in
and about the ruins. The grand entrance faces North,
looking down towards Karnak. The twin towers of the
great propylon, dilapidated as they are, stripped of
their cornices, encumbered with débris, are magnificent
still. In front of them, one on each side of the central
gateway, sit two helmeted colossi, battered, and feature-
less, and buried to the chin, like two of the Proud in
the doleful Fifth Circle. A few yards in front of these
again stands a solitary obelisk, also half-buried. The
colossi are of black granite; the obelisk is of red,
highly polished, and covered on all four sides with
superb hieroglyphs in three vertical columns. These
hieroglyphs are engraved with the precision of the
finest gem. They are cut to a depth of about two
inches in the outer columns, and five inches in the
central column of the inscription. The true height of
this wonderful monolith is over seventy feet, between
thirty and forty of which are hidden under the accumulated soil of many centuries. Its companion
obelisk, already scaling away by imperceptible degrees
under the skyey influences of an alien climate, looks
down with melancholy indifference upon the petty re-
volutions and counter-revolutions of the Place de la
Concorde. On a line with the two black colossi, but
some fifty feet or so farther to the West, rises a third

and rather smaller head of chert or limestone, the fellow to which is doubtless hidden among the huts that encroach half-way across the face of the eastern tower. The whole outer surface of these towers is covered with elaborate sculptures of gods and men, horses and chariots, the pageantry of triumph and the carnage of war. The King in his chariot draws his terrible bow, or slays his enemies on foot, or sits enthroned, receiving the homage of his court. Whole regiments armed with lance and shield march across the scene. The foe flies in disorder. The King, attended by his fan-bearers, returns in state, and the priests burn incense before him.

This king is Rameses the Second, called Sesostris and Osymandias by ancient writers, and best known to history as Rameses the Great. His actual names and titles as they stand upon the monuments are Ra-user-ma Setp-en-Ra Ra-messou Mer-Amen; that is to say, "Sun strong in Truth, Approved of the Sun, Son of the Sun, Beloved of Ammon."

The battle-scenes here represented relate to that memorable campaign against the Khetas which forms the subject of the famous Third Sallier Papyrus,* and is commemorated upon the walls of almost every temple built by this monarch. Separated from his army and surrounded by the enemy, the King, attended only by his chariot-driver, is said to have six times charged the foe—to have hewn them down with his sword of might—to have trampled them like straw beneath his horses' feet—to have dispersed them single-handed, like a God.

---

* Translated into French by the late Vicomte de Rougé under the title of *Le Poëme de Pentaour*, 1856; into English by Mr. Goodwin, 1858; and again by Professor Lushington in 1874. See *Records of the Past*, vol. II.

Two thousand five hundred chariots were there, and he overthrew them; one hundred thousand warriors, and he scattered them. Those that he slew not with his hand, he chased unto the water's edge, causing them to leap to destruction as leaps the crocodile. Such was the immortal feat of Rameses, and such the chronicle written by the Royal Scribe, Pentaour.

Setting aside the strain of Homeric exaggeration that runs through this narrative, there can be no doubt that it records some brilliant deed of arms actually performed by the King within sight, though not within reach, of his army. The hieroglyphic texts interspersed among these tableaux state that the events depicted took place on the fifth day of the month Epiphi, in the fifth year of his reign. If, therefore, as it appears from an inscription* found at Dakkeh in Nubia, Rameses II. came to the throne at about ten years of age, "while yet he wore the plaited sidelock," he can scarcely have been more than fifteen at the time of his great exploit.

More sculptures and many precious inscriptions are doubtless hidden on the lower part of these towers, some twenty or thirty feet below the present level of the ground.

The mutilated colossi are portrait statues of the conqueror. The obelisk, in the pompous style of Egyptian dedications, proclaims that "The Lord of the World, Guardian-Sun of Truth, approved of Phra, has built

---

* It is, however, by no means certain that the data given in this inscription are correct. A great obscurity, which the latest researches tend rather to increase than to diminish, overhangs everything connected with the childhood and accession of Rameses II. According to records discovered within the last three or four years at Abydos, he would seem to have been in some sense King from his birth; as if the right to the throne of Egypt came to him through his mother, and as if his father, Seti I., had reigned for him during his infancy as King-Regent. Some of the inscriptions of Abydos, indeed, show him to have received homage even *before* his birth.

this edifice in honour of his Father Ammon-Ra, and has erected to him these two great obelisks of stone in face of the house of Rameses in the City of Ammon."

So stately was the approach made by Rameses the Great to the temple founded about a hundred and fifty years before by Amenhotep III. He built also the courtyard upon which this pylon opened, joining it to the older part of the building in such wise that the original first court became now the second court, while next in order came the portico, the hall of assembly, and the sanctuary. By and by, when the long line of Rameses had passed away, other and later kings put their hands to the work. The names of Sabaco, of Ptolemy Philopater, and of Alexander the Younger, appear among the later inscriptions; while those of Amenhotep IV. (Khoo-en-Aten), Horus, and Seti, the father of Rameses the Great, are found in the earlier parts of the building. It was in this way that an Egyptian temple grew from age to age, owing a colonnade to this King and a pylon to that, till it came in time to represent the styles of many periods. Hence, too, that frequent irregularity of plan which, unless it could be ascribed to the caprices of successive builders, would form so unaccountable a feature in Egyptian architecture. In the present instance, the pylon and courtyard of Rameses II. are set at an angle of five degrees to the courtyard and sanctuary of Amenhotep III. This has evidently been done to bring the temple of Luxor into a line with the temple of Karnak, in order that the two might be connected by means of that stupendous avenue of sphinxes, the scattered remains of which yet strew the course of the ancient roadway.

As I have already said, these half-buried pylons

this solitary obelisk, those giant heads rising in ghastly
resurrection before the gates of the temple, are magnificent still. But it is as the magnificence of a splendid
prologue to a poem of which only garbled fragments
remain. Beyond that entrance lies a smoky, filthy, intricate labyrinth of lanes and passages. Mud hovels,
mud pigeon-towers, mud yards, and a mud mosque,
cluster like wasps' nests in and about the ruins. Architraves sculptured with royal titles support the roofs of
squalid cabins. Stately capitals peep out from the midst
of sheds in which buffaloes, camels, donkeys, dogs, and
human beings herd together in unsavoury fellowship.
Cocks crow, hens cackle, pigeons coo, turkeys gobble,
children swarm, women bake and gossip, and all the
sordid routine of Arab life goes on amid winding
alleys that mask the colonnades and deface the inscriptions of the Pharaohs. To trace the plan of this
part of the building is now impossible; while to
excavate it would involve the demolition of half the
village.

All communication being now cut off between the
courts and the portico, one has to go round outside
and through a door at the farther end of the Temple,
in order to reach the sanctuary and the adjoining
chambers. The Arab who keeps the key provides an
inch or two of candle. For it is very dark in here;
the roof being still perfect, with a large, rambling,
modern house built on the top of it—so that if this
part of the Temple was ever partially lighted, as at
Denderah and elsewhere, by small wedge-like openings in the roof, even those faint gleams are now excluded.

The sanctuary, which was rebuilt in the reign of

Alexander Ægus; some small side chambers; and a large hall, which was perhaps the hall of assembly, are all that remain under cover of the original roofing-stones. Some half-buried and broken columns, however, on the side next the river, show that this end was surrounded by a colonnade. The sanctuary—an oblong granite chamber with its own separate roof—stands enclosed in a larger hall, like a box within a box, and is covered inside and outside with bas-reliefs. These sculptures (among which I observed a curious kneeling figure of the king, offering a kneeling image to Ammon Ra) are executed in the mediocre style of the Ptolemies. That is to say, the forms are more natural but less refined than those of the Pharaonic period. The limbs are fleshy, the joints large, the features insignificant. Of actual portraiture one cannot detect a trace; while every face wears the objectionable smirk of a fashion-book beauty.

In the large hall, however, which I have called the hall of assembly, one is carried back to the time of the founder. Between Amenhotep III. and Alexander Ægus there lies a great gulf of 1200 years; and their styles are as widely separated as their reigns. The merest novice could not possibly mistake the one for the other. Nothing is, of course, more common than to find Egyptian and Græco-Egyptian work side by side in the same temple; but nowhere are the distinctive characteristics of each brought into stronger contrast than in these dark chambers of Luxor. In the sculptures that line the hall of Amenhotep we find the pure lines, the severe and slender forms, the characteristic heads, of a period when the art, having as yet neither gained nor lost by foreign influences, was entirely Egyptian. The subjects

relate chiefly to the infancy of the king; but it is difficult to see anything properly by the light of a candle
tied to the end of a stick; and here, where the bas-
relief is so low and the walls are so high, it is almost
impossible to distinguish the details of the upper
tableaux.

I could make out, however, that Ammon Ra, Maut,
and their son Khonsu, the three personages of the
Theban triad, are the presiding deities of these scenes;
and that they are in some way identified with the fortunes of Thothmes IV., his queen, and their son Amenhotep III. Amenhotep is born, apparently, under the
especial protection of Maut, the Divine Mother; brought
up with the youthful god Khonsu; and received by
Ammon Ra as the brother and equal of his own divine
son. I think it was in this hall that I observed a singular group representing Ammon Ra and Maut in an
attitude symbolical perhaps of troth-plight, or marriage.
They sit face to face, the goddess holding in her right
hand the left hand of the god, while in her left hand
she supports his right elbow. Their thrones, meanwhile,
rest on the heads, and their feet are upheld on the hands,
of two female genii. It is significant that Rameses III.
and one of the symbolical goddesses of Hades are depicted in the same attitude in one of the famous subjects sculptured on the upper storeys of the Pavilion at
Medinet Haboo.

We saw this interesting Temple much too cursorily;
yet gave more time to it than the majority of those
who year after year anchor for days together close under
its majestic columns. If the whole building could be
transported bodily to some point between Memphis and
Siout where the river is bare of ruins, it would be

enthusiastically visited. Here it is eclipsed by the wonders of Karnak and the western bank, and gets undeservedly neglected. Those parts of the original building which yet remain are, indeed, peculiarly precious; for Amenhotep (or Amunoph) the Third was one of the great builder-kings of Egypt, and we have here one of the few extant specimens of his architectural work.

The Coptic quarter of Luxor lies north of the great pylon, and partly skirts the river. It is cleaner, wider, more airy than that of the Arabs. The Prussian Consul is a Copt; the polite postmaster is a Copt; and in a modest lodging built half beside and half over the Coptic church lives the Coptic Bishop. The postmaster (an ungainly youth in a European suit so many sizes too small that his arms and legs appeared to be sprouting out at the ends of his garments) was profuse in his offers of service. He undertook to forward letters to us at Assouan, Korosko, and Wady Halfah, where post-offices had lately been established. And he kept his promise, I am bound to say, with perfect punctuality;—always adding some queer little complimentary message on the outer wrapper, such as "I hope you well my compliments;" or "Wishes you good news pleasant voyage." As a specimen of his literary style I copied the following notice, of which it was evident that he was justly proud:—

"NOTICE: On the commandation, We have ordered the post stations in lower Egypt from Assiut to Cartoom. Belonging to the Post Kedevy Egyptian in a good order. Now to pay for letters in lower Egypt is as in upper Egypt twice. Means that the letters which goes from here far than Asiut; must pay for it two piastres per ten grs. Also that which goes far than Cartoom. The letters which goes between Asiut and Cartoom; must pay only one piastre per ten grs. This and that is, to buy stamps from the Post and put it upon the letter. Also if somebody wishes to send letters insuranced, must pay two piastres more for any letter. There is orderation in the Post to receive the letters which goes to Europe, America and Asia, as England, France, Italy, Germany, Syria, Constantinople etc. Also to send newspapers patterns and other things. Luxor the 1st January 1874. *L'Ispettore*, M. ADDA."

This young man begged for a little stationery and a pen-knife at parting. We had, of course, much pleasure in presenting him with such a modest testimonial. We afterwards learned that he levied the same little tribute on every Dahabeeyah that came up the river; so I conclude that he must by this time have quite an interesting collection of small cutlery.

From the point where the railroad ends, the Egyptian and Nubian mails are carried by runners stationed at distances of four miles all along the route. Each man runs his four miles, and at the end thereof finds the next man ready to snatch up his bag and start off at full speed immediately. The next man transfers it in like manner to the next; and so it goes by day and night without a break, till it reaches the first railway station. Each runner is supposed to do his four miles in half an hour, and the mail which goes out every morning from Luxor reaches Cairo in six days. Considering that Cairo was 450 miles away; that 268 miles of this distance had to be done on foot; and that the trains went only once a day, we thought this a very creditable speed.

In the afternoon we took donkeys, and rode out to Karnak. Our way lay through the bazaar, which was the poorest we had yet seen. It consisted of only a few open sheds, in one of which, seated on a mud-built divan, cross-legged and turbanless like a row of tumbler mandarins, we saw five of our sailors under the hands of the Luxor barber. He had just lathered all five heads, and was complacently surveying the effect of his work, much as an artistic cook might survey a dish of particularly successful méringues à la crême. The méringues looked very sheepish when we laughed and passed by.

Next came the straggling suburb where the dancing girls most do congregate. These damsels, in gaudy garments of emerald green, bright rose, and flaming yellow, were squatting outside their cabins or lounging unveiled about the thresholds of two or three dismal dens of cafés in the market-place. They showed their teeth, and laughed familiarly in our faces. Their eyebrows were painted to meet on the bridge of the nose; their eyes were blackened round with kohl; their cheeks were extravagantly rouged; their hair was gummed, and greased, and festooned upon their foreheads, and plaited all over in innumerable tails. Never before had we seen anything in female form so hideous. One of these houris was black; and she looked quite beautiful in her blackness, compared with the painting and plastering of her companions.

We now left the village behind, and rode out across a wide plain, barren and hillocky in some parts; overgrown in others with coarse halfeh grass; and dotted here and there with clumps of palms. The Nile lay low and out of sight, so that the valley seemed to

stretch away uninterruptedly to the mountains on both
sides. Now leaving to the left a Sheykh's tomb, topped
by a little cupola and shaded by a group of tamarisks;
now following the bed of a dry watercourse; now skirting shapeless mounds that indicated the site of ruins
unexplored, the road, uneven but direct, led straight to
Karnak. At every rise in the ground we saw the huge
propylons towering higher above the palms. Once, but
for only a few moments, there came into sight a confused and wide-spread mass of ruins, as extensive,
apparently, as the ruins of a large town. Then our
way dipped into a sandy groove bordered by mud-walls
and plantations of dwarf-palms. All at once this groove
widened, became a stately avenue guarded by a double
file of shattered sphinxes, and led towards a lofty pylon
standing up alone against the sky.

Close beside this grand gateway, as if growing there
on purpose, rose a thicket of sycamores and palms;
while beyond it were seen the twin pylons of a Temple.
The sphinxes were colossal, and measured about ten
feet in length. One or two were ram-headed. Of the
rest—some forty or fifty in number—all were headless,
some split asunder, some overturned, others so mutilated
that they looked like torrent-worn boulders. This avenue
once reached from Luxor to Karnak. Taking into account the distance (which is just two miles from Temple
to Temple) and the short intervals at which the sphinxes
are placed, there cannot originally have been fewer than
five hundred of them; that is to say two hundred and
fifty on each side of the road.

Dismounting for a few minutes, we went into the
Temple; glanced round the open courtyard with its
colonnade of pillars; peeped hurriedly into some ruinous

side-chambers; and then rode on. Our books told us that we had seen the small Temple of Rameses the Third. It would have been called large anywhere but at Karnak.

I seem to remember the rest as if it had all happened in a dream. Leaving the Temple, we turned towards the river, skirted the mud-walls of the native village, and approached the Great Temple by way of its main entrance. Here we entered upon what had once been another great avenue of sphinxes, ram-headed, couchant on plinths deep cut with hieroglyphic. legends, and leading up from some grand landing-place beside the Nile.

And now the towers that we had first seen as we sailed by in the morning rose straight before us, magnificent in ruin, glittering to the sun, and relieved in creamy light against blue depths of sky. One was nearly perfect; the other, shattered as if by the shock of an earthquake, was still so lofty that an Arab clambering from block to block midway of its vast height looked no bigger than a squirrel.

On the threshold of this tremendous portal we again dismounted. Shapeless crude-brick mounds, marking the limits of the ancient wall of circuit, reached far away on either side. An immense perspective of pillars and pylons leading up to a very distant obelisk opened out before us. We went in, the great walls towering up like cliffs above our heads, and entered the First Court. Here, in the midst of a large quadrangle open to the sky, stands a solitary column, the last of a central avenue of twelve, some of which, disjointed by the shock, lie just as they fell, like skeletons of vertebrate monsters left stranded by the Flood.

Crossing this Court in the glowing sunlight, we came to a mighty doorway between two more propylons —the doorway splendid with coloured bas-reliefs; the propylons mere cataracts of fallen blocks piled up to right and left in grand confusion. The cornice of the doorway is gone. Only a jutting fragment of the lintel stone remains. That stone, when perfect, measured forty feet and ten inches across. The doorway must have been full a hundred feet in height.

We went on. Leaving to the right a mutilated colossus engraven on arm and breast with the cartouche of Rameses II., we crossed the shade upon the threshold, and passed into the famous Hypostyle Hall of Seti the First.

It is a place that has been much written about and often painted; but of which no writing and no art can convey more than a dwarfed and pallid impression. To describe it, in the sense of building up a recognisable image by means of words, is impossible. The scale is too vast; the effect too tremendous; the sense of one's own dumbness, and littleness, and incapacity, too complete and crushing. It is a place that strikes you into silence; that empties you, as it were, not only of words but of ideas. Nor is this a first effect only. Later in the year, when we came back down the river and moored close by, and spent long days among the ruins, I found I never had a word to say in the Great Hall. Others might measure the girth of those tremendous columns; others might climb hither and thither, and find out points of view, and test the accuracy of Wilkinson and Zincke; but I could only look, and be silent.

Yet to look is something, if one can but succeed in remembering; and the Great Hall of Karnak is photographed in some dark corner of my brain for as long as I have memory. I shut my eyes, and see it as if I were there—not all at once, as in a picture; but bit by bit, as the eye takes note of large objects and travels over an extended field of vision. I stand once more among those mighty columns which radiate into avenues from whatever point one takes them. I see them swathed in coiled shadows and broad bands of light. I see them sculptured and painted with shapes of Gods and Kings, with blazonings of royal names, with sacrificial altars, and forms of sacred beasts, and emblems of wisdom and truth. The shafts of these columns are enormous. I stand at the foot of one—or of what seems to be the foot; for the original pavement lies buried seven feet below. Six men standing with extended arms, finger-tip to finger-tip, could barely span it round. It casts a shadow twelve feet in breadth—such a shadow as might be cast by a tower. The capital that juts out so high above my head looks as if it might have been placed there to support the heavens. It is carved in the semblance of a full-blown lotus, and glows with undying colours—colours that are still fresh, though laid on by hands that have been dust these three thousand years and more. It would take not six men, but a dozen to measure round the curved lip of that stupendous lily.

Such are the twelve central columns. The rest (one hundred and twenty-two in number) are gigantic too; but smaller. Of the roof they once supported, only the beams remain. Those beams are stones — huge monoliths * carved and painted, that bridge the space

* The size of these stones not being given in any of our books, I paced the length of one of the shadows, and (allowing for so much more at each end as

from pillar to pillar, and pattern the trodden soil with
bands of shadow.

Looking up and down the central avenue, we see
at the one end a flame-like obelisk; at the other, a
solitary palm against a background of glowing mountain.
To right, to left, showing transversely through long files
of columns, we catch glimpses of colossal bas-reliefs
lining the roofless walls in every direction. The King,
as usual, figures in every group, and performs the
customary acts of worship. The Gods receive and ap-
prove him. Half in light, half in shadow, these slender,
fantastic forms stand out sharp, and clear, and colour-
less; each figure some eighteen or twenty feet in
height. They could scarcely have looked more weird
when the great roof was in its place and perpetual
twilight reigned. But it is difficult to imagine the roof
on, and the sky shut out. It all looks right as it is;
and one feels, somehow, that such columns should have
nothing between them and the infinite blue depths
of heaven.

The great central avenue was, however, sufficiently
lighted by means of a double row of clerestory windows,
some of which are yet standing. Certain writers have
suggested that they may have been glazed; but this
seems improbable, for two reasons. Firstly, because
one or two of these huge window-frames yet contain
the solid stone gratings which in the present instance

would be needed to reach to the centres of the two capitals on which it rested)
found the block above must measure at least 25 feet in length. The measurements of the Great Hall are, in plain figures, 170 feet in length by 329 in
breadth. It contains 134 columns, of which the central twelve stand 62 feet
high in the shaft (or about 70 with the plinth and abacus), and measure 34 feet
6 inches in circumference. The smaller columns stand 42 feet 5 inches in the
shaft, and measure 28 feet in circumference. All are buried to a depth of between six or seven feet in the alluvial deposits of between three and four thousand annual inundations.

seem to have done duty for a translucent material: and, secondly, because we have no evidence to show that the early Egyptians, though familiar since the days of Cheops with the use of the blow-pipe, ever made glass in sheets, or introduced it in this way into their buildings.

How often has it been written, and how often must it be repeated, that the Great Hall at Karnak is the noblest architectural work ever designed and executed by human hands? One writer tells us that it covers four times the area occupied by the Cathedral of Notre Dame in Paris. Another measures it against St. Peter's. All admit their inability to describe it; yet all attempt the description. To convey a concrete image of the place to one who has not seen it, is however, as I have already said, impossible. If it could be likened to this place or that, the task would not be so difficult; but there is, in truth, no building in the wide world to compare with it. The Pyramids are more stupendous. The Colosseum covers more ground. The Parthenon is more beautiful. Yet in nobility of conception, in vastness of detail, in majestic beauty of the highest order, the Hall of Pillars exceeds them every one. This doorway, these columns, are the wonder of the world. How was that lintel-stone raised? How were those capitals lifted? Entering among those mighty pillars, says a recent observer, "you feel that you have shrunk to the dimensions and feebleness of a fly." But I think you feel more than that. You are stupified by the thought of the mighty men who made them. You say to yourself:—"There were indeed giants in those days."

It may be that the traveller who finds himself for

13*

the first time in the midst of a grove of *Wellingtonia gigantea* feels something of the same overwhelming sense of awe and wonder; but the great trees, though they have taken three thousand years to grow, lack the pathos and the mystery that comes of human labour. They do not strike their roots through six thousand years of history. They have not been watered with the blood and tears of millions.* Their leaves know no sounds less musical than the singing of birds, or the moaning of the night-wind as it sweeps over the highlands of Calaveros. But every breath that wanders down the painted aisles of Karnak seems to echo back the sighs of those who perished in the quarry, at the oar, and under the chariot-wheels of the conqueror.

The Hypostyle Hall, though built by Seti, the father of Rameses II., is supposed by some Egyptologists to have been planned, if not begun, by that same Amen-hotep III. who founded the Temple of Luxor and set up the famous Colossi of the Plain. However this may be, the cartouches so lavishly sculptured on pillar and architrave contain no names but those of Seti, who undoubtedly executed the work *en bloc*, and of Rameses, who completed it.

And now would it not be strange if we knew the name and history of the architect who superintended the building of this wondrous Hall, and planned the huge doorway by which it was entered, and the mighty pylons that lie shattered on either side? Would it not be interesting to look upon his portrait, and see what manner of man he was? Well, the Egyptian room in the Glyptothek Museum at Munich contains a

---

* It has been calculated that every stone of these huge Pharaonic temples cost at least one human life.

statue found nearly sixty years ago at Thebes, which almost certainly represents that man, and is inscribed with his history. His name was Bak-en-Khonsu. He sits upon the ground, bearded, robed, and in an attitude of meditation. That he was a man of unusual ability is shown by the inscriptions engraved upon the back of the statue. These inscriptions record his promotion step by step to the highest grade of the hierarchy. Having attained the dignity of High Priest and First Prophet of Ammon during the reign of Seti the First, he became Chief Architect of the Thebaid under Rameses II., and received a royal commission to superintend the embellishment of the Temples. When Rameses II. "erected a monument to his Divine Father Ammon Ra," the building thereof was executed under the direction of Bak-en-Khonsu. Here the inscription, as translated by M. Deveria, goes on to say that "he made the sacred edifice in the upper gate of the Abode of Ammon.* He erected obelisks of granite. He made golden flagstaffs. He added very, very great colonnades."

M. Deveria suggests that the temple of Goornah may here be indicated; but to this it might be objected that Goornah is situated in the lower, and not the upper part of Thebes; that at Goornah there are no great colonnades and no obelisks; and that, moreover, for some reason at present unknown to us, the erection of obelisks seems to have been confined to the Eastern bank of the Nile. It is, however, possible that the works here enumerated may not all have been executed

* *i.e. Per Amen*, or *Pa-Amen;*—the ancient name of Thebes, which was the city especially dedicated to Ammon. It was also written *Api*, or *Abpi*, or *Apetou*, by some ascribed to an Indo-Germanic root signifying Abode.

for one and the same Temple. The "sacred edifice in the upper gate of the Abode of Ammon" might be the Temple of Luxor, which Rameses did in fact adorn with the only obelisks we know to be his in Thebes; the monument erected by him to his Divine Father Ammon (evidently a new structure) would scarcely be any other than the Ramesseum; while the "very, very great colonnades," which are expressly specified as additions, would seem as if they could only belong to the Hypostyle Hall of Karnak. The question is at all events interesting; and it is pleasant to believe that in the Munich statue we have not only a portrait of one who at Karnak played the part of Michael Angelo to some foregone and forgotten Bramante, but who was also the Ictinus of the Ramesseum. For the Ramesseum is the Parthenon of Thebes.

The sun was sinking and the shadows were lengthening when, having made the round of the principal ruins, we at length mounted our donkeys and turned towards Luxor. To describe all that we saw after leaving the Great Hall would fill a chapter. Huge obelisks of shining granite—some yet erect, some shattered and prostrate; vast lengths of sculptured walls covered with wondrous battle subjects, sacerdotal processions, and elaborate chronicles of the deeds of Kings; ruined courtyards surrounded by files of headless statues; a sanctuary* built all of polished granite, and

* M. Alphonse Mariette's excellent translation of his brother's *Itinéraire* (*Monuments of Upper Egypt*: London: Trübner & Co. Alexandria and Cairo, Mourès, 1877) contains some new and valuable matter on Karnak, and the best small plan of the ruins yet given to the public. Apropos of the granite Sanctuary, the following is noteworthy as being the latest utterance of M. Mariette's opinion: "It is a mistake to consider the granite chamber as the actual sanctuary of the great temple of Karnak. The sanctuary of the great temple was anterior to Philip, anterior even to Thothmes; it ranked among the oldest

engraven like a gem; a second Hall of Pillars dating
back to the early days of Thothmes the Third; labyrinths of roofless chambers; mutilated colossi, shattered
pylons, fallen columns, unintelligible foundations and
hieroglyphic inscriptions without end, were glanced at,
passed by, and succeeded by fresh wonders. I dare
not say how many small outlying temples we saw in
the course of that rapid survey. In one place we came
upon an undulating tract of coarse halfeh grass, in the
midst of which, battered, defaced, forlorn, sat a weird
company of green granite Sphinxes and lioness-headed
Pashts. In another, we saw a magnificent colossal
hawk upright on his pedestal in the midst of a bergfall
of ruins. More avenues of Sphinxes, more pylons,
more colossi were passed before the road we took in
returning brought us round to that by which we had
come. By the time we reached the Sheyhk's tomb, it
was nearly dusk. We rode back across the plain,
silent and bewildered. Have I not said that it was
like a dream?

edifices in Egypt, since it dated from the second King of the XIIth dynasty.
It was built of sandstone, and stood in the centre of the large court to the East.
Its renown, its antiquity, and probably also its riches, had the effect of attract-
ing more than any other part of the temple, the attention of every conqueror
who invaded Thebes, and it has disappeared to its very foundations. With
the exception of two or three shafts of shattered columns, on which may still
be traced the legend of Usurtasen 1. nothing remains to recall its memory."
Monuments of Upper Egypt. p. 177.

CHAPTER IX.

Thebes to Assouan.

HURRYING close upon the serenest of Egyptian sunsets came a night of storms. The wind got up about ten. By midnight, the river was racing in great waves and our Dahabeeyah rolling at her moorings like a ship at sea. The sand, driving in furious gusts from the Lybian desert, dashed like hail against our cabin windows. Every moment we were either bumping against the bank, or being rammed by our own felucca. At length, a little before dawn, a huge slice of the bank gave way, thundering like an avalanche upon our decks; whereupon Reïs Hassan, being alarmed for the safety of the boat, hauled us up to a little sheltered nook a few hundred yards higher. Taking it altogether, we had not had such a lively night since leaving Benisouef.

The look-out next morning was dismal—the river running high in yeasty waves; the boats all huddled together under the shore; the Western bank hidden in clouds of sand. To get under way was impossible, for the wind was dead against us; and to go anywhere by land was equally out of the question. Karnak in a sandstorm would have been grand to see; but one would have needed a diving helmet to preserve eyes and ears from destruction.

Towards afternoon, the fury of the wind so far subsided that we were able to cross the river and ride to Medinet Haboo and the Ramesseum. As we achieved only a passing glimpse of these wonderful ruins, I will for the present say nothing about them. We came to know them so well hereafter that no mere first impression would be worth record.

A light but fitful breeze helped us on next day as far as Erment, the Ptolemaic Hermonthis; once the site of a goodly temple, now of an important sugar-factory. Here we moored for the night, and after dinner received a visit of ceremony from the Bey —a tall, slender, sharp-featured, bright-eyed man in European dress, remarkably dignified and well bred—who came attended by his secretary, Kawass, and pipe-bearer. Now the Bey of Erment is a great personage in these parts. He is governor of the town and province, as well as superintendent of the sugar-factory; holds a military command; has his palace and gardens close by, and his private steamer on the river; and is, like most high officials in Egypt, a Turk of distinction. The secretary, who was the Bey's younger brother, wore a brown Inverness cape over a long white petticoat, and left his slippers at the saloon-door. He sat all the time with his toes curiously doubled under, so that his feet looked like clenched fists in stockings. Both gentlemen wore the tarboosh, or fez; and each carried a visiting cane. The visiting cane, by the way, plays a conspicuous part in modern Egyptian life. It measures about two and a half feet in length, is tipped at both ends with gold or silver, and is supposed to add the last touch of elegance to the bearer.

We entertained our guests with coffee and lemonade, and, as well as we could, with conversation. The Bey, who spoke only Turkish and Arabic, gave a flourishing account of the sugar-works, and despatched his pipe-bearer for a bundle of fresh canes and some specimens of raw and candied sugars. He said he had an English foreman and several English workmen, and that for the English as a nation he had the highest admiration and regard; but that the Arabs "had no heads." To our inquiries about the ruins, his replies were sufficiently discouraging. Of the large Temple every vestige had long since disappeared; while of the smaller one only a few columns and part of the walls were yet standing. They lay out beyond the town and a long way from the river. There was very little to see. It was all "soghéer" (small); "moosh-taïb" (bad); not worth the trouble of the walk. As for "antichi," they were rarely found here, and when found were of slight value.

A scarab which he wore in a ring was then passed round and admired. It fell to our Little Lady's turn to examine it last, and restore it to the owner. But the owner, with a bow and a deprecating gesture, would have none of it. The ring was a toy—a nothing—the lady's—his no longer. She was obliged to accept it, however unwillingly. To decline would have been to offend. But it was the way in which the thing was done that made the charm of this little incident. The grace, the readiness, the courtesy, the lofty indifference of it, were alike admirable. Macready in his best days could have done it with as princely an air; but even he would probably have missed something of the Oriental reticence of the Bey of Erment.

He then invited us to go over the sugar-factory (which we declined on account of the lateness of the hour), and presently took his leave. About ten minutes after, came a whole posse of presents—three large bouquets of roses for the Sittàt (ladies), two scarabæi,

a small funereal statuette in the rare green porcelain,
and a live turkey. We in return sent a complicated
English knife with all sorts of blades, and some pots
of English jam.

The wind rose next morning with the sun, and by
breakfast-time we had left Erment far behind. All
that day the good breeze served us well. The river
was alive with cargo-boats. The Philæ put on her
best speed. The little Bagstones kept up gallantly.
And the Fostat, a large iron Dahabeeyah full of
English gentlemen, kept us close company all the
afternoon. We were all alike bound for Esneh, which
is a large trading town, and lies twenty-six miles
South of Erment.

Now at Esneh the men were to bake again. Great,
therefore, was Reïs Hassan's anxiety to get in first,
secure the oven, and buy the flour before dusk. The
Reïs of the 'Fostat' and he of the 'Bagstones' were
equally anxious, and for the same reasons. Our men,
meanwhile, were wild with excitement, watching every
manœuvre of the other boats; hanging on to the shoghool like a swarm of bees; and obeying the word of
command with unwonted alacrity. As we neared the
goal, the race grew hotter. The honour of the boats
was at stake, and the bread question was for the moment
forgotten. Finally all three Dahabeeyahs ran in abreast,
and moored side by side in front of a row of little
open cafés just outside the town.

Esneh (of which the old Egyptian civil name was
Sni, and the Roman name Latopolis) stands high upon
the mounds of the ancient city. It is a large place—
as large, apparently, as Minieh; and, like Minieh, is
the capital of a province. Here dragomans lay in pro-

vision of limes, charcoal, flour, and live stock, for the Nubian journey; and crews bake for the last time before their return to Egypt. For in Nubia food is scarce, and prices are high, and there are no public ovens.

It was about five o'clock on a market-day when we reached Esneh, and the market was not yet over. Going up through the usual labyrinth of windowless mud-alleys where the old men crouched, smoking, under every bit of sunny wall, and the children swarmed like flies, and the cry for backsheesh buzzed incessantly about our ears, we came to an open space in the upper part of the town, and found ourselves all at once in the midst of the market. Here were peasant folk selling farm-produce; stall-keepers displaying combs, looking-glasses, gaudy printed handkerchiefs and cheap bracelets of bone and coloured glass; camels lying at ease and snarling at every passer by; patient donkeys; ownerless dogs; veiled women; blue and black-robed men; and all the common sights and sounds of a native market. Here, too, we found Reïs Hassan bargaining for flour; Talhamy haggling with a charcoal-dealer; the M. B.'s buying turkeys and geese for themselves and a huge store of tobacco for their crew. Most welcome sight of all, however, was a dingy chemist's shop about the size of a sentry-box, over the door of which was suspended an Arabic inscription; while inside, robed all in black, sat a lean and grizzled Arab, from whom we bought a big bottle of rose water to make eye-lotion for L.'s ophthalmic patients.

Meanwhile there was a Temple to be seen at Esneh; and this Temple, as we had been told, was to be found close against the market-place. We looked round in vain, however, for any sign of pylon or portico. The chemist said it was "kureiyib," which means "near by." A camel-driver pointed to a dilapidated wooden gateway in a recess between two neighbouring houses. A small boy volunteered to lead the way. We were greatly puzzled. We had expected to see the Temple towering above the surrounding houses, as at Luxor, and could by no means understand how any large building to which that gateway might give access, should not be visible from without.

The boy, however, ran and thumped upon the gate, and shouted "Abbas! Abbas!" Mehemet Ali, who was doing escort, added some thundering blows with his staff; a little crowd gathered; but no Abbas came.

The bystanders, as usual, were liberal with their advice; recommending the boy to climb over, and the sailor to knock louder, and suggesting that Abbas the absent might possibly be found in a certain neighbouring café. At length I somewhat impatiently expressed my opinion that there was "Mafeesh Birbeh" (no Temple at all); whereupon a dozen voices were raised to assure me that the Birbeh was no myth— that it was "kebeer" (big)—that it was "kwy-ees" (beautiful)—and that all the "Ingleez" came to see it.

In the midst of the clamour, however, and just as we are about to turn away in despair, the gate creaks open; the gentlemen of the Fostat troop out in puggeries and knickerbockers; and we are at last admitted.

This is what we see—a little yard surrounded by

mud-walls; at the farther end of the yard a dilapidated
doorway; beyond the doorway, a strange-looking stu-
pendous·mass of yellow limestone masonry, long, and
low, and level, and enormously massive. A few steps
farther, and this proves to be the curved cornice of a
mighty Temple—a Temple neither ruined nor defaced,
but buried to the chin in the accumulated rubbish of
a score of centuries. This part is evidently the portico.
We stand close under a row of huge capitals. The
columns that support them are buried beneath our
feet. The ponderous cornice juts out above our heads.
From the level on which we stand to the top of that
cornice may measure about twenty-five feet. A high
mud-wall runs parallel to the whole width of the
façade, leaving a passage of about twelve feet in
breadth between the two. A low mud-parapet and a
hand-rail reach from capital to capital. All beyond
is vague, cavernous, mysterious—a great shadowy gulf,
in the midst of which dim ghosts of many columns
are darkly visible. From an opening between two of
the capitals, a flight of brick steps leads down into
a vast hall so far below the surface of the outer world,
so gloomy, so awful, that it might be the portico of
Hades.

Going down these steps we come to the original
level of the Temple. We tread the ancient pavement.
We look up to the massive ceiling, recessed, and
sculptured, and painted, like the ceiling at Denderah.
We could almost believe, indeed, that we are again
standing in the portico of Denderah. The number of
columns is the same. The arrangement of the intercolumnar screen is the same. The general effect and
the main features of the plan are the same. In some

respects, however, Esneh is even more striking. The columns, though less massive than those of Denderah, are more elegant, and look loftier. Their shafts are covered with figures of gods, and emblems, and lines of hieroglyphed inscription, all cut in low relief. Their capitals, in place of the huge draped Hathor-heads of Denderah, are studied from natural forms—from the lotus-lily, the papyrus-blossom, the plumy date-palm. The wall-sculpture, however, is inferior to that at Denderah, and immeasurably inferior to the wall-sculpture at Karnak. The figures are of the meanest Ptolemaic type, and all of one size. The inscriptions, instead of being grouped wherever there happened to be space, and so producing the richest form of wall-decoration ever devised by man, are disposed in symmetrical columns, the effect of which, when compared with the florid style of Karnak, is as the methodical neatness of an engrossed deed to the splendid freedom of an illuminated manuscript.

The steps occupy the place of the great doorway. The jambs and part of the cornice, the intercolumnar screen, the shafts of the columns under whose capitals we came in, are all there, half-projecting from, and half-imbedded in, the solid mound beyond. The light, however, comes in from so high up and through so narrow a space, that one's eyes need to become accustomed to the darkness before any of these details can be distinguished. Then, by degrees, forms of deities familiar and unfamiliar emerge from the gloom.

The Temple is dedicated to Kneph, the Soul of the World, whom we now see for the first time. He is ram-headed, and holds in his hand the tau, or

emblem of life.* Another new acquaintance, is Bes, **
the grotesque god of mirth and jollity.

Two singular little erections, built in between the
columns to right and left of the steps, next attract our
attention. They are like stone sentry-boxes. Each is
in itself complete, with roof, sculptured cornice, doorway, and, if I remember rightly, a small square window in the side. The inscriptions upon two similar
structures in the portico at Edfoo show that the right-
hand closet contained the sacred books belonging to
the Temple, while in the closet to the left of the main
entrance the King underwent the ceremony of purification. It may therefore be taken for granted that these
at Esneh were erected for the same purposes.

And now we look round for the next hall—and
look in vain. The doorway which should lead to it is
walled up. The portico was excavated by Mohammed
Ali in 1842; not in any spirit of antiquarian zeal, but
in order to provide a safe underground magazine for
gunpowder. Up to that time, as may be seen by one
of the illustrations to Wilkinson's "Thebes and General
View of Egypt," the interior was choked to within a
few feet of the capitals of the columns, and used as a
cotton-store. Of the rest of the building, nothing is

* "A ram was the emblem of Kneph, and the asp was sacred to him,
being frequently represented as rising up from between his horns. A ram is
also the hieroglyphic sign for Soul, and the asp is an emblem of dominion; so
the asp-crowned, ram-headed figure of Kneph in his mysterious boat represents
the all-pervading spirit moving upon the face of the waters." — *Keary's
Egyptian History*. Kneph was also one of the Gods of the Cataract, and chief
of the Triad worshipped at Elephantine. An inscription at Philæ styles him
" Maker of all that is, Creator of all beings, First existent, the Father of
Fathers, the Mother of Mothers."
** *Bes*. "La culte de Bes parait être une importation Asiatique. Quelque-
fois le dieu est armé d'une épée qu'il brandit au-dessus de sa tête; dans ce rôle-
il semble le dieu des combats. Plus souvent c'est le dieu de la danse, de la
musique, des plaisirs."—*Mariette Bey*.

known; nothing is visible. It is as large, probably, as Denderah or Edfoo, and in as perfect preservation. So, at least, says local tradition; but not even local tradition can point out to what extent it underlies the foundations of the modern houses that swarm above its roof. An inscription first observed by Champollion states that the sanctuary was built by Thothmes III. Is that antique sanctuary still there? Has the Temple grown step by step under the hands of successive Kings, as at Luxor? Or has it been re-edified *ab ovo*, as at Denderah? These are "puzzling questions," only to be resolved by the demolition of a quarter of the town. Meanwhile, what treasures of sculptured history, what pictured chambers, what buried bronzes and statues may here await the pick of the excavator!

All next day, while the men were baking, the Writer sat in a corner of the outer passage, and sketched the portico of the Temple. The sun rose upon the one horizon and set upon the other before that drawing was finished; yet for scarcely more than one hour did it light up the front of the Temple. At about half-past nine A.M. it first caught the stone fillet at the angle. Then, one by one, each massy capital became outlined with a thin streak of gold. As this streak widened, the cornice took fire, and presently the whole stood out in light against the sky. Slowly then, but quite perceptibly, the sun travelled across the narrow space overhead; the shadows became vertical; the light changed sides; and by ten o'clock, there was shade for the remainder of the day. Towards noon, however, the sun being then at its highest and the air transfused with light, the inner columns, swallowed up till now in darkness, became illumined

with a wonderful reflected light, and glowed from out
the gloom like pillars of fire.

Never to go on shore without an escort is one of
the rules of Nile life; and Salame has by this time
become my exclusive property. He is a native of
Assouan, young, active, intelligent, full of fun, hot-
tempered withal, and as thorough a gentleman as I
have ever had the pleasure of knowing. For a sample
of his good breeding, take this day at Esneh—a day
which he might have idled away in the bazaars and
cafés, and which it must have been dull work to spend
cooped up between a mud-wall and an outlandish
Birbeh, built by the Djinns who reigned before Adam.
Yet Salame betrays no discontent. Curled up in a
shady corner, he watches me like a dog; is ready with
an umbrella as soon as the sun comes round; and
replenishes a water-bottle or holds a colour-box as
deftly as though he had been to the manner born.
At one o'clock arrives my luncheon, enshrined in a
pagoda of plates. Being too busy to leave off work,
however, I put the pagoda aside, and despatch Salame
to the market, to buy himself some dinner; for which
purpose, wishing to do the thing handsomely, I present
him with the magnificent sum of two silver piastres, or
about fivepence English. With this he contrives to
purchase three or four cakes of flabby native bread, a
black-looking rissole of chopped meat and vegetables,
and about a pint of dried dates.

Knowing this to be a better dinner than my friend
gets every day, knowing also that our sailors habitually
eat at noon, I am surprised to see him leave these
dainties untasted. In vain I say "Bismillah" (in the
name of God); pressing him to eat in vocabulary

phrases eked out with expressive pantomime. He laughs, shakes his head, and, asking permission to smoke a cigarette, protests he is not hungry. Thus three more hours go by. Accustomed to long fasting and absorbed in my sketch, I forget all about the pagoda; and it is past four o'clock when I at length set to work to repair tissue at the briefest possible cost of time and daylight. And now the faithful Salame falls to with an energy that causes the cakes, the rissole, the dates, to vanish as if by magic. Of what remains from my luncheon, he also disposes in a trice. Never, unless in a pantomime, have I seen mortal man display so prodigious an appetite.

I made Talhamy scold him, by and by, for this piece of voluntary starvation.

"By my Prophet!" said he, "am I a pig or a dog, that I should eat when the Sitt was fasting?"

It was at Esneh, by the way, that that hitherto undiscovered curiosity, an ancient Egyptian coin, was offered to me for sale. The finder was digging for nitre, and turned it up at an immense depth below the mounds on the outskirts of the town. He volunteered to show the precise spot, and told his artless tale with child-like simplicity. Unfortunately, however, for the authenticity of this remarkable relic, it bore, together with the familiar profile of George IV., a superscription of its modest value, which was precisely one farthing. On another occasion, when we were making our long stay at Luxor, a coloured glass button of honest Birmingham make was brought to the boat by a Fellah who swore that he had himself found it upon a mummy in the Tombs of the Queens at Koornet Murraee. The same man came to my tent one day when I was

14*

sketching, bringing with him a string of more than doubtful scarabs—all veritable "antichi," of course, and all backed up with undeniable pedigrees.

"Là, là, (no, no),—bring me no more antichi," I said, gravely. "They are old and worn out, and cost much money. Have you no imitation scarabs, new and serviceable, that one might wear without the fear of breaking them?"

"These are imitations, O Sitt!" was the ready answer.

"But you told me a moment ago they were genuine antichi."

"That was because I thought the Sitt wanted to buy antichi," he said, quite shamelessly.

"See now," I said, "if you are capable of selling me new things for old, how can I be sure that you would not sell me old things for new?"

To this he replied by declaring that he had made the scarabs himself. Then, fearing I should not believe him, he pulled a scrap of coarse paper from his bosom, borrowed one of my pencils, and drew an asp, an ibis, and some other common hieroglyphic forms, with tolerable dexterity.

"Now you believe?" he asked, triumphantly.

"I see that you can make birds and snakes," I replied; "but that neither proves that you can cut scarabs, nor that these scarabs are new."

"Nay, Sitt," he protested, "I made them with these hands. I made them but the other day. By Allah! they cannot be newer."

Here Talhamy interposed.

"In that case," he said, "they are too new, and will crack before a month is over. The Sitt would do better to buy some that are well seasoned."

Our honest Fellah touched his brow and breast.

"Now in strict truth, O Dragoman!" he said, with an air of the most engaging candour, "these scarabs were made at the time of the inundation. They are new; but not too new. They are thoroughly seasoned. If they crack, you shall denounce me to the governor, and I will eat stick for them!"

Now it has always seemed to me that the most curious feature in this little scene was the extraordinary simplicity of the Arab. With all his cunning, with all his disposition to cheat, he suffered himself to be turned inside-out as unsuspiciously as a baby. It never occurred to him that his untruthfulness was being put to the test, or that he was committing himself more and more deeply with every word he uttered. The fact is, however, that the Fellah is half a savage. Notwithstanding his mendacity—(and it must be owned that he is the most brilliant liar under heaven)—he remains a singularly transparent piece of humanity; easily amused, easily deceived, easily angered, easily pacified. He steals a little, cheats a little, lies a great deal; but on the other hand he is patient, hospitable, affectionate, trustful. He suspects no malice, and bears none. He commits no great crimes. He is incapable of revenge. In short, his good points outnumber his bad ones; and what man or nation need hope for a much better character?

To generalise in this way may seem like presumption on the part of a passing stranger; yet it is more excusable as regards Egypt than it would be of any other equally accessible country. In Europe, and indeed in most parts of the East, one sees too little of the people to be able to form an opinion about them;

but it is not so on the Nile. Cut off from hotels, from
railways, from Europeanised cities, you are brought
into continual intercourse with natives. The sick who
come to you for medicines, the country gentlemen and
government officials who visit you on board your boat
and entertain you on shore, your guides, your donkey-
boys, the very dealers who live by cheating you, furnish
endless studies of character, and teach you more of
Egyptian life than all the books of Nile-travel that
ever were written.

Then your crew, part Arab, part Nubian, are a
little world in themselves. One man was born a slave,
and will carry the dealer's brand-marks to his grave.
Another has two children in Miss Whateley's school at
Cairo. A third is just married, and has left his young
wife sick at home. She may be dead by the time he
gets back, and he will hear no news of her meanwhile.
So with them all. Each has his simple story—a story
in which the local oppressor, the dreaded conscription,
and the still more dreaded *corvée*, form the leading incidents. The poor fellows are ready enough to pour
out their hopes, their wrongs, their sorrows. Through
sympathy with these, one comes to know the men;
and through the men, the nation. For the life of the
Beled repeats itself with but little variation wherever
the Nile flows and the Khedive rules. The characters
are the same; the incidents are the same. It is only
the *mise en scène* that differs.

Thus it comes to pass that the mere traveller who
spends but half-a-year on the Nile may, if he takes
an interest in Egypt and the Egyptians, learn more of
both in that short time than would be possible in a

country less singularly narrowed in all ways—politically, socially, geographically.

And this reminds me that the traveller on the Nile really sees the whole land of Egypt. Going from point to point in other countries, one follows a thin line of road, railway, or river, leaving wide tracts unexplored on either side; but there are few places in Middle or Upper Egypt, and none at all in Nubia, where one may not, from any moderate height, survey the entire face of the country from desert to desert. It is well to do this frequently. It helps one, as nothing else can help one, to an understanding of the wonderful mountain waste through which the Nile has been scooping its way for uncounted cycles. And it enables one to realise what a mere slip of alluvial deposit is this famous land which is "the gift of the river."

A dull grey morning, a faint and fitful breeze, carried us slowly on our way from Esneh to Edfoo. The new bread—a heavy boat-load when brought on board —lay in a huge heap at the end of the upper deck. It took four men one whole day to cut it up. Their incessant gabble drove us nearly distracted.

"Uskoot, Khaleefeh! Uskoot, Ali!" (Silence, Khaleefeh! Silence, Ali!) Talhamy would say from time to time. "You are not on your own deck. The Howadji can neither read nor write for the clatter of your tongues."

And then, for about a minute and a half, they would be quiet.

But you could as easily keep a monkey from chattering, as an Arab. Our men talked incessantly; and their talk was always about money. Listen to them when we might, such words as "Khámsa guroosh" (five piastres), "noos reyal" (half-a-dollar), "ethneen shilling" (two shillings), were perpetually coming to the surface. We never could understand how it was that money, which played so small a part in their lives, should play so large a part in their conversation.

It was about midday when we passed El Kab, the ancient Eileithyias. A rocky valley narrowing inland; a Sheykh's tomb on the mountain-ridge above; a few clumps of date-palms; some remains of what looked like a long crude-brick wall running at right angles to the river; and an isolated mass of hollowed limestone rock left standing apparently in the midst of an exhausted quarry, were all we saw of El Kab as the Dahabeeyah glided by.

And now, as the languid afternoon wears on, the propylons of Edfoo loom out of the misty distance. We have been looking for them long enough before they come into sight—calculating every mile of the way; every minute of the daylight. The breeze, such as it was, has dropped now. The river stretches away before us, smooth and oily as a pond. Nine of the men are tracking. Will they pull us to Edfoo in time to see the Temple before nightfall?

Reïs Hassan looks doubtful; but takes refuge as usual in "Inshallah!" (God willing). Talhamy talks of landing a sailor to run forward and order donkeys. Meanwhile the Philæ creeps lazily on; the sun declines unseen behind a filmy veil; and those two shadowy towers, rising higher and ever higher on the horizon, look grey, and ghostly, and far distant still.

Suddenly the trackers stop, look back, shout to those on board, and begin drawing the boat to shore. Reïs Hassan points joyously to a white streak breaking across the smooth surface of the river about half-a-mile behind. The Fostat's sailors are already swarming aloft —the Bagstones' trackers are making for home—our own men are preparing to fling in the rope and jump on board as the Philæ nears the bank.

For the capricious wind, that always springs up when we don't want it, is coming!

And now the Fostat, being hindmost, flings out her big sail and catches the first puff; the Bagstones' turn comes next; the Philæ shakes her wings free, and shoots ahead; and in fewer minutes than it takes to tell, we are all three scudding along before a glorious breeze.

The great towers that showed so far away half-an-hour ago, are now close at hand. There are palm-woods about their feet, and clustered huts, from the midst of which they tower up against the murky sky, magnificently. Soon they are passed and left behind, and the grey twilight takes them, and we see them no more. Then night comes on, cold and starless; yet not too dark for going as fast as wind and canvas will carry us.

And now, with that irrepressible instinct of rivalry that flesh—especially flesh on the Nile—is heir to, we quickly turn our good going into a trial of speed. It is no longer a mere business-like devotion to the matter in hand. It is a contest for glory. It is the Philæ against the Fostat, and the Bagstones against both. In plain English, it is a race. The two leading Daha-beeyahs are pretty equally matched. The Philæ is larger than the Fostat; but the Fostat has a bigger mainsail. On the other hand, the Fostat is an iron boat; whereas the Philæ, being wooden-built, is easier

to pole off a sandbank, and lighter in hand. The Bagstones carries a capital mainsail, and can go as fast as
either upon occasion.   Meanwhile the race is one of
perpetually varying fortunes.   Now the Fostat shoots
ahead; now the Philæ. We pass and re-pass; take the
wind out of one another's sails; economise every curve;
hoist every stitch of canvas; and, having identified ourselves with our boats, are as eager to win as if a great
prize depended on it.   Under these circumstances, to
dine is difficult—to go to bed superfluous—to sleep
impossible. As to mooring for the night, it is not to
be thought of for a moment.   Having begun the contest, we can no more help going than the wind can
help blowing; and our crew are as keen about winning
as ourselves.

As night advances, the wind continues to rise, and
our excitement with it.   Still the boats chase each
other along the dark river, scattering spray from their
bows and flinging out broad foam-tracks behind them.
Their cabin-windows, all alight within, cast flickering
flames upon the waves below.   The coloured lanterns
at their mast-heads, orange, purple, and crimson, burn
through the dusk like jewels. Presently the mist blows
off; the sky clears; the stars come out; the wind howls;
the casements rattle; the tiller scroops; the sailors
shout, and race, and bang the ropes about overhead;
while we, sitting up in our narrow berths, spend half
the night watching from our respective windows.

In this way some hours go by.   Then, about three
in the morning, with a shock, a recoil, a yell, and a
scuffle, we all three rush headlong upon a sandbank!
The men fly to the rigging, and furl the flapping sail.
Some seize punting poles. Others, looking like full-

grown imps of darkness, leap overboard and set their shoulders to the work. A strophe and antistrophe of grunts are kept up between those on deck and those in the water. Finally, after some ten minutes' frantic struggle, the Philæ slips off, leaving the other two aground in the middle of the river.

Towards morning, the noisy night having worn itself away, we all fall asleep—only to be roused again by Talhamy's voice at seven, proclaiming aloud that the Bagstones and Fostat are once more close upon our heels; that Silsilis and Kom Ombo are passed and left behind; that we have already put forty-six miles between ourselves and Edfoo; and that the good wind is still blowing.

We are now within fifteen miles of Assouan. The Nile is narrow here, and the character of the scenery has quite changed. Our view is bounded on the Arabian side by a near range of black granitic mountains; while on the Libyan side lies a chain of lofty sand-hills, each curiously capped by a crown of dark boulders. On both banks the river is thickly fringed with palms.

Meanwhile the race goes on. Last night it was sport; to day it is earnest. Last night we raced for glory; to day we race for a stake.

"A guinée for Reïs Hassan, if we get first to Assouan!"

Reïs Hassan's eyes glisten. No need to call up the dragoman to interpret between us. The look, the tone, are as intelligible to him as the choicest Arabic; and the magical word 'guinée' stands for a sovereign now, as it stood for one pound one in the days of Nelson and Abercrombie. He touches his head and breast; casts a backward glance at the pursuing Dahabeeyahs,

a forward glance in the direction of Assouan; kicks off
his shoes; ties a handkerchief about his waist; and
stations himself at the top of the steps leading to the
upper deck.   By the light in his eye and the set look
about his mouth, Reïs Hassan means winning.

Now to be first in Assouan means to be first on
the governor's list, and first up the Cataract.   And as
the passage of the Cataract is some two or three days'
work, this little question of priority is by no means un-
important.   Not for five times the promised 'guinée'
would we have the Fostat slip in first, and so be kept
waiting our turn on the wrong side of the frontier.

And now, as the sun rises higher, so the race waxes
hotter.   At breakfast time we were fifteen miles from
Assouan.   Now the fifteen miles have gone down to
ten; and when we reach yonder headland, they will
have dwindled to seven.   It is plain to see, however,
that as the distance decreases between ourselves and
Assouan, so also it decreases between ourselves and
the Fostat.   Reïs Hassan knows it.   I see him measuring the space by his eye.   I see the frown settling
on his brow.   He is calculating how much the Fostat
gains in every quarter of an hour, and how many quarters we are yet distant from the goal.   For no Arab
sailor counts by miles.   He counts by time, and by
the reaches in the river; and these may be taken at a
rough average of three miles each.   When, therefore,
our captain, in reply to an oft-repeated question, says
we have yet two bends to make, we know that we are
about six miles from our destination.

Six miles—and the Fostat creeping closer every
minute!   Just now we were all talking eagerly; but as
the end draws near, even the sailors are silent.   Reïs

Hassan stands motionless at his post, on the look-out for shallows. The words "Shamàl—Yemeen" (left—right), delivered in a short, sharp tone, are the only sounds he utters. The steersman, all eye and ear, obeys him like his hand. The sailors squat in their places, quiet and alert as cats.

And now it is no longer six miles but five—no longer five, but four. The Fostat, thanks to her bigger sail, well-nigh overtakes us; and the Bagstones is not more than a hundred yards behind the Fostat. On we go, however, past palm-woods of nobler growth than any we have yet seen; past forlorn homeward-bound Dahabeeyahs lying-to against the wind; past native boats, and river-side huts, and clouds of driving sand; till the corner is turned, and the last reach gained, and the minarets of Assouan are seen as through a shifting fog in the distance. The ruined tower crowning yonder promontory stands over against the town; and those black specks midway in the bed of the river are the first outlying rocks of the Cataract. The channel there is hemmed in between reefs and sandbanks, and to steer it is difficult in even the calmest weather. Still our canvas strains to the wind, and the Philæ rushes on full-tilt, like a racer at the hurdles.

Every eye now is turned upon Reïs Hassan; and Reïs Hassan stands rigid, like a man of stone. The rocks are close ahead—so close that we can see the breakers pouring over them, and the swirling eddies between. Our way lies through an opening between the boulders. Beyond that opening, the channel turns off sharply to the left! It is a point at which everything will depend on the shifting of a sail. If done too soon, we miss the mark; if too late, we strike upon the rocks.

Suddenly our Captain flings up his hand, takes the stairs at a bound, and flies to the prow. The sailors spring to their feet, gathering some round the Shoghool, and some round the end of the yard. The Fostat is up beside us. The moment for winning or losing is come.

And now, for a couple of breathless seconds, the two Dahabeeyahs plunge onward side by side, making for that narrow passage which is only wide enough for one. Then the iron boat, shaving the sandbank to get a wider berth, shifts her sail first, and shifts it clumsily, breaking or letting go her Shoghool. We see the sail flap, and the rope fly, and all hands rushing to retrieve it.

In that moment Reïs Hassan gives the word. The Philæ bounds forward—takes the channel from under the very bows of the Fostat—changes her sail without a hitch—and dips right away down the deep water, leaving her rival hard and fast among the shallows.

The rest of the way is short and open. In less than five minutes we have taken in our sail, paid Reïs Hassan his well-earned guinée, and found a snug corner to moor in. So ends our memorable race of nearly sixty-eight miles from Edfoo to Assouan.

CHAPTER X.

Assouan and Elephantine.

THE green island of Elephantine, which is about a mile in length, lies opposite Assouan and divides the Nile in two channels. The Libyan and Arabian deserts —smooth amber sand-slopes on the one hand; rugged granite cliffs on the other—come down to the brink on either side. On the Libyan shore a Sheykh's tomb, on the Arabian shore a bold fragment of Moorish architecture with ruined arches open to the sky, crown two opposing heights, and keep watch over the gate of the Cataract. Just under the Moorish ruin, and separated from the river by a slip of sandy beach, lies Assouan.

A few scattered houses, a line of blank wall, the top of a minaret, the dark mouths of one or two gloomy alleys, are all that one sees of the town from the mooring-place below. The black boulders close against the shore, some of which are superbly hiero- glyphed, glisten in the sun like polished jet. The beach is crowded with bales of goods; with camels laden and unladen; with turbaned figures coming and going; with damaged cargo-boats lying up high and dry, and half heeled over, in the sun. Others, moored close together, are taking in or discharging cargo. A little apart from these lie some three or four Daha- beeyahs flying English, American, and Belgian flags. Another has cast anchor over the way at Elephantine. Small row-boats cross and re-cross, meanwhile, from shore to shore; dogs bark; camels snort and snarl; donkeys bray; and clamorous curiosity-dealers scream, chatter, hold their goods at arm's length, battle and implore to come on board, and are only kept off the landing plank by means of two big sticks in the hands of two stalwart sailors.

The things offered for sale at Assouan are altogether new and strange. Here are no scarabæi, no funereal gods, no relics of a past civilisation; but, on the contrary, such objects as speak only of a rude and barbarous present—ostrich eggs and feathers, silver trinkets of rough Nubian workmanship, spears, bows, arrows, bucklers of rhinoceros-hide, ivory bracelets cut solid from the tusk, porcupine quills, baskets of stained and plaited reeds, gold nose-rings, and the like. One old woman has a Nubian lady's dressing-case for sale —an uncouth, Fetish-like object with a cushion for its body, and a top-knot of black feathers. The cushion contains two Kohl-bottles, a bodkin, and a bone comb.

But the noisiest dealer of the lot is an impish boy blessed with the blackest skin and the shrillest voice ever brought together in one human being. His simple costume consists of a tattered shirt and a white cotton skull-cap; his stock in trade, of a greasy leather fringe tied to the end of a stick. Flying from window to window of the saloon on the side next the shore, scrambling up the bows of a neighbouring cargo-boat so as to attack us in the rear, thrusting his stick and fringe in our faces whichever way we turn, and pursuing us with eager cries of "Madame Nubia! Madame Nubia!" he skips, and screams, and grins like an ubiquitous goblin, and throws every competitor into the shade.

Having seen a similar fringe in the collection of a friend at home, I at once recognised in "Madame

Nubia" one of those curious girdles which, with the addition of a necklace and a few bracelets, form the entire wardrobe of little girls south of the Cataract. They vary in size according to the age of the wearer; the largest being about twelve inches in depth and twenty-five in length. A few are ornamented with beads and small shells; but these are *parures de luxe.* The ordinary article is cheaply and unpretentiously trimmed with castor-oil. That is to say, the girdle when new is well soaked in the oil, which softens and darkens the leather, besides adding a perfume dear to native nostrils.

For to the Nubian, who grows his own plants and bruises his own berries, this odour is delicious. He reckons castor-oil among his greatest luxuries. He eats it as we eat butter. His wives saturate their plaited locks in it. His little girls perfume their fringes with it. His boys anoint their bodies with it. His home, his breath, his garments, his food, are redolent of it. It pervades the very air in which he lives and has his being. Happy the European traveller who, while his lines are cast in Nubia, can train his degenerate nose to delight in the aroma of castor-oil!

The march of civilisation is driving these fringes out of fashion on the frontier. At Assouan, they are chiefly in demand among English and American visitors. Most people purchase a "Madame Nubia" for the entertainment of friends at home. L., who is given to vanities in the way of dress, bought one so steeped in fragrance that it scented the Philæ for the rest of the voyage, and retains its odour to this day.

Almost before the mooring-rope was made fast, our

Painter, arrayed in a gorgeous kefiah * and armed with the indispensable visiting-cane, had sprung ashore and hastened to call upon the Governor. A couple of hours later, the Governor (having promised to send at once for the Sheykh of the Cataract and to forward our going by all means in his power) returned the visit. He brought with him the Mudeer ** and Kadee *** of Assouan, each attended by his pipe-bearer.

We received our guests with due ceremony in the saloon. The great men placed themselves on one of the side-divans; and the Painter opened the conversation by offering them champagne, claret, port, sherry, curaçoa, brandy, whiskey, and Angostura bitters. Talhamy interpreted.

The Governor laughed. He was a tall young man, graceful, lively, good-looking, and black as a crow. The Kadee and Mudeer, both elderly Arabs, yellow, wrinkled, and precise, looked shocked at the mere mention of these unholy liquors. Somebody then proposed lemonade.

The Governor turned briskly towards the speaker. "Gazzoso?" he said, interrogatively.

To which Talhamy replied:—"Aïwah (Yes), Gazzoso."

Aërated lemonade and cigars were then brought. The Governor watched the process of uncorking with a face of profound interest, and drank with the undisguised greediness of a schoolboy. Even the Kadee and Mudeer relaxed somewhat of the gravity of their demeanour. To men whose habitual drink consists

---

* *Kefiah:* Head-shawl.
** *Mudeer:* Chief Magistrate,
*** *Kadee:* Judge.

òf lime-water and sugar, bottled lemonade represents champagne mousseux of the choicest brand.

Then began the usual attempts at conversation; and only those who have tried small-talk by proxy know how hard it is to supply topics, suppress yawns, and keep up an animated expression of countenance, while the civilities on both sides are being interpreted by a dragoman.

We began, of course, with the temperature; for in Egypt, where it never rains and the sun is always shining, the thermometer takes the place of the weather as a useful platitude. Knowing that Assouan enjoys the hottest reputation of any town on the surface of the globe, we were agreeably surprised to find it no warmer than England in September. The Governor accounted for this by saying that he had never known so cold a winter. We then asked the usual questions about the crops, the height of the river, and so forth; to all of which he replied with the ease and *bonhomie* of a man of the world. Nubia, he said, was healthy— the date-harvest had been abundant—the corn promised well—the Soudan was quiet and prosperous. Referring to the new postal arrangements, he congratulated us on being able to receive and post letters at the Second Cataract. He also remarked that the telegraphic wires were now in working order as far as Khartoom. We then asked how soon he expected the railway to reach Assouan; to which he replied—"In two years, at latest."

At length our little stock of topics came to an end, and the entertainment flagged.

"What shall I say next?" asked the dragoman.

15*

"Tell him we particularly wish to see the slave-market."

The smile vanished from the Governor's face. The Mudeer set down a glass of fizzing lemonade, untasted. The Kadee all but dropped his cigar. If a shell had burst in the saloon, their consternation could scarcely have been greater.

The Governor, looking very grave, was the first to speak.

"He says there is no slave-trade in Egypt, and no slave-market in Assouan," interpreted Talhamy.

Now we had been told in Cairo, on excellent authority, that slaves were still bought and sold here, though less publicly than of old; and that of all the sights a traveller might see in Egypt, this was the most curious and pathetic.

"No slave-market!" we repeated, incredulously.

The Governor, the Kadee, and the Mudeer shook their heads, and lifted up their voices, and said all together, like a trio of Mandarins in a comic opera:—

"Là, là, là! Mafeesh bazaar—mafeesh bazaar!" (No, no, no! No bazaar—no bazaar!)

We endeavoured to explain that in making this inquiry we desired neither the gratification of an idle curiosity, nor the furtherance of any political views. Our only object was sketching. Understanding, therefore, that a private bazaar still existed in Assouan....

This was too much for the judicial susceptibilities of the Kadee. He would not let Talhamy finish.

"There is nothing of the kind," he interrupted, puckering his face into an expression of such virtuous horror as might become a reformed New Zealander on the subject of cannibalism. "It is unlawful—unlawful."

An awkward silence followed. We felt we had committed an enormous blunder, and were disconcerted accordingly.

The Governor saw, and with the best grace in the world took pity upon, our embarrassment. He rose, opened the piano, and asked for some music; whereupon the Little Lady played the liveliest thing she could remember, which happened to be a waltz by Verdi.

The Governor, meanwhile, sat beside the piano, smiling and attentive. With all his politeness, however, he seemed to be looking for something—to be not altogether satisfied. There was even a shade of disappointment in the tone of his "Ketther-khayrik keteer," when the waltz finally exploded in a shower of arpeggios. What could it be? Was it that he wished for a song? Or would a pathetic air have pleased him better?

Not a bit of it. He was looking for what his quick eye presently detected—namely some printed music, which he seized triumphantly and placed before the player. What he wanted was "music played from a book."

Being asked whether he preferred a lively or a plaintive melody, he replied that "he did not care, so long as it was *difficult.*"

Now it chanced that he had pitched upon a volume of Wagner; so the Little Lady took him at his word, and gave him a dose of "Tannhaüser." Strange to say, he was delighted. He showed his teeth; he rolled his eyes; he uttered the long-drawn "Ah!" which in Egypt signifies applause. The more crabbed, the more

far-fetched, the more unintelligible the movement, the
better, apparently, he liked it.

I never think of Assouan but I remember that
curious scene—our Little Lady at the piano; the black
Governor grinning in ecstasies close by; the Kadee in
his magnificent shawl-turban; the Mudeer half-asleep;
the air thick with tobacco-smoke; and above all—
dominant, tyrannous, overpowering—the crash and
clang, the involved harmonies, and the multitudinous
combinations of Tannhäuser.

The linked sweetness of an Oriental visit is generally
drawn out to a length that sorely tries the patience
and politeness of European hosts. A native gentleman,
if he has any business to attend to, gets through his
work before noon, and has nothing to do but smoke,
chat, and doze away the remainder of the day. For
time, which hangs heavily on his hands, he has absolutely no value. His main object in life is to consume
it, if possible, less tediously. He pays a visit, therefore, with the deliberate intention of staying as long
as possible. Our guests on the present occasion
remained the best part of two hours; and the Governor,
who talked of going to England shortly, asked for all
our names and addresses, that he might come and see
us at home.

Leaving the cabin, he paused to look at our roses,
which stood near the door. We told him they had
been given to us by the Bey of Erment.

"Do they grow at Erment?" he asked, examining
them with great curiosity. "How beautiful! Why will
they not grow in Nubia?"

We suggested that the climate was probably too
hot for them.

He stooped, inhaling their perfume. He looked puzzled.

"They are very sweet," he said. "Are they roses?"

The question gave us a kind of shock. We could hardly believe we had reached a land where roses were unknown. Yet the Governor, who had smoked a rose-water narghilé, and drunk rose-sherbet, and eaten conserve of roses all his days, recognised them by their perfume only. He had never been out of Assouan in his life; not even as far as Erment. And he had never seen a rose in bloom.

We had hoped to begin the passage of the Cataract on the morning of the day following our arrival at the frontier; but some other Dahabeeyah, it seemed, was in the act of fighting its way up to Philæ; and till that boat was through, neither the Sheykh nor his men would be ready for us. At eight o'clock in the morning of the next day but one, however, they promised to take us in hand. We were to pay £12 English for the double journey; that is to say, nine pounds down, and the remaining three pounds on our return to Assouan.

Such was the treaty concluded between ourselves and the Sheykh of the Cataract at a solemn conclave over which the Governor, assisted by the Kadee and Mudeer, presided.

Having a clear day to spend at Assouan, we of course gave part thereof to Elephantine, which in the inscriptions is called Abu, or the Ivory Island. There may perhaps have been a depôt, or "treasure-city," here for the precious things of the Upper Nile country; the gold of Nubia and the elephant-tusks of Cush.

It is a very beautiful island—rugged and lofty to the South; low and fertile to the North; with an exquisitely varied coast-line full of wooded creeks and miniature beaches, in which one might expect at any moment to meet Robinson Crusoe with his goat-skin umbrella, or man Friday bending under a load of faggots. They are all Fridays here, however; for Elephantine, being the first Nubian outpost, is peopled by Nubians only. It contains two Nubian villages, and the mounds of a very ancient city which was the capital of all Egypt under the Pharaohs of the VIth Dynasty, between three and four thousand years before Christ. Two Temples, one of which dated from the reign of Amenhotep III., were yet standing here some sixty years ago. They were seen by Belzoni in 1815, and had just been destroyed to build a palace and barracks when Champollion went up in 1829. A ruined gateway of the Ptolemaic period and a forlorn-looking sitting statue of Menephtah, the Pharaoh of the Exodus, alone remain to identify the sites on which they stood.

Thick palm-groves and carefully-tilled patches of the castor-oil and cotton plant, lentils and dourra, make green the heart of the island. The western shore is wooded to the water's edge. One may walk here in the shade at hottest noon, listening to the murmur of the Cataract and seeking for wild flowers— which, however, would seem to blossom nowhere save in the sweet Arabic name of Gezeeret-el-Zahr, the Island of Flowers.

Upon the high ground at the Southern extremity of the island, among rubbish heaps, and bleached bones, and human skulls, and the sloughed skins of

Snakes, and piles of particoloured potsherds, we picked up several bits of inscribed terra-cotta—evidently fragments of broken vases. The writing was very faint, and in part obliterated. We could see that the characters were Greek; but not even our Idle Man was equal to making out a word of the sense. Believing them to be mere disconnected scraps to which it would be impossible to find the corresponding pieces, taking it for granted, also, that they were of comparatively modern date, we brought away some three or four as souvenirs of the place, and thought no more about them.

We little dreamed that Dr. Birch, in his cheerless official-room at the British Museum so many thousand miles away, was at this very time occupied in deciphering a collection of similar fragments, nearly all of which had been brought from this same spot.* Of the curious interest attaching to these illegible scrawls,

---

* The results of Dr. Birch's labour were given to the public in his "Guide to the First and Second Egyptian Rooms," published by order of the Trustees of the British Museum in May 1874. Of the contents of case 99, in the Second Room, he says, "The use of potsherds for documents received a great extension at the time of the Roman Empire, when receipts for the taxes were given on these fragments by the collectors of revenue at Elephantine or Syene, on the frontier of Egypt. These receipts commenced in the reign of Vespasian, A.D. 77, and are found as late as M. Aurelius and L. Verus, A.D. 165. It appears from them that the capitation and trades tax, which was 16 drachms in A.D. 77, rose to 20 in A.D. 165, having steadily increased. The dues were paid in instalments called *merismoi*, at three periods of the year. The taxes were farmed out to publicans, *misthotai*, who appear from their names to have been Greeks. At Elephantine the taxes were received by tax-gatherers, *prakteres*, who seem to have been appointed as early as the Ptolemies. Their clerks were Egyptians, and they had a chest and treasurer, *phylax.*" See p. 109, *as above*, also Birch's *History of Ancient Pottery*, chap. i. p. 45.

These barren memoranda are not the only literary curiosities found at Elephantine. Among the Egyptian MSS. of the Louvre may be seen some fragments of the XVIIIth book of the Iliad, discovered in a tomb upon the island. How they came to be buried there no one knows. A lover of poetry would like to think, however, that some Greek or Roman officer, dying at his post upon this distant station, desired, perhaps, to have his Homer laid with him in his grave.

of the importance they were shortly to acquire in the
eyes of the learned, of the possible value of any chance
additions to their number, we knew, and could know,
nothing. Six months later, we lamented our ignorance,
and our lost opportunities.

For the Egyptians, it seems, used potsherds, instead
of papyrus, for short memoranda; and each of these
fragments that we had picked up contained a record
complete in itself. I fear we should have laughed, if
any one had suggested that they might be tax-gatherer's
receipts. Yet that is just what they were—receipts for
government dues collected on the frontier during the
period of Roman rule in Egypt. They were written in
Greek, because the Romans deputed Greek scribes to
perform the duties of this unpopular office; but the
Greek is so corrupt and the penmanship so clownish,
that only Dr. Birch, and one or two other eminent
scholars, can read them.

Not all the inscribed fragments found at Elephantine, however, are tax-receipts, or written in bad Greek.
The British Museum contains several in the demotic,
or current script of the people, and a few in the more
learned hieratic, or priestly, hand. These have not
yet been translated. They are probably business
memoranda and short private letters of Egyptians of
the same period.

But how came these fragile documents to be preserved when the city in which their writers lived, and
the Temples in which they worshipped, and the tombs
to which their mummies were consigned, have disappeared and left scarce a trace behind? Who cast
them down among the potsherds on this barren hill-
side? Are we to suppose that some kind of Public

Record-Office once occupied the site, and that the receipts here stored were duplicates of those given to the payers? Or is it not even more probable that this place was the Monte Testaccio of the ancient city, to which all broken pottery, written as well as unwritten, found its way sooner or later?

With the exception of a fine fragment of Roman quay nearly opposite Assouan, the ruined gateway of Alexander and the battered statue of Menephtah are the only objects of archæological interest in the island. But the charm of Elephantine is the everlasting charm of natural beauty—of rocks, of palm-woods, of quiet waters.

The streets of Assouan are just like the streets of every other mud town on the Nile. The Bazaars reproduce the Bazaars of Minieh and Siout. The environs are noisy with cafés and dancing girls, like the environs of Esneh and Luxor. Into the mosque, where some kind of service was going on, we peeped without entering. It looked cool, and clean, and spacious; the floor being covered with fine matting, and some scores of ostrich-eggs depending from the ceiling. In the bazaars we bought baskets and mats of Nubian manufacture, woven with the same reeds, dyed with the same colours, shaped after the same models, as those found in the tombs at Thebes. A certain oval basket with a vaulted cover, of which specimens are preserved in the British Museum, seems still to be the pattern most in demand at Assouan. The basket-makers have neither changed their fashion nor the buyers their taste, since the days of Rameses the Great.

Here also, at a little cupboard of a shop near the

Shoe Bazaar, we were tempted to spend a few pounds
in ostrich feathers, which are conveyed to Assouan by
traders from the Soudan.   The merchant brought out
a feather at a time, and seemed in no haste to sell.
We also affected indifference.   The haggling on both
sides was tremendous.   The bystanders, as usual, were
profoundly interested, and commented on every word
that passed.   At last we carried away an armful of
splendid plumes, most of which measured from two
and a half to three feet in length.   Some were pure
white; others, white tipped with brown. · They had
been neither cleaned nor curled, but were just as they
came from the hands of the ostrich-hunters.

By far the most amusing sight in Assouan was the
traders' camp down near the landing-place. Here were
Abyssinians like slender-legged baboons; wild-looking
Bishareeyah and Ababdeh Arabs with flashing eyes and
flowing hair; sturdy Nubians the colour of a Bar-
bedienne bronze; and natives of all tribes and shades,
from Kordofan and Sennar, the deserts of Bahuda and
the banks of the Blue and White Niles.   Some were
returning from Cairo; others were on their way thither.
Some, having disembarked their merchandise at Mahatta,
(a village on the other side of the Cataract) had come
across the desert to re-embark it at Assouan.   Others
had just disembarked theirs at Assouan, in order to re-
embark it at Mahatta.   Meanwhile, they were living
sub Jove; each entrenched in his own little redoubt
of piled-up bales and packing-cases, like a spider
in the centre of his web; each provided with his
kettle and coffee-pot, and a rug to sleep and pray
upon.   One sulky old Turk had fixed up a roof of
matting, and furnished his den with a *Kafas,* or palm-

wood couch; but he was a self-indulgent exception to the rule.

Some smiled, some scowled, when we passed through the camp. One offered us coffee. Another, more obliging than the rest, displayed the contents of his packages. Great bundles of lion and leopard skins, bales of cotton, sacks of henna-leaves, elephant-tusks swathed in canvas and matting, strewed the sandy bank. Of gum-arabic alone there must have been several hundred bales; each bale sewn up in a raw hide and tied with thongs of hippopotamus leather. Towards dusk, when the camp-fires were alight and the evening meal was in course of preparation, the scene became wonderfully picturesque. Lights gleamed; shadows deepened; strange figures stalked to and fro, or squatted in groups amid their merchandise. Some were baking flat cakes; others stirring soup, or roasting coffee. A hole scooped in the sand, a couple of stones to support the kettle, and a handful of dry sticks, served for kitchen-range and fuel, Meanwhile all the dogs in Assouan prowled round the camp, and a jargon of barbaric tongues came and went with the breeze that followed the sunset.

I must not forget to add that among this motley crowd we saw two brothers, natives of Khartoom. We met them first in the town, and afterwards in the camp. They wore voluminous white turbans, and flowing robes of some kind of creamy cashmere cloth. Their small proud heads and delicate aristocratic features were modelled on the purest Florentine type; their eyes were long and liquid; their complexions, free from any taint of Abyssinian blue or Nubian bronze, were intensely, lustrously, magnificently black.

We agreed that we had never seen two such handsome men. They were like young and beautiful
Dantes carved in ebony; Dantes unembittered by the
world, unsicklied by the pale cast of thought, and
glowing with the life of the warm South.

Having explored Elephantine and ransacked the
bazaars, our party dispersed in various directions.
Some gave the remainder of the day to letter-writing.
The Painter, bent on sketching, started off in search
of a jackal-haunted ruin up a wild ravine on the
Libyan side of the river. The Writer and the Idle
Man boldly mounted camels and rode out into the
Arabian desert.

Now the camel-riding that is done at Assouan is
of the most commonplace description, and bears to
genuine desert travelling about the same relation that
half-an-hour on the Mer de Glace bears to the passage
of the Mortaretsch glacier or the ascent of Monte
Rosa. The short cut from Assouan to Philæ, or at
least the ride to the granite quarries, forms part of
every dragoman's programme, and figures as the
crowning achievement of every Cook's tourist. The
Arabs themselves perform these little journeys much
more pleasantly and expeditiously on donkeys. They
take good care, in fact, never to scale the summit of
a camel if they can help it. But for the impression-
able traveller, the Assouan camel is *de rigueur*. In
his interests are those snarling quadrupeds be-tasselled
and be-rugged, taken from their regular work, and
paraded up and down the landing-place. To transport
cargoes disembarked above and below the Cataract is
their vocation. Taken from this honest calling to
perform in an absurd little drama got up especially

for the entertainment of tourists, it is no wonder if the beasts are more than commonly ill-tempered. They know the whole proceeding to be essentially cockney, and they resent it accordingly.

The ride, nevertheless, has its advantages; not the least being that it enables one to realise the kind of work involved in any of the regular desert expeditions. At all events, it entitles one to claim acquaintance with the ship of the desert, and (bearing in mind the probable inferiority of the specimen) to form an *ex pede* judgment of his qualifications.

The camel has his virtues—so much at least must be admitted; but they do not lie upon the surface. My Buffon tells me, for instance, that he carries a fresh-water cistern in his stomach; which is meritorious. But the cistern ameliorates neither his gait nor his temper—which are abominable. Irreproachable as a beast of burden, he is open to many objections as a steed. It is unpleasant, in the first place, to ride an animal that not only objects to being ridden, but cherishes a strong personal antipathy to his rider. Such, however, is his amiable peculiarity. You know that he hates you, from the moment you first walk round him, wondering when and how to begin the ascent of his hump. He does not in fact, hesitate to tell you so in the roundest terms. He swears freely while you are taking your seat; snarls if you but move in the saddle; and stares you angrily in the face, if you attempt to turn his head in any direction save that which he himself prefers. Should you persevere, he tries to bite your feet. If biting your feet does not answer, he lies down.

Now the lying-down and getting-up of a camel are

performances designed for the express purpose of in-
flicting grievous bodily harm upon his rider. Thrown
twice forward and twice backward, punched in his
"wind" and damaged in his spine, the luckless novice
receives four distinct shocks, each more violent and
unexpected than the last. For this "execrable hunch-
back" is fearfully and wonderfully made. He has a
superfluous joint somewhere in his legs, and uses it to
revenge himself upon mankind.

His paces, however, are more complicated than his
joints and more trying than his temper. He has four:
—a short walk, like the rolling of a small boat in a
chopping sea; a long walk which dislocates every bone
in your body; a trot that reduces you to imbecility;
and a gallop that is sudden death. One tries in vain
to imagine a crime for which the *peine forte et dure*
of sixteen hours on camel-back would not be a full
and sufficient expiation. It is a punishment to which
one would not willingly be the means of condemning
any human being—not even a reviewer.

They had been down on the bank for hire all day
long—brown camels and white camels, shaggy camels
and smooth camels; all with gay worsted tassels on
their heads, and rugs flung over their high wooden
saddles, by way of housings. The gentlemen of the
Fostat had ridden away hours ago, cross-legged and
serene; and we had witnessed their demeanour with
mingled admiration and envy. Now, modestly conscious of our own daring, we prepared to do likewise.
It was a solemn moment when, having chosen our
beasts, we prepared to encounter the unknown perils
of the desert. What wonder if the Happy Couple exchanged an affecting farewell at parting?

We mounted and rode away; two imps of darkness
following at the heels of our camels, and Salame performing the part of bodyguard. Thus attended, we
found ourselves pitched, swung, and rolled along at a
pace that carried us rapidly up the slope, past a
suburb full of cafés and grinning dancing girls, and
out into the desert. Our way for the first half-mile or
so lay among tombs. A great Mohammedan necropolis, part ancient, part modern, lies behind Assouan,
and covers more ground than the town itself. Some
scores of tiny mosques, each topped by its little
cupola, and all more or less dilapidated, stand here
amid a wilderness of scattered tombstones. Some are
isolated; some grouped picturesquely together. Each
covers, or is supposed to cover, the grave of a Moslem
Santon; but some are mere commemorative chapels
dedicated to saints and martyrs elsewhere buried. Of
simple head-stones defaced, shattered, overturned,
propped back to back on cairns of loose stones, or
piled in broken and dishonoured heaps, there must
be many hundreds. They are for the most part
rounded at the top like ancient Egyptian steles, and
bear elaborately-carved inscriptions, some of which
are in the Cufic character, and more than a thousand
years old. Seen when the sun is bending Westward
and the shadows are lengthening, there is something
curiously melancholy and picturesque about this City
of the Dead in the dead desert.

Leaving the tombs, we now strike off towards the
quarries. The horizon beyond Assouan is bounded on
all sides by rocky heights, bold and picturesque in
form, yet scarcely lofty enough to deserve the name of
mountains. The sandy bottom under our camels' feet

is strewn with small pebbles, and tolerably firm. Clustered rocks of black and red granite profusely inscribed with hieroglyphed records crop up here and there, and serve as landmarks just where landmarks are needed. For nothing would be easier than to miss one's way among these tawny slopes, and to go wandering off, like lost Israelites, into the desert.

Winding in and out among undulating hillocks and tracts of rolled boulders deposited by pre-historic floods, we come at last to a little group of cliffs, at the foot of which our camels halt unbidden. Here we dismount, climb a short slope, and find the huge monolith at our feet.

Being cut horizontally, it lies half buried in drifted sand, with nothing to show that it is not wholly disengaged and ready for transport. Our books tell us, however, that the under-cutting has never been done, and that it is yet one with the granite bottom on which it seems to lie. Both ends are hidden; but one can pace some sixty feet of its yet visible surface. That surface bears the tool-marks of the workmen. A slanting groove pitted with wedge-holes indicates where it was intended to taper towards the top. Another shows where it was to be reduced at the side. Had it been finished, this would have been the largest obelisk in the world. The great obelisk of Queen Hatasu at Karnak, which, as its inscriptions record, came also from Assouan, stands ninety-two * feet high, and measures eight feet square at the base; but this

---

* These are the measurements given in *Murray's Handbook,* 1873. The new English translation, however, of Mariette Bey's *Itinéraire de la Haute Egypte* gives the obelisk of Hatasu 108 feet 10 inches in height. See *The Monuments of Upper Egypt,* translated by Alphonse Mariette: London, 1877,

which lies sleeping in the desert would have stood ninety-five feet in the shaft, and have measured over eleven feet square at the base. We can never know now why it was left here, * nor guess with what royal name it should have been inscribed. Had the king said in his heart that he would set up a mightier obelisk than was ever yet seen by eyes of men, and did he die before the block could be extracted from the quarry? Or were the quarrymen driven from the desert, and the Pharaoh from his throne, by the hungry hordes of Ethiopia, or Syria, or the islands beyond the sea? The great stone may be older than Rameses the Great, or as modern as the last of the Romans; but to give it a date, or to divine its history, is impossible. Egyptology, which has solved the enigma of the Sphinx, is powerless here. The obelisk of the quarry holds its secret safe, and holds it for ever.

Ancient Egyptian quarrying is seen under its most striking aspect among extensive limestone or sandstone ranges, as at Toora and Silsilis; but the process by which the stone was extracted can nowhere be more distinctly traced than at Assouan. In some respects, indeed, the quarries here, though on a smaller scale than those lower down the river, are even more interesting. Nothing surprises one at Silsilis, for instance, more than the economy with which the sandstone has been cut from the heart of the mountain; but at Assouan, as the material was more precious, so does the economy seem to have been still greater. At Silsilis, the yellow cliffs have been sliced as neatly as the cheeses in a cheesemonger's window. Smooth, up-

---

* There is a considerable fissure in the block, which might well have accounted for its abandonment; were not the flaw comparatively modern.

right walls alone mark the place where the work has been done; and the amount of débris is altogether insignificant. But at Assouan, when extracting granite for sculptural purposes, they attacked the form of the object required, and cut it out roughly to shape. The great obelisk is but one of many cases in point. In the same group of rocks, or one very closely adjoining, we saw a rough-hewn column, erect and three-parts detached, as well as the semi-cylindrical hollow from which its fellow had been taken. One curious recess from which a quadrant-shaped mass had been cut away puzzled us immensely. In other places the blocks appeared to have been coffer-shaped. We sought in vain, however, for the broken sarcophagus mentioned in Murray.

But the drifted sands, we may be sure, hide more precious things than these. Inscriptions are probably as abundant here as in the breccia of Hamamat. The great obelisk must have had a fellow, if we only knew where to look for it. The obelisks of Queen Hatasu, and the sarcophagi of many famous Kings, might possibly be traced to their beds in these quarries. So might the casing stones of the Pyramid of Menkara, the massive slabs of the Temple of the Sphinx, and the walls of the sanctuary of Philip Aridæus at Karnak. Above all, the syenite Colossus of the Ramesseum, which was the largest detached statue in the world, must have left its mighty matrix among the rocks close by. But these, like the song of the sirens or the alias of Achilles, though "not beyond all conjecture," are among the things that will never now be discovered.

As regards the process of quarrying at Assouan, it seems that rectangular granite blocks were split off here, as the softer limestone and sandstone elsewhere, by means of wooden wedges. These were fitted to holes already cut for their reception; and, being saturated with water, split the hard rock by mere force of expansion. Every quarried mass hereabouts is marked with rows of these wedge-holes.

Passing by the way a tiny oasis where there were camels, and a well, and an idle water-wheel, and a patch of emerald-green barley, we next rode back nearly to the outskirts of Assouan, where, in a dismal hollow on the verge of the desert, may be seen a small, half-buried Temple of Ptolemaic times. Traces of colour are still visible on the winged globe under the cornice, and on some mutilated bas-reliefs at either side of the principal entrance. Seeing that the interior was choked with rubbish, we made no attempt to go inside; but rode away again without dismounting.

And now, there being still an hour of daylight, we signified our intention of making for the top of the nearest hill, in order to see the sun set. This, clearly, was an unheard-of innovation. The camel-boys stared, shook their heads, protested there was "mafeesh sikkeh," (no road) and evidently regarded us as lunatics. The camels planted their splay feet obstinately in the sand, tried to turn back, and, when obliged to yield to the force of circumstances, abused us all the way. Arrived at the top, we found ourselves looking down upon the island of Elephantine, with the Nile, the town, and the Dahabeeyahs, at our feet. A prolongation of the ridge on which we were now standing, led, however, to another height crowned by a ruined tomb; and seemed to promise a view of the Cataract. Seeing us prepare to go on, the camel-boys broke into a *furore* of re-

monstrance, which, but for Salame's big stick, would
have ended in downright mutiny. Still we pushed forward, and, still dissatisfied, insisted on attacking a third
summit. The boys now trudged on in sullen despair.
The sun was sinking; the way was steep and difficult;
the night would soon come on. If the Howadji chose
to break their necks, it concerned nobody but themselves; but if the camels broke theirs, who was to pay
for them?

Such—expressed half in broken Arabic, half in
gestures—were the sentiments of our youthful Nubians.
Nor were the camels themselves less emphatic. They
grinned; they sniffed; they snorted; they snarled; they
disputed every foot of the way. As for mine (a gawky,
supercilious beast with a bloodshot eye and a battered
Roman nose), I never heard any dumb animal make
use of so much bad language in my life.

The last hill was very steep and stony; but the
view from the top was magnificent. We had now
gained the highest point of the ridge that divides the
valley of the Nile from the Arabian desert. The Cataract,
widening away reach after reach and studded with innumerable rocky islets, looked more like a lake than a
river. Of the Libyan desert we could see nothing
beyond the opposite sand-slopes, gold-rimmed against
the sunset. The Arabian desert, a boundless waste
edged by a serrated line of purple peaks, extended
Eastward to the remotest horizon. We looked down
upon it as on a raised map. The Moslem tombs, some
five hundred feet below, showed like toys. To the
right, in a wide valley opening away Southwards, we
recognised that ancient bed of the Nile which serves
for the great highway between Egypt and Nubia. At

the end of the vista, some very distant palms against a rocky background pointed the way to Philæ.

Meanwhile, the sun was fast sinking—the lights were crimsoning—the shadows were lengthening. All was silent; all was solitary. We listened, but could scarcely hear the murmur of the rapids. We looked in vain for the quarry of the obelisk. It was but one group of rocks among scores of others, and to distinguish it at this distance was impossible.

Presently, a group of three or four black figures mounted on little grey asses, came winding in and out among the tombs, and took the road to Philæ. To us they were moving specks; but our lynx-eyed camel-boys at once recognised the "Sheykh el Shellâl" (Sheykh of the Cataract) and his retinue. More Dahabeeyahs had come in; and the worthy man, having spent all day in Assouan, visiting, palavering, bargaining, was now going home to Mahatta for the night. We watched the retreating riders for some minutes, till twilight stole up the ancient channel like a flood, and drowned them in warm shadows.

The afterglow had faded off the heights when we at length crossed the last ridge, descended the last hill-side, and regained the level from which we had started. Here once more we met the Fostat party. They had ridden to Philæ and back by the desert, and were apparently all the worse for wear. Seeing us, they urged their camels to a trot, and tried to look as if they liked it. The Idle Man and the Writer wreathed their countenances in ghastly smiles, and did likewise. Not for worlds would they have admitted that they found the pace difficult. Such is the moral influence of the camel. He acts as a tonic; he promotes the Spartan virtues; and if not himself heroic, is at least the cause of heroism in others.

It was nearly dark when we reached Assouan. The cafés were all alight and astir. There were smoking and coffee-drinking going on outside; there were sounds of music and laughter within. A large private house on the opposite side of the road was being decorated, as if for some festive occasion. Flags were flying from the roof, and two men were busy putting up a gaily-painted inscription over the doorway. Asking, as was natural, if there was a marriage or a fantasia afoot, it was not a little startling to be told that these were signs of mourning, and that the master of the house had died during the interval that elapsed between our riding out and riding back again.

In Egypt, where the worship of ancestry and the preservation of the body were once among the most sacred duties of the living, they now make short work with their dead. He was to be buried, they said, tomorrow morning, three hours after sunrise.

CHAPTER XI.

The Cataract and the Desert.

AT Assouan one bids good-bye to Egypt, and enters
Nubia through the gates of the Cataract,—which is, in
truth, no cataract, but a succession of rapids extending
over two-thirds of the distance between Elephantine
and Philæ. The Nile—diverted from its original
course by some unrecorded catastrophe, the nature of
which has given rise to much scientific conjecture—
here spreads itself over a rocky basin, bounded by
sand slopes on the one side, and by granite cliffs on
the other. Studded with numberless islets, divided
into numberless channels, foaming over sunken rocks,
eddying among water-worn boulders, now shallow, now
deep, now loitering, now hurrying, here sleeping in the
ribbed hollow of a tiny sand-drift, there circling above
the vortex of a hidden whirlpool, the river, whether
looked upon from the deck of the Dahabeeyah or the
heights along the shore, is seen everywhere to be fighting its way through a labyrinth, the paths of which
have never yet been mapped or sounded.

Those paths are everywhere difficult, and everywhere dangerous; and to that labyrinth the Shellalee,
or Cataract-Arab, alone possesses the key. At the
time of the inundation, when all but the highest rocks
are under water, and navigation is as easy here as
elsewhere, the Shellalee's occupation is gone. But as
the floods subside and travellers begin to reappear, his

work commences. To haul Dahabeeyahs up those treacherous rapids by sheer stress of rope and muscle; to steer skilfully down again through channels bristling with rocks and boiling with foam, becomes now, for some five months of the year, his principal industry. It is hard work; but he gets well paid for it, and his profits are always on the increase. From forty to fifty Dahabeeyahs are now annually taken up between November and March; and every year brings a larger influx of travellers. Meanwhile, accidents rarely happen; prices tend continually upwards; and the Cataract Arabs make a little fortune by their singular monopoly.

The scenery of the First Cataract is like nothing else in the world—except the scenery of the Second. It is altogether new, and strange, and beautiful. It is incomprehensible that travellers should have written of it in general with so little admiration. They seem to have been impressed by the wildness of the waters, by the quaint forms of the rocks, by the desolation and grandeur of the landscape as a whole; but scarcely at all by its beauty—which is paramount.

The Nile here widens to a lake. Of the islands, which it would hardly be an exaggeration to describe as some hundreds in number, no two are alike. Some are piled up like the rocks at the Land's End in Cornwall, block upon block, column upon column, tower upon tower, as if reared by the hand of man. Some are green with grass; some golden with slopes of drifted sand; some planted with rows of blossoming lupins, purple and white. Others again are mere cairns of loose blocks, with here and there a perilously balanced top-boulder. On one, a singular upright monolith, like a menhir, stands conspicuous, as if placed there to commemorate a date, or to point the way to Philæ. Another mass rises out of the water squared and buttressed, in the likeness of a fort. A third, humped and shining like the wet body of some amphibious beast, lifts what seems to be a horned head above the surface of the rapids. All these blocks and boulders and fantastic rocks are granite; some red, some purple, some black. Their forms are rounded by the friction of ages. Those nearest the brink reflect the sky like mirrors of burnished steel. Royal ovals and hieroglyphed inscriptions, fresh as of yesterday's cutting, start out here and there from those glittering surfaces with startling distinctness. A few of the larger islands are crowned with clumps of palms; and one, the loveliest of any, is completely embowered in gum-trees and acacias, dôm and date palms, and feathery tamarisks, all festooned together under a hanging canopy of yellow-blossomed creepers.

On a brilliant Sunday morning, with a favourable wind, we entered on this fairy archipelago. Sailing steadily against the current, we glided away from Assouan, left Elephantine behind, and found ourselves at once in the midst of the islands. From this moment every turn of the tiller disclosed a fresh point of view, and we sat on deck, spectators of a moving panorama. The diversity of subjects was endless. The combinations of form and colour, of light and shadow, of foreground and distance, were continually changing. A boat or a few figures alone were wanting to complete the picturesqueness of the scene; but in all those channels, and among all those islands, we saw no sign of any living creature.

Meanwhile the Sheykh of the Cataract — a flat-faced, fishy-eyed old Nubian, with his head tied up in a dingy yellow silk handkerchief—sat apart in solitary grandeur at the stern, smoking a long chibouque. Behind him squatted some five or six dusky strangers; and a new steersman, black as a negro, had charge of the helm. This new steersman was our pilot for Nubia. From Assouan to Wady Halfeh, and back again to Assouan, he alone was now held responsible for the safety of the Dahabeeyah and all on board.

At length a general stir among the crew warned us of the near neighbourhood of the first rapid. Straight ahead, as if ranged along the dyke of a weir, a chain of small islets barred the way; while the current, divided into three or four headlong torrents, came rushing down the slope, and reunited at the bottom in one tumultuous race.

That we should ever get the Philæ up that hill of moving water, seemed at first sight impossible. Still our steersman held on his course, making for the widest channel. Still the Sheykh smoked imperturbably. Presently, without removing the pipe from his mouth, he delivered the one word—"Roóhh!" (Forward!)

Instantly, evoked by his nod, the rocks swarmed with natives. Hidden till now in all sorts of unseen corners, they sprang out shouting, gesticulating, laden with coils of rope, leaping into the thick of the rapids, splashing like water-dogs, bobbing like corks, and making as much show of energy as if they were going to haul us up Niagara. The thing was evidently a *coup de théâtre*, like the apparition of Clan Alpine's warriors in the Donna del Lago—with backsheesh in the background.

The scene that followed was curious enough. Two ropes were carried from the Dahabeeyah to the nearest .island, and there made fast to the rocks. Two ropes from the island were also brought on board the Dahabeeyah. A double file of men on deck, and another double file on shore, then ranged themselves along the ropes; the Sheykh gave the signal; and, to a wild chanting accompaniment and a movement like a barbaric Sir Roger de Coverley dance, a system of double hauling began, by means of which the huge boat slowly and steadily ascended. We may have been a quarter of an hour going up the incline; though it seemed much longer. Meanwhile, as they warmed to their work, the men chanted louder and pulled harder, till the boat went in at last with a rush, and swung over into a pool of comparatively smooth water.

Having moored here for an hour's rest, we next repeated the performance against a still stronger current a little higher up. This time, however, a rope broke. Down went the haulers, like a row of cards suddenly tipped over—round swung the Philæ, receiving the whole rush of the current on her beam! Luckily for us, the other rope held fast against the strain. Had it also broken, we must have been wrecked then and there, ignominiously.

Our Nubian auxiliaries struck work after this. Fate, they said, was adverse; so they went home, leaving us moored for the night in the pool at the top of the first rapid. The Sheykh promised, however, that his people should begin work next morning at dawn, and get us through before sunset. Next morning came, however, and not a man appeared upon the scene. At about mid-day they began dropping in, a few at a time; hung about in a languid, lazy way for a couple of hours or so; moved us into a better position for attacking the next rapid; and then melted away mysteriously by twos and threes among the rocks, and were no more seen.

We now felt that our time and money were being recklessly squandered, and we resolved to bear it no longer. Our Painter therefore undertook to remonstrate with the Sheykh, and to convince him of the error of his ways. The Sheykh listened; smoked; shook his head; replied that in the Cataract, as elsewhere, there were lucky and unlucky days, days when men felt inclined to work, and days when they felt disinclined. To-day, as it happened, they felt disinclined. Being reminded that it was unreasonable to keep us three days going up five miles of river, and that there was a governor at Assouan to whom we should appeal to-morrow unless the work went on in earnest, he smiled, shrugged his shoulders, and muttered something about "destiny."

Now the Painter, being of a practical turn, had compiled for himself a little vocabulary of choice Arabic maledictions, which he carried in his note-book for reference when needed. Having no faith in its possible usefulness, we were amused by the industry with which he was constantly adding to this collection. We looked upon it, in fact, as a harmless pleasantry—just as we looked upon his pocket-revolver, which was never loaded; or his brand-new fowling-piece, which he was never known to fire.

But the Sheykh of the Cataract had gone too far. The fatuity of that smile would have exasperated the meekest of men; and our Painter was not the meekest

of men. So he whipped out his pocket-book, ran his
finger down the line, and delivered an appropriate
quotation. His accent may not have been faultless;
but there could be no mistake as to the energy of his
style, or the vigour of his language. The effect of
both was instantaneous. The Sheykh sprang to his
feet as if he had been shot—turned pale with rage
under his black skin—vowed the Philæ might stay
where she was till doomsday, for aught that he or his
men would do to help her a foot farther—bounded into
his own rickety sandal, and rowed away, leaving us to
our fate.

We stood aghast. It was all over with us. We
should never see Aboo Simbel now—never write our
names on the Rock of Abooseer, nor slake our thirst at
the waters of the Second Cataract. What was to be
done? Must the Sheykh be defied, or propitiated?
Should we appeal to the Governor, or should we im-
molate the Painter? The majority were for immolat-
ing the Painter.

We went to bed that night, despairing; but lo!
next morning at sunrise appeared the Sheykh of the
Cataract, all smiles, all activity, with no end of ropes
and a force of two hundred men. We were his dearest
friends now. The Painter was his brother. He had
called out the ban and arrière ban of the Cataract in
our service. There was nothing, in short, that he
would not do to oblige us.

The dragoman vowed that he had never seen
Nubians work as these Nubians worked this day. They
fell to like giants, tugging away from morn till dewy
eve, and never giving over till they brought us round
the last corner, and up the last rapid. The sun had

set, the afterglow had faded, the twilight was closing in, when our Dahabeeyah slipped at last into level water, and the two hundred, with a parting shout, dispersed to their several villages.

We were never known to make light of the Painter's repertory of select abuse after this. If that note-book of his had been the drowned book of Prospero, or the magical Papyrus of Thoth fished up anew from the bottom of the Nile, we could not have regarded it with a respect more nearly bordering upon awe.

Though there exists no boundary line to mark where Egypt ends and Nubia begins, the nationality of the races dwelling on either side of that invisible barrier is as sharply defined as though an ocean divided them. Among the Shellalee, or Cataract villagers, one comes suddenly into the midst of a people that have apparently nothing in common with the population of Egypt. They belong to a lower ethnological type; and they speak a language derived from purely African sources. Contrasting with our Arab sailors the sulky-looking, half-naked, muscular savages that thronged about the Philæ during her passage up the Cataract, one could not but perceive that they were to this day as distinct and inferior a people as when their Egyptian conquerors, massing together in one contemptuous epithet all nations south of the frontier, were wont to speak of them as "the vile race of Cush." Time has done little to change them since those early days. Some Arabic words have crept into their vocabulary. Some modern luxuries—as tobacco, coffee, soap, and gunpowder—have come to be included in the brief catalogue of their daily wants. But in most other respects they are living to this day as they lived in the time of the Pharaohs; cultivating lentils and doorah, brewing barley beer, plaiting mats and baskets of stained reeds, tracing rude patterns upon bowls of gourd-rind, flinging the javelin, fashioning bucklers of crocodile-skin and bracelets of ivory, and supplying Egypt with henna. The dexterity with which, sitting as if in a wager boat, they balance themselves on a palm-log, and paddle to and fro about the river, is really surprising. This barbaric substitute for a boat is probably as ancient as the pyramids.

Having witnessed the passage of the first few rapids, we were glad to escape from the Dahabeeyah, and spend our time sketching here and there on the borders of the desert, and among the villages and islands round about. In all Egypt and Nubia there is no scenery richer in picturesque bits than the scenery of the Cataract. An artist might pass a winter there, and not exhaust the pictorial wealth of those five miles that divide Assouan from Philæ. Of tortuous creeks shut in by rocks fantastically piled—of sand-slopes golden to the water's edge—of placid pools low-lying in the midst of lupin-fields and tracts of tender barley—of creeking Sakkiehs, half hidden among palms and dropping water as they turn—of mud dwellings, here clustered together in hollows, there perched separately on heights among the rocks, and perpetuating to this day the form and slope of Egyptian pylons—of rude boats drawn up in sheltered coves, or going to pieces high and dry upon the sands—of water-washed boulders of crimson, and black, and purple granite, on which the wild fowl cluster at mid-day and the fisher spreads his nets to dry at sunset—of camels, and caravans, and camps on shore—of

cargo-boats and cangias on the river—of wild figures
of half-naked athletes—of dusky women decked with
barbaric ornaments, unveiled, swift-gliding, trailing long
robes of deepest gentian blue—of ancient crones, and
little naked children like live bronzes—of these, and
a hundred other subjects, in infinite variety and combination, there is literally no end. It is all so picturesque, indeed, so biblical, so poetical, that one is
almost in danger of forgetting that the places are
something more than beautiful backgrounds, and that
the people are not merely appropriate figures placed
there for the delight of sketchers, but are made of
living flesh and blood, and moved by hopes, and fears,
and sorrows, like our own.

Mahatta—green with sycamores and tufted palms;
nestled in the hollow of a little bay; half-islanded in
the rear by an arm of backwater, curved and glittering
like the blade of a Turkish scimetar—is by far the
most beautifully situated village on the Nile. It is the
residence of the principal Sheykh, and, if one may say
so, is the capital of the Cataract. The houses lie
some way back from the river. The bay is thronged
with native boats of all sizes and colours. Men and
camels, women and children, donkeys, dogs, merchandise,
and temporary huts put together with poles and matting, crowd the sandy shore. It is Assouan over again;
but on a larger scale. The shipping is tenfold more
numerous. The traders' camp is in itself a village.
The beach is half a mile in length, and a quarter of a
mile in the slope down to the river. Mahatta is, in
fact, the twin port to Assouan. It lies, not precisely
at the other extremity of the great valley between Assouan and Philæ, but at the nearest accessible point

THE CATARACT AND THE DESERT.   259

above the Cataract. It is here that the Soudan traders
disembark their goods for re-embarkation at Assouan.
Such rickety, barbaric-looking craft as these Nubian
cangias we had not yet seen on the river. They
looked as old and obsolete as the Ark. Some had
curious carved verandahs outside the cabin-entrance.
Others were tilted up at the stern like Chinese junks.
Most of them had been slavers in the palmy days of
Defterdar Bey; plying then as now between Wady
Halfeh and Mahatta; discharging their human cargoes
at this point for re-shipment at Assouan; and rarely
passing the Cataract, even at the time of inundation. If their wicked old timbers could have spoken,
they might have told us many a black and bloody
tale.

Going up through the village and the palm-gardens,
and turning off in a north-easterly direction towards the
desert, one presently comes out about midway of that
valley to which I have made allusion more than once
already. No one, however unskilled in physical geo-
graphy, could look from end to end of that huge furrow and not see that it was once a river-bed. We
know not for how many tens of thousands, or hundreds
of thousands, of years the Nile may have held on its
course within those original bounds. Neither can we
tell when it deserted them. It is, however, quite certain that the river flowed that way within historic times;
that is to say, in the days of Amenemhat III. (*circa*
B.C. 2800). So much is held to be proven by certain
inscriptions* which record the maximum height of the

---

* "The most important discovery which we have made here, and which I
shall only mention briefly, is a series of short rock-inscriptions, which mark the
highest rises of the Nile during a series of years under the government of

17*

inundation at Semneh during various years of that King's reign. The Nile then rose in Ethiopia to a level 27 feet and 3 inches in excess of the highest point to which it is ever known to attain at the present day. I am not aware what relation the height of this ancient bed bears to the levels recorded at Semneh, or to those now annually self-registered upon the furrowed banks of Philæ; but one sees at a glance, without aid of measurements or hydrographic science, that if the river were to come down again next summer in a mighty 'bore,' the crest of which rose 27 feet above the highest ground now fertilised by the annual overflow, it would at once refill its long-deserted bed, and convert Assouan into an island.

Granted, then, that the Nile flowed through the desert in the time of Amenemhat III., there must at some later period have come a day when it suddenly ran dry. This catastrophe is supposed to have taken place about the time of the expulsion of the Hyksos (*circa* B.C. 1703), when a great disruption of the rocky bar-

Amenemhat III. and of his immediate successors. . . . They prove that the river, above 4000 years ago, rose more than 24 feet higher than now, and thereby must have produced totally different conditions in the inundation and in the whole surface of the ground, both above and below this spot."—Lepsius's *Letters from Egypt, etc.*, Letter xxvi.

"The highest rise of the Nile in each year at Semne was registered by a mark indicating the year of the king's reign, cut in the granite, either on one of the blocks forming the foundation of the fortress, or on the cliff, and particularly on the east or right bank, as best adapted for the purpose. Of these markings eighteen still remain, thirteen of them having been made in the reign of Mœris (Amenemhat III.) and five in the time of his next two successors. . . . We have here presented to us the remarkable facts that the highest of the records now legible, viz. that of the thirtieth year of the reign of Amenemhat, according to exact measurements which I made, is 8.17 metres (26 feet 8 inches) higher than the highest level to which the Nile rises in years of the greatest floods; and, further, that the lowest mark, which is on the east bank and indicated the fifteenth year of the same king, is still 4.14 metres (13 feet 6½ inches); and the single mark on the west bank indicating the ninth year, is 2.77 metres (9 feet) above the highest level."—Lepsius's *Letter to Professor Ehrenberg.* See Appendix to the above.

rier at Silsilis is thought to have taken place; so drain-
ing Nubia, which till now had played the part of a
vast reservoir, and dispersing the pent-up floods over
the plains of Southern Egypt. It would, however, be
a mistake to conclude that the Nile was by this catastrophe turned aside in order to be precipitated in the
direction of the Cataract. One arm of the river must
always have taken the present lower and deeper course;
while the other must of necessity have run low—perhaps very nearly dry—as the inundation subsided every
spring.

There remains no monumental record of this event;
but the facts speak for themselves. The great channel
is there. The old Nile-mud is there—buried for the
most part in sand, but still visible on many a rocky
shelf and plateau between Assouan and Philæ. There
are even places where the surface of the mass is seen
to be scooped out, as if by the sudden rush of the departing waters. Since that time, the tides of war and
commerce have flowed in their place. Every conquering Thothmes and Rameses bound for the land of
Cush, led his armies that way. Sabacon, at the head
of his Ethiopian hordes, took that short cut to the
throne of all the Pharaohs. The French under Desaix,
pursuing the Memlooks after the battle of the Pyramids, swept down that pass to Philæ. Meanwhile the
whole trade of the Soudan, however interrupted at
times by the ebb and flow of war, has also set that
way. We never crossed those five miles of desert
without encountering a train or two of baggage-camels
laden either with European goods for the far South, or
with Oriental treasures for the north.

I shall not soon forget an Abyssinian caravan that

we met one day just coming out from Mahatta. It consisted of seventy camels laden with elephant tusks. The tusks, which were about fourteen feet in length, were packed in half-dozens and sewn up in buffalo hides. Each camel was slung with two loads, one at either side of the hump. There must have been about 840 tusks in all. Beside each shambling beast strode a bare-footed Nubian. Following these, on the back of a gigantic camel, came a hunting leopard in a wooden cage, and a wild cat in a basket. Last of all marched a coal-black Abyssinian nearly seven feet in height, magnificently shawled and turbaned, with a huge scimetar dangling by his side, and in his belt a pair of enormous inlaid seventeenth-century pistols, such as would have become the holsters of Prince Rupert. This elaborate warrior represented the guard of the caravan. The hunting leopard and the wild cat were for Prince Hassan, the third son of the Viceroy. The ivory was for exportation. Anything more picturesque than this procession, with the dust driving before it in clouds, and the children following it out of the village, it would be difficult to conceive. One longed for Gerôme to paint it on the spot.

The rocks on either side of the ancient river-bed are profusely hieroglyphed. These inscriptions, together with others found in the adjacent quarries, range over a period of between three and four thousand years, beginning with the early reigns of the ancient empire, and ending with the Ptolemies and Cæsars. Some are mere autographs. Others run to a considerable length. Many are headed with figures of gods and worshippers. These, however, are for the most part mere graffiti, ill drawn and carelessly sculptured. The records they illustrate are chiefly votive. The passer-by adores the gods of the Cataract; implores their protection; registers his name, and states the object of his journey. The votaries are of various ranks, periods, and nationalities; but the formula in most instances is pretty much the same. Now it is a citizen of Thebes performing the pilgrimage to Philæ; or a general at the head of his troops returning from a foray in Ethiopia; or a tributary Prince doing homage to Rameses the Great, and associating his suzerain with the divinities of the place. Occasionally we come upon a royal cartouche and a pompous catalogue of titles, setting forth how the Pharaoh himself, the Golden Hawk, the Son of the Sun, the Mighty, the Invincible, the Godlike, passed that way.

It is curious to see how royalty, so many thousand years ago, set the fashion in names, just as it does to this day. Nine-tenths of the ancient travellers who left their signatures upon these rocks were called Rameses or Thothmes or Usertasen. Others, still more ambitious, took the names of gods. Ampère, who hunted diligently for inscriptions both here and among the islands, found the autographs of no end of merely mortal Ammons and Hathors.

Our three days' detention in the Cataract was followed by a fourth of glassy calm. There being no breath of air to fill our sails and no footing for the trackers, we could now get along only by dint of hard punting; so that it was past midday before the Philæ lay moored at last in the shadow of the holy island to which she owed her name.

CHAPTER XII.

Philæ.

HAVING been for so many days within easy reach of Philæ, it is not to be supposed that we were content till now with only an occasional glimpse of its towers in the distance. On the contrary, we had found our way thither towards the close of almost every day's excursion. We had approached it by land from the desert; by water in the felucca; from Mahatta by way of the path between the cliffs and the river. When I add that we moored here for a night and the best part of two days on our way up the river, and again for a week when we came down, it will be seen that we had time to learn the lovely island by heart.

The approach by water is quite the most beautiful. Seen from the level of a small boat, the island, with its palms, its colonnades, its pylons, seems to rise out of the river like a mirage. Piled rocks frame it in on either side, and purple mountains close up the distance. As the boat glides nearer between glistening boulders, those sculptured towers rise higher and ever higher against the sky. They show no sign of ruin or of age. All looks solid, stately, perfect. One forgets for the moment that anything is 'changed. If a sound of antique chanting were to be borne along the quiet air— if a procession of white-robed priests bearing aloft the veiled ark of the God, were to come sweeping round between the palms and the pylons—we should not think it strange.

Most travellers land at the end nearest the Cataract; so coming upon the principal temple from behind, and seeing it in reverse order. We, however, bid our Arabs row round to the southern end, where was once a stately landing-place with steps down to the river. We skirt the steep banks, and pass close under the beautiful little roofless Temple commonly known as Pharaoh's Bed—that Temple which has been so often painted, so often photographed, that every stone of it, and the platform on which it stands, and the tufted palms that cluster round about it, have been since childhood as familiar to our mind's eye as the Sphinx or the Pyramids. It is larger, but not one jot less beautiful than we had expected. And it is exactly like the photographs. Still, one is conscious of perceiving a shade of difference too subtle for analysis; like the difference between a familiar face and the reflection of it in a looking-glass. Anyhow, one feels that the real Pharaoh's Bed will henceforth displace the photographs in that obscure mental pigeon-hole where till now one has been wont to store the well-known image; and that even the photographs have undergone some kind of change.

And now the corner is rounded; and the river widens away southwards between mountains and palm-groves; and the prow touches the débris of a ruined quay. The bank is steep here. We climb; and a wonderful scene opens before our eyes. We are standing at the lower end of a courtyard leading up to the propylons of the great Temple. The courtyard is irregular in shape, and enclosed on either side by covered colonnades.   The colonnades are of unequal lengths and set at different angles.   One is simply a covered walk; the other opens upon a row of small chambers, like a monastic cloister opening upon a row of cells. The roofing-stones of these colonnades are in part displaced, while here and there a pillar or a capital is missing; but the twin towers of the propylon, standing out in sharp unbroken lines against the sky and covered with colossal sculptures, are as perfect, or very nearly as perfect, as in the days of the Ptolemies who built them.

The broad area between the colonnades is honeycombed with crude-brick foundations; vestiges of a Coptic village of early Christian time.   Among these we thread our way to the foot of the principal propylon, the entire width of which is 120 feet.   The towers measure 60 feet from base to parapet.   These dimensions are insignificant for Egypt; yet the propylon, which would look small at Luxor or Karnak, does not look small at Philæ.   The keynote here is not magnitude, but beauty.   The island is small—that is to say it covers an area about equal to the summit of the Acropolis at Athens; and the scale of the buildings has been determined by the size of the island.   As at Athens, the ground is occupied by one principal Temple of moderate size and several subordinate Chapels. Perfect grace, exquisite proportion, most varied and capricious grouping, here take the place of massiveness; so lending to Egyptian forms an irregularity of treatment that is almost Gothic, and a lightness that is almost Greek.

And now we catch glimpses of an inner court, of a second propylon, of a pillared portico beyond; while, looking up to the colossal bas-reliefs above our heads, we see the usual mystic forms of kings and deities, crowned, enthroned, worshipping and worshipped. These sculptures which, as we first saw them, looked no less perfect than the towers, prove to be as laboriously mutilated as those of Denderah. The hawk-head of Horus and the cow-head of Hathor have here and there escaped destruction; but the human-faced deities are literally "sans eyes, sans nose, sans ears, sans everything."

We enter the inner court—an irregular quadrangle enclosed on the east by an open colonnade, on the west by a chapel fronted with Hathor-headed columns, and on the north and south sides by the second and first propylons. In this quadrangle a cloistral silence reigns. The blue sky burns above—the shadows sleep below—a tender twilight lies about our feet. Inside the chapel there sleeps perpetual gloom. It was built by Ptolemy Euergetes II., and is one of that order to which Champollion gave the name of Mammisi. It is a most curious place, dedicated to Hathor and commemorative of the nurture of Horus. On the blackened walls within, dimly visible by the faint light that struggles through screen and doorway, we see Isis, the wife and sister of Osiris, giving birth to Horus. On the screen panels outside we trace the story of his infancy, education, and growth. As a babe at the breast, he is nursed in the lap of Hathor, the divine foster-mother. As a young child, he stands at his mother's knee and listens to the playing of a female harpist (we saw a barefooted boy the other day in Cairo thrumming upon a harp of just the same shape, and with precisely as many strings); as a youth, he sows grain in honour of Isis, and offers a jewelled collar to Hathor. This Isis, with her long aquiline nose, thin lips, and haughty aspect, looks like one of the complimentary portraits so often introduced among the temple sculptures of Egypt. It may represent one of the two Cleopatras wedded to Ptolemy Physcon.

Two greyhounds with collars round their necks are sculptured on the outer wall of another small chapel adjoining. These also look like portraits. Perhaps they were the favourite dogs of some high priest of Philæ.

Close against the greyhounds and upon the same wall-space, is engraven that famous copy of the inscription of the Rosetta Stone first observed here by Lepsius in A.D. 1843. It neither stands so high nor looks so illegible as Ampère (with all the jealousy of a Champollionist and a Frenchman) is at such pains to make out. One would have said that it was in a state of more than ordinarily good preservation.

As a reproduction of the Rosetta decree, however, the Philæ version is incomplete. The Rosetta text, after setting forth with official pomposity the victories and munificence of the King, Ptolemy V., the Ever-living, the Avenger of Egypt, concludes by ordaining that the record thereof shall be engraven in hieroglyphic, demotic, and Greek characters, and set up in all temples of the first, second, and third class throughout the Empire. Broken and battered as it is, the precious black basalt*

---

* M. Mariette, at the end of his *Aperçu de l'Histoire d'Egypte*, gives the following succinct account of the Rosetta Stone, and the discovery of Champollion:—

"Découverte, il y a 65 ans environ, par des soldats français qui creusaient un retranchment près d'une redoute située à Rosette, la pierre qui porte ce nom a joué le plus grand rôle dans l'archéologie égyptienne. Sur la face prin-

of the British Museum fulfils these conditions. The three writings are there. But at Philæ, though the original hieroglyphic and demotic texts are reproduced almost verbatim, the priceless Greek transcript is want-

cipale sont gravées *trois* inscriptions. Les deux premières sont en langue égyptienne et écrites dans les deux écritures qui avaient cours à cette époque. L'une est en écriture hiéroglyphique réservée aux prêtres : elle ne compte plus que 14 lignes tronquées par la brisure de la pierre. L'autre est en une écriture cursive appliquée principalement aux usages du peuple et comprise par lui : celle-ci offre 32 lignes de texte. Enfin, la troisième inscription de la stèle est en langue grecque et comprend 54 lignes. C'est dans cette dernière partie que réside l'intérêt du monument trouvé à Rosette. Il résulte, en effet, de l'interprétation du texte grec de la stèle que ce texte n'est qu'une version de l'original transcrit plus haut dans les deux écritures égyptiennes. La Pierre de Rosette nous donne donc, dans une langue parfaitement connue (le grec) la traduction d'un texte conçu dans une autre langue encore ignorée au moment où la stèle a été découverte. Qui ne voit l'utilité de cette mention ? Remonter du connu à "inconnu n'est pas une opération en dehors des moyens d'une critique prudente, et déjà l'on devine que si la Pierre de Rosette a acquis dans la science la célébrité dont elle jouit aujourd'hui, c'est qu'elle a fourni la vraie clef de cette mystérieuse écriture dont l'Égypte a si longtemps gardé le secret. Il ne faudrait pas croire cependant que le déchiffrement des hiéroglyphes au moyen de la Pierre de Rosette ait été obtenu du premier coup et sans tâtonnements. Bien au contraire, les savants s'y essayèrent sans succès pendant 20 ans. Enfin, Champollion parut. Jusqu'à lui, on avait cru que chacune des lettres qui composent l'écriture hiéroglyphique était un *symbole;* c'est à dire, que dans une seule de ces lettres était exprimée une *idée* complète. Le mérite de Champollion a été de prouver qu'au contraire l'écriture égyptienne contient des signes qui expriment véritablement des *sons.* En d'autres termes qu'elle est *Alphabétique.* Il remarqua, par exemple, que partout où dans le texte grec de Rosette se trouve le nom propre *Ptolémée,* on rencontre à l'endroit correspondant du texte égyptien un certain nombre de signes enfermés dans un encadrement elliptique. Il en conclut : 1°, que les noms des rois étaient dans le système hiéroglyphique signalé à l'attention par une sorte d'écusson qu'il appela *cartouche:* 2°, que les signes contenus dans cet écusson devaient être lettre pour lettre le nom de Ptolémée. Déjà donc en supposant les voyelles omises, Champollion était en possession de cinq lettres—P, T, L, M. S. D'un autre côté, Champollion savait, d'après une seconde inscription grecque gravée sur une obélisque de Philæ, que sur cet obélisque un cartouche hiéroglyphique qu'on y voit devait être celui de Cléopâtre. Si sa première lecture était juste, le P, le L, et le T. de Ptolémée devaient se retrouver dans le second nom propre; mais en même temps ce second nom propre fournissait un K et un R nouveaux. Enfin, appliqué à d'autres cartouches, l'alphabet encore très-imparfait révélé à Champollion par les noms de Cléopâtre et de Ptolémée le mit en possession d'à peu près toutes les autres consonnes. Comme *prononciation* des signes, Champollion n'avait donc pas à hésiter, et dès le jour où cette constatation eut lieu, il put certifier qu'il était en possession de l'alphabet égyptien. Mais restait la langue; car prononcer des mots n'est rien si l'on ne sait pas ce que ces mots veulent dire. Ici le génie de Champollion se donna libre cours. Il s'aperçut en effet que son alphabet tiré des noms propres et appliqué aux

ing. It is provided for, as upon the Rosetta Stone, in the preamble. Space has been left for it at the bottom of the tablet. We even fancied we could here and there distinguish traces of red ink where the lines should come. But not one word of it has ever been cut into the surface of the stone.

Taken by itself, there is nothing strange in this omission; but taken in connection with a precisely similar omission in another inscription a few yards distant, it becomes something more than a coincidence.

This second inscription is cut upon the face of a block of living rock which forms part of the foundation of the easternmost tower of the second propylon. Having enumerated certain grants of land made to the Temple by the VIth and VIIth Ptolemies, it concludes, like the first, by decreeing that this record of the royal bounty shall be engraven in the hieroglyphic, demotic, and Greek:—that is to say, in the ancient sacred writ-

---

mots de la langue donnait tout simplement du *Copte*. Or, le Copte à son tour est une langue qui, sans être aussi explorée que le grec, n'en était pas moins depuis longtemps accessible. Cette fois le voile était donc complétement levé. La langue égyptienne n'est que du Copte écrit en hiéroglyphes; ou, pour parler plus exactement, le Copte n'est que la langue des anciens Pharaons, écrite, comme nous l'avons dit plus haut, en lettres grecques. Le reste se devine. D'indices en indices, Champollion procéda véritablement du connu à l'inconnu, et bientôt l'illustre fondateur de l'égyptologie put poser les fondements de cette belle science qui a pour object l'interprétation des hiéroglyphes. Tel est la Pierre de Rosette."—*Aperçu de l'histoire d'Egypte*: Mariette Bey, p. 189 *et seq.*: 1872.

In order to have done with this subject, it may be as well to mention that another trilingual tablet was found by M. Mariette while conducting the excavations at Sân (Tanis) in 1865. It dates from the ninth year of Ptolemy Euergetes, and the text ordains the deification of Berenice, a daughter of the king, then just dead (B.C. 254). This stone, preserved in the museum at Boulak, is known as the Stone of Sân, or the Decree of Canopus. Had the Rosetta Stone never been discovered, we may fairly conclude that the Canopic Decree would have furnished some later Champollion with the necessary key to hieroglyphic literature, and that the great discovery would only have been deferred till the present time.

ing of the priests, the ordinary script of the people, and the language of the Court. But here again the sculptor has left his work unfinished. Here again the inscription breaks off at the end of the demotic, leaving a blank space for the third transcript. This second omission suggests intentional neglect; and the motive for such neglect would not be far to seek. The tongue of the dominant race is likely enough to have been unpopular among the old noble and sacerdotal families; and it may well be that the priesthood of Philæ, secure in their distant, solitary isle, could with impunity evade a clause which their brethren of the Delta were obliged to obey.

It does not follow that the Greek rule was equally unpopular. We have reason to believe quite otherwise. The conqueror of the Persian invader was in truth the deliverer of Egypt. Alexander restored peace to the country, and the Ptolemies identified themselves with the interests of the people. A dynasty that not only lightened the burdens of the poor but respected the privileges of the rich; that honoured the priesthood, endowed the Temples, and compelled the Tigris to restore the spoils of the Nile, could scarcely fail to win the suffrages of all classes. The priests of Philæ might despise the language of Homer while honouring the descendants of Philip of Macedon. They could naturalise the King. They could disguise his name in hieroglyphic spelling. They could depict him in the traditional dress of the Pharaohs. They could crown him with the double crown, and represent him in the act of worshipping the gods of his adopted country. But they could neither naturalise nor disguise his language. Spoken or written, it was an alien thing. Carven in high places, it stood for a badge of servitude. What could a conservative hierarchy do but abhor, and, when possible, ignore it?

There are other sculptures in this quadrangle which one would like to linger over; as, for instance, the capitals of the Eastern colonnade, no two of which are alike, and the grotesque bas-reliefs of the frieze of the Mammisi. Of these, a quasi-heraldic group, representing the sacred hawk sitting in the centre of a fan-shaped persea tree between two supporters, is one of the most curious; the supporters being on the one side a maniacal lion, and on the other a Typhonian hippopotamus, each grasping a pair of shears.

Passing now through the doorway of the second propylon, we find ourselves in the portico—the famous painted portico of which we had seen so many sketches that we fancied we knew it already. That second-hand knowledge goes for nothing, however, in presence of the reality; and we are as much taken by surprise as if we were the first travellers to set foot within these enchanted precincts.

For here is a place in which time seems to have stood as still as in that immortal palace where everything went to sleep for a hundred years. The bas-reliefs on the walls, the intricate paintings on the ceilings, the colours upon the capitals, are incredibly fresh and perfect. These exquisite capitals have long been the wonder and delight of travellers in Egypt. They are all studied from natural forms—from the lotus in bud and blossom, the papyrus, and the palm. Conventionalised with consummate skill, they are at the same time so justly proportioned to the height and girth 'of the columns as to give an air of wonderful lightness to the whole structure. But above all, it is with the colour—

colour conceived in the tender and pathetic minor of Watteau and Lancret and Greuze—that one is most fascinated. Of those delicate half-tones, not even the careful facsimile in the "Grammar of Ornament" conveys the remotest idea. Every tint is softened, intermixed, degraded. The pinks are coralline; the greens are tempered with verditer; the blues are of a greenish turquoise, like the western half of an autumnal evening sky.*

Architecturally, this portico is unlike any we have yet seen, being open to the sky in the centre, like the atrium of a Roman house. The light thus admitted glows overhead, lies in a square patch on the ground below, and is reflected upon the pictured recesses of the ceiling. At the upper end, where the pillars stand two deep, there was originally an intercolumnar screen. The rough sides of the columns show where the connecting blocks have been torn away. The pavement, too, has been pulled up .by treasure-seekers, and the ground is strewn with broken slabs and fragments of shattered cornice.

These are the only signs of ruin—signs traced not

* The famous capitals are not the only specimens of admirable colouring in Philæ. Among the battered bas-reliefs of the great colonnade at the south end of the island, there yet remain some isolated patches of uninjured and very lovely ornament. See, more particularly, the mosaic pattern upon the throne of a divinity just over the second doorway in the western wall; and the designs upon a series of other thrones a little farther along towards the north, all most delicately drawn in uniform compartments, picked out in the three primary colours, and laid on in flat tints of wonderful purity and delicacy. Among these a lotus between two buds, an exquisite little sphinx on a pale red ground, and a series of sacred hawks, white upon red, alternating with white upon blue, all most exquisitely conventionalised, may be cited as examples of absolutely perfect treatment and design in polychrome decoration. A more instructive and delightful task than the copying of these precious fragments can hardly be commended to students and sketchers on the Nile.

by the finger of Time, but by the hand of the spoiler. So fresh, so fair is all the rest, that we are fain to cheat ourselves for a moment into the belief that what we see is work not marred, but arrested. Those columns, depend on it, are yet unfinished. That pavement is about to be relaid. It would not surprise us to find the masons here to-morrow morning, or the sculptor, with mallet and chisel, carrying on that band of lotus buds and bees. Far more difficult is it to believe that they all struck work for ever some two-and-twenty centuries ago.

Here and there, where the foundations have been disturbed, one sees that the columns are constructed of sculptured blocks, the fragments of some earlier Temple; while, at a height of about six feet from the ground, a Greek cross cut deep into the side of the shaft stamps upon each pillar the seal of Christian worship.

For the Copts who choked the colonnades and courtyards with their hovels seized also on the Temples. Some they pulled down for building material; others they appropriated. We can never know how much they destroyed; but two large convents on the Eastern bank a little higher up the river, and a small basilica at the north end of the island, would seem to have been built with the magnificent masonry of the Southern quay, as well as with blocks taken from a structure that once occupied the South-eastern corner of the great colonnade. As for this beautiful painted portico, they turned it into a chapel. A little rough-hewn niche in the East wall, and an overturned credence-table fashioned from a single block of granite,* mark the site of the chancel. The Arabs, taking this last for a gravestone, have pulled it up, according to their usual practice, in search of treasure buried with the dead. On the front of the credence-table, and over the niche which some unskilled but pious hand has decorated with rude Byzantine carvings, the Greek cross is again conspicuous.

The religious history of Philæ is so curious that it is a pity it should not find an historian. It shared with Abydos and some other places the reputation of being the burial-place of Osiris. It was called "the Holy Island." Its very soil was sacred. None might land upon its shores, or even approach them too nearly, without permission. To obtain that permission and perform the pilgrimage to the tomb of the God, was to the pious Egyptian what the Mecca pilgrimage is to the pious Mussulman of to-day. The most solemn oath to which he could give utterance was "By Him who sleeps in Philæ."

When and how the island first came to be regarded as the resting-place of the most beloved of the Gods does not appear; but its reputation for sanctity seems to have been of comparatively modern date. It probably rose into importance as Abydos declined. Herodotus, who went as far as Elephantine and made minute enquiry concerning the river above that point, relates that the Cataract was in the occupation of "Ethiopian nomads;" but makes no mention of Philæ

---

* A late writer in *The Saturday Review* is of opinion that this credence-table was fashioned with part of a shrine destined for one of the captive hawks sacred to Horus.

or its Temples. This omission on the part of one who, wherever he went, sought the society of the priests and paid particular attention to the religious observances of the country, may be taken as good negative proof that the island had not yet become the home of the Osirian mysteries. Four hundred years later, however, Diodorus Siculus describes it as the holiest of holy places; while Strabo, writing about the same time, relates that Abydos had then dwindled to a mere village. It seems possible, therefore, that at some period subsequent to the visit of Herodotus and prior to that of Diodorus or Strabo, the priests of Isis may have migrated from Abydos to Philæ; in which case there would have been a formal transfer not only of the relics of Osiris, but of the sanctity which had attached for ages to their original resting-place. Nor is the motive for such an exodus wanting. The ashes of the God were no longer safe at Abydos. Situated in the midst of a rich corn country on the high road to Thebes, no city south of Memphis lay more exposed to the hazards of war. Cambyses had already passed that way. Other invaders might follow. To seek beyond the frontier that security which might no longer be found in Egypt, would seem therefore to be the obvious course of a priestly guild devoted to its trust. This, of course, is mere conjecture; to be taken for what it may be worth. The decadence of Abydos coincides, at all events, with the growth of Philæ; and it is only by help of some such assumption that one can understand how a new site should have suddenly arisen to such a height of holiness.

The earliest Temple here, of which only a small

propylon remains, would seem to have been built by
the last of the native Pharaohs (Nectanebo II., B.C. 361);
but the high and palmy days of Philæ belong to the
period of Greek and Roman rule. It was in the time
of the Ptolemies that the Holy Island became the seat
of a Sacred College and the stronghold of a powerful
hierarchy. Visitors from all parts of Egypt, travellers
from distant lands, court functionaries from Alexandria
charged with royal gifts, came annually in crowds to
pay their vows at the tomb of the God. They have
cut their names by hundreds all over the principal
Temple, just like tourists of to-day. Some of these
antique autographs are written upon and across those
of preceding visitors; while others—palimpsests upon
stone, so to say—having been scratched on the yet
unsculptured surface of doorway and pylon, are seen
to be older than the hieroglyphic texts which were
afterwards carved over them. These inscriptions cover
a period of several centuries, during which time successive Ptolemies and Cæsars continued to endow the
island. Rich in lands, in temples, in the localisation
of a great national myth, the Sacred College was yet
strong enough in A.D. 379 to oppose a practical resistance to the Edict of Theodosius. At a word from
Constantinople, the whole land of Egypt was forcibly
Christianised. Priests were forbidden under pain of
death to perform the sacred rites. Hundreds of temples
were plundered. Forty thousand statues of divinities
were destroyed at one fell swoop. Meanwhile the
brotherhood of Philæ, entrenched behind the Cataract
and the desert, survived the degradation of their order
and the ruin of their immemorial faith. It is not known

with certainty for how long they continued to transmit
their hereditary privileges; but two of the above-men-
tioned votive inscriptions show that so late as A.D. 453
the priestly families were still in occupation of the
island, and still celebrating the mysteries of Osiris and
Isis.   There even seems reason for believing that the
ancient worship continued to hold its own till the end
of the sixth century, at which time, according to an
inscription at Kalabsheh, of which I shall have more
to say hereafter, Silco, "King of all the Ethiopians,"
himself apparently a Christian, twice invaded Lower
Nubia, where God, he says, gave him the victory, and
the vanquished swore to him *by their idols*" to observe
the terms of peace.

There is nothing in this record to show that the
invaders went beyond Tafa, the ancient Taphis, which
is twenty-seven miles above Philæ; but it seems reason-
able to conclude that so long as the old gods yet
reigned in any part of Nubia, the island sacred to
Osiris would maintain its traditional sanctity.

At length, however, there must have come a day
when for the last time the tomb of the God was
crowned with flowers and the "Lamentations of Isis"
were recited on the threshold of the sanctuary.   And
there must have come another day when the cross was
carried in triumph up those painted colonnades, and
the first Christian mass was chanted in the precincts
of the heathen.   One would like to know how these
changes were brought about; whether the old faith
died out for want of worshippers, or was expelled with
clamour and violence.   But upon this point, history is

vague * and the graffiti of the time are silent. We only know for certain that the old went out, and the new came in; and that where the resurrected Osiris was wont to be worshipped according to the most sacred mysteries of the Egyptian ritual, the resurrected Christ was now adored after the simple fashion of the primitive Coptic Church.

And now the Holy Island, near which it was believed no fish had power to swim or bird to fly, and upon whose soil no pilgrim might set foot without permission, became all at once the common property of a populous community. Courts, colonnades, even terraced roofs, were overrun with little crude-brick dwellings. A small basilica was built at the lower end of the island. The portico of the Great Temple was converted into a Chapel, and dedicated to Saint Stephen. "This good work," says a Greek inscription traced there by some monkish hand of the period, "was done by the well-beloved of God, the Abbot-Bishop Theodore." Of this same Theodore, whom another inscription styles "the very holy father," we know nothing but his name.

The walls hereabout are full of these fugitive records. "The cross has conquered, and will ever conquer," writes one anonymous scribe. Others have left simple signatures; as, for instance—"I, Joseph," in one place, and "I, Theodosius of Nubia," in another. Here and there an added word or two give a more human interest to the autograph. So, in the pathetic scrawl

---

* The Emperor Justinian is credited with the mutilation of the sculptures of the large Temple: but the ancient worship was probably only temporarily suspended in his time.

of one who writes himself "Johannes, a slave," we seem
to read the story of a life in a single line. These
Coptic signatures are all followed by the sign of the
cross.

The foundations of the little basilica, with its apse
towards the East and its two doorways to the West,
are still traceable. We set a couple of our sailors one
day to clear away the rubbish at the lower end of the
nave, and found the font—a rough stone basin at the
foot of a broken column.

It is not difficult to guess what Philæ must have
been like in the days of Abbot Theodore and his flock.
The little basilica, we may be sure, had a cluster of
mud domes upon the roof; and I fancy, somehow, that
the Abbot and his monks installed themselves in that
row of cells on the East side of the great colonnade,
where the priests of Isis dwelt before them. As for
the village, it must have been just like Luxor—swarming with dusky life; noisy with the babble of children,
the cackling of poultry, and the barking of dogs; send-
ing up thin pillars of blue smoke at noon; echoing to
the measured chime of the prayer-bell at morn and
even; and sleeping at night as soundly as if no ghost-
like, mutilated Gods were looking on mournfully in the
moonlight.

The Gods are avenged now. The creed that dethroned them is dethroned. Abbot Theodore, and his
successors, and the religion they taught, and the simple
folk that listened to their teaching, are gone and forgotten. For the church of Christ, which still languishes
in Egypt, is extinct in Nubia. It lingered long; though
doubtless in some such degraded and barbaric form as

it wears in Abyssinia to this day. But it was absorbed by Islamism at last; and only a ruined convent perched here and there upon some solitary height, or a few crosses rudely carved on the walls of a Ptolemaic Temple, remain to show that Christianity once passed that way.

The mediæval history of Philæ is almost a blank. The Arabs, having invaded Egypt towards the middle of the seventh century, were long in the land before they began to cultivate literature; and for more than three hundred years history is silent. It is not till the tenth century that we once again catch a fleeting glimpse of Philæ. The frontier is now removed to the head of the Cataract. The Holy Island has ceased to be Christian; ceased to be Nubian; contains a mosque and garrison, and is the last fortified outpost of the Moslems. It still retains, and apparently continues to retain for some centuries longer, its ancient Egyptian name. That is to say (P being as usual converted into B) the Pilak of the hieroglyphic inscriptions becomes in Arabic Belak;* which is much more like the original than the Philæ of the Greeks.

The native Christians, meanwhile, would seem to have relapsed into a state of semi-barbarism. They make perpetual inroads upon the Arab frontier, and

* These and the following particulars about the Christians of Nubia are found in the famous work of Makrizi, an Arab historian of the fifteenth century, who quotes largely from earlier writers. See Burckhardt's *Travels in Nubia*, 4to, 1819, Appendix III. Although Belak is distinctly described as an island in the neighbourhood of the Cataract, distant four miles from Assouan, Burckhardt persisted in looking for it among the islets below Mahatta, and believed Philæ to be the first Nubian town beyond the frontier. The hieroglyphic alphabet, however, had not then been deciphered. Burckhardt died at Cairo in 1817, and Champollion's discovery was not given to the world till 1822.

suffer perpetual defeat. Battles are fought; tribute is
exacted; treaties are made and broken. Towards the
close of the thirteenth century, their king being slain
and their churches plundered, they lose one fourth of
their territory, including all that part which borders
upon Assouan. Those who remain Christians are also
condemned to pay an annual capitation tax, in addition to the usual tribute of dates, cotton, slaves, and
camels. After this we may conclude that they accepted Islamism from the Arabs, as they had accepted
Osiris from the Egyptians and Christ from the Romans.
As Christians, at all events, we hear of them no more;
for Christianity in Nubia perished root and branch,
and not a Copt, it is said, may now be found above
the frontier.

Philæ was still inhabited in A.D. 1799, when a de-
tachment of Desaix's army under General Beliard took
possession of the island, and left an inscription* on
the soffit of the doorway of the great pylon to commemorate the passage of the Cataract. Denon, describing the scene with his usual vivacity, relates how
the natives first defied and then fled from the French;
flinging themselves into the river, drowning such of
their children as were too young to swim, and escap-
ing into the desert. They appear at this time to have
been mere savages—the women ugly and sullen; the
men naked, agile, quarrelsome, and armed not only

---

* This inscription, which M. About considers the most interesting thing in
Philæ, runs as follows:—"L'An VI. de la République, le 15 Messidor, une
Armée Française commandée par Bonaparte est descendue à Alexandrie.
L'Armée ayant mis, vingt jours après, les Mamelouks en fuite aux Pyramides,
Desaix, commandant la première division, les a poursuivis au dela des Cata-
ractes, où il est arrivé le 18 Ventôse de l'an VII."

with swords and spears, but with matchlock guns, which they used to keep up "a brisk and well-directed fire."

Their abandonment of the island probably dates from this time; for when Burckhardt went up in A.D. 1813, he found it, as we find it to this day, deserted and solitary. One poor old man—if indeed he still lives — is now the one inhabitant of Philæ; and I suspect he only crosses over from Biggeh in the tourist-season. He calls himself, with or without authority, the guardian of the island; sleeps in a nest of rags and straw in a sheltered corner behind the great Temple; and is so wonderfully wizened and bent and knotted up, that nothing of him seems quite alive except his eyes. We gave him fifty copper piastres * for a parting present when on our way back to Egypt; and he was so oppressed by the consciousness of wealth, that he immediately buried his treasure and implored us to tell no one what we had given him.

With the French siege and the flight of the native population closes the last chapter of the local history of Philæ. The Holy Island has done henceforth with wars of creeds or kings. It disappears from the domain of history, and enters the domain of science. To have contributed to the discovery of the hieroglyphic alphabet is a high distinction; and in no sketch of Philæ, however slight, should the obelisk ** that furnished Champollion with the name of Cleopatra be allowed to pass unnoticed. This monument, second only to the Rosetta Stone in point of philological interest, was,

* About two-and-sixpence English.
** See previous note, p. 268.

with the assistance of Belzoni, carried off by Mr. J. W. Bankes, the discoverer of the first Tablet of Abydos, and is now in Dorsetshire. The material of this obelisk, which stands 22 feet high, is the red granite of Syene.

And now—for we have lingered over long in the portico—it is time we glanced at the interior of the Temple. So we go in at the central door, beyond which open some nine or ten halls and side-chambers leading, as usual, to the sanctuary. Here all is dark, earthy, oppressive. In rooms unlighted by the faintest gleam from without, we find smoke-blackened walls covered with elaborate bas-reliefs. Mysterious passages, pitch-dark, thread the thickness of the walls and communicate by means of trap-like openings with vaults below. In the sanctuary lies an overthrown altar; while in the corner behind it stands the very niche in which Strabo must have seen that poor sacred hawk of Ethiopia which he describes as "sick, and nearly dead."

But in this Temple dedicated not only to Isis, but to the memory of Osiris and the worship of Horus their son, there is one chamber which we may be quite sure was shown neither to Strabo nor Diodorus, nor to any stranger of alien faith, be his repute or station what it might; a chamber holy above all others; holier even than the sanctuary;—the chamber sacred to Osiris. We, however, unrestricted, unforbidden, are free to go where we list; and our books tell us that this mysterious chamber is somewhere overhead. So, emerging once again into the daylight, we go up a well-worn staircase that leads out upon the roof.

This roof is an intricate, up-and-down place; and the room is not easy to find. It lies at the bottom of a little flight of steps—a small stone cell some twelve feet square, lighted only from the doorway. The walls are covered with sculptures representing the shrines, the mummification, and the resurrection of Osiris. *

* The story of Osiris—the beneficent God, the friend of man, slain and dismembered by Typhon; buried in a score of graves; sought by Isis; recovered limb by limb; resuscitated in the flesh; transferred from earth to reign over the dead in the world of Shades—is one of the most complex of Egyptian legends. Osiris under some aspects is the Nile. He personifies Abstract Good. He appears as a Myth of the Solar Year. He bears a notable likeness to Prometheus, and to the Indian Bacchus. The following extract is taken from that modest, learned, and eloquent little volume, the Catalogue of the Boulak Museum, by Mariette Bey:—

"Originairement Osiris est le soleil nocturne; il est la nuit primordiale; il précède la lumière; il est par conséquent antérieur à *Ra*, le soleil diurne.

"De ce rôle principal découlent une multitude d'allégories qui se groupent autour d'Osiris, et font de ce personnage un des types divines les plus curieux à étudier.

"La vie de l'homme a été assimilée par les Égyptiens à la course du soleil au-dessus de nos têtes; le soleil qui se couche et disparaît à l'horizon occidental est l'image de sa mort. A peine le moment suprême est-il arrivé, qu'Osiris s'empare de l'âme qu'il est chargé de conduire à la lumière éternelle. Osiris, dit-on, était autrefois descendu sur la terre. Être bon par excellence, il avait adouci les mœurs des hommes par la persuasion et la bienfaisance. Mais il avait succombé sous les embûches de Typhon, son frère, le génie du mal, et pendant que ses deux sœurs, Isis et Nephthys, recueillaient son corps qui avait été jeté dans le fleuve, le dieu ressuscitait d'entre les morts et apparaissait à son fils Horus, qu'il instituait son vengeur. C'est ce sacrifice qu'il avait autrefois accompli en faveur des hommes qu'Osiris renouvelle ici en faveur de l'âme dégagée de ses liens terrestres. Non seulement il devient son guide, mais il s'identifie à elle; il l'absorbe en son propre sein. C'est lui alors qui, devenu le défunt lui-même, se soumet à toutes les épreuves qui celui-ci doit subir avant d'être proclamé juste; c'est lui qui, à chaque âme qu'il doit sauver, fléchit les gardiens des demeures infernales et combat les monstres compagnons de la nuit et de la mort; c'est lui enfin qui, vainqueur des ténèbres, avec l'assistance d'Horus, s'assied au tribunal de la suprême justice et ouvre à l'âme déclarée pure les portes du séjour éternel. L'image de la mort aura été empruntée au soleil qui disparaît à l'horizon du soir: le soleil resplendissant du matin sera la symbole de cette seconde naissance à une vie qui, cette fois, ne connaîtra pas la mort.

"Osiris est donc le principe du bien. . . . Chargé de sauver les âmes de la mort définitive, il est l'intermédiaire entre l'homme et Dieu; il est le type et le sauveur de l'homme." *Notice des Monuments à Boulaq*—AUG. MARIETTE-BEY, 1872, pp. 105 *et seq.*

"The astronomical and physical elements are too obvious to be mistaken.

These shrines, containing each some part of his body, are variously fashioned. His head, for instance, rests on a Nilometer; his arm is enclosed in what would seem to be a high-shouldered bottle of a form much used in Roman times, and here surmounted by one of the head-dresses peculiar to the God; his legs and feet lie at full length in a pylon-shaped mausoleum. Upon another shrine stands the mitre-shaped crown which he wears as Judge of the Lower World. Two female genii keep guard over each shrine. In a lower frieze we see the mummy of the god laid upon a bier, with the four so-called canopic jars* ranged underneath. A little farther on, he lies in state, surrounded, as in a *chapelle ardente*, by rows of lighted torches. Finally, he is depicted lying on a couch; his limbs reunited; his head, left hand, and left foot upraised, as in the act of returning to consciousness. Nephthys, in the guise of a winged genius, fans him with the breath of life. Isis, with outstretched arms, stands at his feet and seems to be calling him back to her embraces. The

---

Osiris and Isis are the Nile and Egypt. The myth of Osiris typifies the solar year—the power of Osiris is the sun in the lower hemisphere, the winter solstice. The birth of Horus typifies the vernal equinox—the victory of Horus the summer solstice—the inundation of the Nile. Typhon is the autumnal equinox." *Egypt's Place in Universal History*—BUNSEN, 1st ed., vol. I. p. 437.

"The Egyptians do not all worship the same gods, excepting Isis and Osiris."—HERODOTUS, Book II.

For a lucid summary of the main features of the Osiris myth under its various aspects, both native and foreign, see Miss Keary's *Early Egyptian History*, 1863, p. 380 *et seq.*

* "These vases made of alabaster, calcareous stone, porcelain, terracotta, and even wood, were destined to hold the soft parts or viscera of the body, embalmed separately and deposited in them. They were four in number, and were made in the shape of the four genii of the Karneter, or Hades, to whom were assigned the four cardinal points of the compass." Birch's *Guide to the First and Second Egyptian Rooms*, 1874, p. 89. See also Birch's *History of Ancient Pottery*, 1873, p. 23 *et seq.*

scene represents, in fact, that supreme moment when Isis pours forth her passionate invocations, and Osiris is resuscitated by virtue of the songs of the divine sisters.*

Ill-modelled and ill-cut as they are, there is a clownish naturalness about these little sculptures which lifts them above the conventional dead level of ordinary Ptolemaic work. The figures tell their tale intelligibly. Osiris seems really struggling to rise, and the action of Isis expresses clearly enough the intention of the artist. Although a few heads have been mutilated and the surface of the stone is somewhat degraded, the subjects are by no means in a bad state of preservation. Osiris in one has lost his foot, and in another his face; the hands of Isis are as shapeless as those of a bran doll; and the naïveté of the treatment verges throughout upon caricature. But the interest attaching to them is altogether apart from the way in which they are executed.

And now, returning to the roof, it is pleasant to breathe the fresher air that comes with sunset—to see the island, in shape like an ancient Egyptian shield, lying mapped out beneath one's feet. From here, we look back upon the way we have come, and forward to the way we are going. Northward lies the Cataract— a network of islets with flashes of river between. Southward, the broad current comes on in one smooth, glassy sheet, unbroken by a single rapid. How eagerly we turn our eyes that way; for yonder lie Aboo Simbel and all the mysterious lands beyond the Cataracts!

* See Mr. P. J. de Horrack's translation of *The Lamentations of Isis and Nephthys*. RECORDS OF THE PAST, vol. II. p. 117 *et seq.*

But we cannot see far, for the river curves away grandly
to the right, and vanishes behind a range of granite
hills. A similar chain hems in the opposite bank; while
high above the palm-groves fringing the edge of the
shore stand two ruined convents on two rocky promi-
nences, like a couple of castles on the Rhine. On the
East bank opposite, a few mud houses and a group of
superb carob trees mark the site of a village, the
greater part of which lies hidden among palms. Behind this village opens a vast sand-valley, like an arm
of the sea from which the waters have retreated. The
old channel along which we rode the other day went
ploughing that way straight across from Philæ. Last
of all, forming the Western side of this fourfold view,
we have the island of Biggeh—rugged, mountainous,
and divided from Philæ by so narrow a channel that
every sound from the native village on the opposite
steep is as audible as though it came from the courtyard at our feet. That village is built in and about
the ruins of a tiny Ptolemaic Temple, of which only a
screen and doorway and part of a small propylon remain. We can see a woman pounding coffee on the
threshold of one of the huts, and some children
scrambling about the rocks in pursuit of a wandering
turkey. Catching sight of us up here on the roof of
the Temple, they come whooping and scampering down
to the water-side, and with shrill cries importune us
for backsheesh. Unless the stream is wider than it
looks, one might almost pitch a piastre into their outstretched hands.

Mr. Hay, it is said, discovered a secret passage of
solid masonry tunnelled under the river from island to

island. The entrance on this side was from a shaft in
the Temple of Isis.* We are not told how far Mr. Hay
was able to penetrate in the direction of Biggeh; but
the passage would lead up, most probably, to the little
Temple opposite.

Perhaps the most entirely curious and unaccustomed
features in all this scene are the mountains. They are
like none that any of us have seen in our diverse wanderings. Other mountains are homogeneous, and thrust
themselves up from below in masses suggestive of pri-
mæval disruption and upheaval. These seem to lie
upon the surface foundationless; rock loosely piled on
rock, boulder on boulder; like stupendous cairns, the
work of demigods and giants. Here and there, on
shelf or summit, a huge rounded mass, many tons in
weight, hangs poised capriciously. Most of these blocks,
I am persuaded, would "log," if put to the test.

But for a specimen stone, commend me to yonder
amazing monolith down by the water's edge opposite,
near the carob trees and the ferry. Though but a
single block of orange-red granite, it looks like three;
and the Arabs, seeing in it some fancied resemblance
to an arm-chair, call it Pharaoh's throne. Rounded and
polished by prehistoric floods, and emblazoned with
royal cartouches of extraordinary size, it seems to have
attracted the attention of pilgrims in all ages. Kings,
conquerors, priests, travellers, have covered it with records of victories, of religious festivals, of prayers, and
offerings, and acts of adoration. Some of these are

* *Operations carried on at the Pyramids of Ghizeh*—COL. HOWARD VYSE,
London, 1840, vol. I. p. 63.

older by a thousand years and more than the temples on the island opposite.

Such, roughly summed up, are the fourfold surroundings of Philæ—the cataract, the river, the desert, the environing mountains. The Holy Island—beautiful, lifeless, a thing of the far past, with all its wealth of sculpture, painting, history, poetry, tradition—sleeps, or seems to sleep, in the midst.

It is one of the world's famous landscapes, and it deserves its fame. Every sketcher sketches it; every traveller describes it. Yet it is just one of those places of which the objective and subjective features are so equally balanced that it bears putting neither into words nor colours. The sketcher must perforce leave out the atmosphere of association that informs his subject; and the writer's description is at best no better than a catalogue raisonnée.

CHAPTER XIII.

Philæ to Korosko.

SAILING gently southward—the river opening wide before us, Philæ dwindling in the rear—we feel that we are now fairly over the border; and that if Egypt was strange and far from home, Nubia is stranger and farther still. The Nile here flows deep and broad. The rocky heights that hem it in so close on either side are still black on the one hand, golden on the other. The banks are narrower than ever. The space in some places is little wider than a towing-path. In others, there is barely room for a belt of date-palms and a slip of alluvial soil, every foot of which produces its precious growth of doorah or barley. The steep verge below is green with lentils to the water's edge. As the river recedes, it leaves each day a margin of fresh, wet soil, in which the careful husbandman hastens to scratch a new furrow and sow another line of seeds. He cannot afford to let so much as an inch of that kindly mud lie idle.

Gliding along with half-filled sail, we observe how entirely the population seems to be regulated by the extent of arable soil. Where the inundation has room to spread, villages come thicker; more dusky figures are seen moving to and fro in the shade of the palms; more children race along the banks, shrieking for backsheesh. When the shelf of soil is narrowed, on the

contrary, to a mere fringe of luminous green dividing
the rock from the river, there is a startling absence of
everything like life. Mile after mile drags its slow
length along, uncheered by any sign of human habitation. When now and then a solitary native, armed with
gun or spear, is seen striding along the edge of the
desert, he only seems to make the general solitude
more apparent.

Meanwhile, it is not only men and women whom
we miss—men labouring by the river-side; women with
babies astride on their shoulders, or water-jars balanced
on their heads—but birds, beasts, boats; everything
that we have been used to see along the river. The
buffaloes dozing at midday in the shallows, the camels
stalking home in single file towards sunset, the water-
fowl haunting the sandbanks, seem suddenly to have
vanished. Even donkeys are now rare; and as for
horses, I do not remember to have seen one during the
seven weeks we spent in Nubia. All night, too, instead
of the usual chorus of dogs barking furiously from
village to village, we hear only the long-drawn wail of
an occasional jackal. It is not wonderful, however,
that animal life should be scarce in a district where
the scant soil yields barely food enough for those who
till it. To realise how very scant it is, one needs only
to remember that about Derr, where it is at its widest,
the annual deposit nowhére exceeds half-a-mile in
breadth; while for the most part of the way between
Philæ and Wady Halfeh—a distance of 210 miles—it
averages from six to sixty yards.

Here, then, more than ever, one seems to see how
entirely these lands which we call Egypt and Nubia

are nothing but the banks of one solitary river in the midst of a world of desert. In Egypt, the valley is often so wide that one forgets the stony waste beyond the corn-lands. But in Nubia, the desert is ever present. We cannot forget it, if we would. The barren mountains press upon our path, showering down avalanches of granite on the one side and torrents of yellow sand on the other. We know that those stones are always falling; that those sands are always drifting; that the river has hard work to hold its own; and that the desert is silently encroaching day by day.

These golden sand-streams are the newest and most beautiful feature in the landscape. They pour down from the high level of the Libyan desert just as the snows of Switzerland pour down from the upper plateaux of the Alps. Through every ravine and gap they find a channel—here trickling in tiny rivulets; flowing yonder in broad torrents that widen to the river.

Becalmed a few miles above Philæ, we found ourselves just at the foot of one of these largest drifts. The M. B.s challenged us to climb the slope, and see the sunset from the desert. It was about six o'clock, and the thermometer was standing at 80° in the coolest corner of the large saloon. We ventured to suggest that the top was a long way up; but the M. B.s would take no refusal. So away we went; panting, breathless, bewailing our hard fate. L. and the Writer had done some difficult walking in their time, over ice and snow, on lava cold and hot, up cinder-slopes and beds of mountain torrents; but this innocent-looking sand-drift proved quite as hard to climb as any of them. The sand lies wonderfully loose and light, and is as hot as if it had been baked in an oven. Into this the foot plunges ankle-deep, slipping back at every step, and leaving a huge hole into which the sand pours down again like water. Looking back, you trace your course by a succession of funnel-shaped pits, each larger than a washhand basin. Though your slipper be as small as Cinderella's, the next comer shall not be able to tell whether it was a lady who went up last, or a camel. It is toilsome work, too; for the foot finds neither rest nor resistance, and the strain upon the muscles is un-remitting.

But the beauty of the sand more than repays the fatigue of climbing it. Smooth, sheeny, satiny; fine as diamond-dust; supple, undulating, luminous, it lies in the most exquisite curves and wreaths, like a snow-drift turned to gold. Remodelled by every breath that blows, its ever-varying surface presents an endless play of delicate lights and shadows. There lives not the sculptor who could render those curves; and I doubt whether Turner himself, in his tenderest and subtlest mood, could have done justice to those complex greys and ambers.

Having paused to rest upon an out-cropping ledge of rock about half-way up, we came at length to the top of the last slope and found ourselves on the level of the desert. Here, faithful to the course of the river, the first objects to meet our eyes were the old familiar telegraph-posts and wires. Beyond them, to North and South, a crowd of peaks closed in the view; but Westward, a rolling waste of hillock and hollow opened away to where the sun, a crimson globe, had already half-vanished below the rim of the world.

One could not resist going a few steps farther, just to touch the nearest of those telegraph posts. It was like reaching out a hand towards home.

When the sun dropped, we turned back. The valley below was already steeped in dusk. The Nile, glimmering like a coiled snake in the shade, reflected the evening sky in three separate reaches. On the Arabian side, a far-off mountain-chain stood out, purple and jagged, against the Eastern horizon.

To come down was easy. Driving our heels well into the sand, we half ran, half glissaded, and soon reached the bottom. Here we were met by an old Nubian woman, who had trudged up in all haste from the nearest village to question our sailors about one Yoosef, her son, of whom she had heard nothing for nearly a year. She was a very poor old woman—a widow, and this Yoosef was her only son. Hoping to better himself, he had worked his passage to Cairo in a cargo-boat some eighteen months ago. Twice since then he had sent her messages and money; but now eleven months had gone by in silence, and she feared he must be dead. Meanwhile her date-palm, taxed to the full value of its produce, had this year yielded not a piastre of profit. Her mud-hut had fallen in, and there was no Yoosef to repair it. Old and sick, she now could only beg; and her neighbours, by whose charity she subsisted, were but a shade less poor than herself.

Our men knew nothing of the missing Yoosef. Reïs Hassan promised when he went back to make inquiries among the boatmen of Boulak:—"But then," he added, "there are so many Yoosefs in Cairo!"

It made one's heart ache to see the tremulous
eagerness with which the poor soul put her questions,
and the crushed look in her face when she turned
away.

And now, being fortunate in respect of the wind,
which for the most part blows steadily from the North
between sunrise and sunset, we make good progress,
and for the next ten days live pretty much on board
our Dahabeeyah. The main features of the landscape
go on repeating themselves with but little variation
from day to day. The mountains wear their habitual
livery of black and gold. The river, now widening,
now narrowing, flows between banks blossoming with
lentils and lupins. With these, and yellow acacia-tufts,
and blue castor-oil berries, and the weird coloquintida,
with its downy leaf and milky juice and puff-bladder
fruit, like a green peach tinged with purple, we make
our daily bouquet for the dinner-table. All other
flowers have vanished, and even these are hard to get
in a land where every green blade is precious to the
grower.

Now, too, the climate becomes sensibly warmer.
The heat of the sun is so great at midday that, even
with the North breeze blowing, we can no longer sit
on deck between twelve and three. Towards sundown,
when the wind drops, it turns so sultry that to take a
walk on shore comes to be regarded as a duty rather
than as a pleasure. Thanks, however, to that indomit-
able Painter who is always ready for an afternoon excursion, we do sometimes walk for an hour before
dinner; striking off generally into the desert; looking
for onyxes and carnelians among the pebbles that here

and there strew the surface of the sand; and watching in vain for jackals and desert-hares.

Sometimes we follow the banks instead of the desert, coming now and then to a creaking Sakkieh turned by a melancholy buffalo; or to a native village hidden behind dwarf-palms. Here each hut has its tiny forecourt, in the midst of which stand the mud-oven and mud-cupboard of the family — two dumpy cones of smooth grey clay, like big chimney-pots—the one capped with a lid, the other fitted with a little wooden door and wooden bolt. Some of the houses have a barbaric ornament palmed off, so to say, upon the walls; the pattern being simply the impression of a human hand dipped in red or yellow ochre, and applied while the surface is moist.

The amount of "bazaar" that takes place whenever we enter one of these villages, is quite alarming. The dogs first give notice of our approach; and presently we are surrounded by all the women and girls of the place, offering live pigeons, eggs, vegetable marrows, necklaces, nose-rings and silver bracelets for sale. The boys pester us to buy wretched half-dead chameleons. The men stand aloof, and leave the bargaining to the women.

And the women not only know how to bargain, but how to assess the relative value of every coin that passes current on the Nile. Rupees, roubles, reyals, dollars and shillings are as intelligible to them as paras or piastres. Sovereigns are not too heavy, nor napoleons too light for them. The times are changed since Belzoni's Nubian, after staring contemptuously at the first piece of money he had ever seen, asked "Who would give anything for that small piece of metal?"

The necklaces consist of onyx, carnelian, bone, silver, and coloured glass beads, with now and then a stray scarab or funereal amulet in the ancient blue porcelain. The arrangement of colour is often very subtle. The brow-pendants in gold repoussée, and the massive old silver bracelets, rough with knobs and bosses, are most interesting in design, and perpetuate patterns of undoubted antiquity. The M. B.s picked up one really beautiful collarette of silver and coral, which might have been worn three thousand years ago by Pharaoh's daughter.

When on board, we begin now to keep a sharp look-out for crocodiles. We hear of them constantly—see their tracks upon the sand-banks in the river—go through agonies of expectation over every black speck in the distance; yet are perpetually disappointed. The farther South we go, the more impatient we become. The E.'s, whose Dahabeeyah, homeward-bound, drifts slowly past one calm morning, report "eleven beauties," seen all together yesterday upon a sand island, some ten miles higher up. Mr. C. B.'s boat, garlanded with crocodiles from stem to stern, fills us with envy. We would give our ears (almost) to see one of these engaging reptiles dangling from either our own main-mast, or that of the faithful Bagstones. Alfred, who has set his heart on bagging at least half-a-dozen, says nothing, but grows gloomier day by day. At night, when the moon is up and less misanthropic folk are in bed and asleep, he rambles moodily into the desert, after jackals.

Meanwhile, on we go, starting at sunrise; mooring at sunset; sailing, tracking, punting; never stopping for an hour by day, if we can help it; and pushing straight for Aboo-Simbel with as little delay as possible. Thus we pass the pylons of Dabod with their background of desert; Gertasseh, a miniature Sunium, seen towards evening against the glowing sunset; Tafah, rich in palms, with white columns gleaming through green foliage by the water-side; the cliffs, islands, and rapids of Kalabsheh, and the huge Temple that rises like a fortress in their midst; Dendoor, a tiny chapel with a single pylon; and Gerf Hossayn, which from this distance might be taken for the mouth of a rock-cut tomb in the face of the precipice.

About half way between Kalabsheh and Dendoor, we enter the Tropic of Cancer. From this day till the day when we repass that invisible boundary, there is a marked change in the atmospheric conditions under which we live. The days get gradually hotter, especially at noon, when the sun is almost vertical; but the freshness of night and the chill of early morning are no more. Unless when a strong wind blows from the North, we no longer know what it is to need a shawl on deck in the evening, or an extra covering on our beds towards dawn. We sleep with our cabin-windows open, and enjoy a delicious equality of temperature from sundown to sunrise. The days and nights, too, are of almost equal length.

Now, also, the Southern Cross and a second group of stars, which we conclude must form part of the Centaur, are visible between two and four every morn-

ing. They have been creeping up, a star at a time, for
the last fortnight; but are still so low upon the Eastern
horizon that we can only see them when there comes
a break in the mountain chain on that side of the river.
At the same time, our old familiar friends of the Northern
hemisphere, looking strangely distorted and out of their
proper place, are fast disappearing on the opposite side
of the heavens.   Orion seems to be lying on his back,
and the Great Bear to be standing on his tail; while
Cassiopeia and a number of others have deserted *en
masse*. The zenith, meanwhile, is but thinly furnished;
so that we seem to have travelled away from the one
hemisphere, and not yet to have reached the other. As
for the Southern Cross, we reserve our opinion till we
get farther South.   It would be treason to hint that
we are disappointed in so famous a constellation.

After Gerf Hossayn, the next place of importance
for which our maps bid us look out, is Dakkeh.   As
we draw near, expecting hourly to see something of
the Temple, the Nile increases in breadth and beauty.
It is a peaceful, glassy morning.   The men have been
tracking since dawn, and stop to breakfast at the foot
of a sandy bank, wooded with tamarisks and gum-trees.
A glistening network of gossamer floats from bough to
bough.   The sky overhead is of a tender luminous
blue, such as we never see in Europe.   The air is
wonderfully still.   The river, which here takes a sudden
bend towards the East, looks like a lake, and seems to
be barred ahead by the desert.   Presently a funeral
passes along the opposite bank; the chief mourner
flourishing a long staff, like a drum-major; the women
·snatching up handfuls of dust, and scattering it upon

their heads. We hear their wild wail long after the procession is out of sight.

Going on again presently, our whole attention becomes absorbed by the new and singular geological features of the Libyan desert. A vast plain covered with isolated mountains of volcanic structure, it looks like some strange transformation of the Puy de Dôme plateau, with all its wind-swept pastures turned to sand, and its grassy craters stripped to barrenness. The more this plain widens out before our eyes, the more it bristles with peaks. As we round the corner, and Dakkeh, like a smaller Edfoo, comes into sight upon the Western bank, the whole desert on that side, as far as the eye can see, presents the unmistakable aspect of one vast field of volcanoes. As in Auvergne, these cones are of all sizes and heights; some low and rounded, like mere bubbles that have cooled without bursting; others ranging apparently from 1000 to 1500 feet in height. The broken craters of several are plainly distinguishable by the help of a field-glass. One in particular is so like our old friend the Puy de Pariou, that in a mere black-and-white sketch, the one might readily be mistaken for the other.

We were surprised to find no account of the geology of this district in any of our books. Murray and Wilkinson pass it in silence; and writers of travels—one or two of whom notice only the "pyramidal" shape of the hills—are for the most part content to do likewise. None seem to have observed their obvious volcanic origin.

Thanks to a light breeze that sprang up in the afternoon, we were able to hoist our big sail again, and to relieve the men from tracking. Thus we glided past the ruins of Maharrakeh, which, seen from the river, looked like a Greek portico set in a hollow waste of burning desert. Next came Wady Sabooah, a temple half buried in sand, near which we met a tiny Daha-beeyah, manned by two Nubians and flying the star and crescent. A shabby Government Inspector, in European dress and a fez, lay smoking on a mat out-side his cabin door; while from a spar overhead there hung a mighty crocodile. This monster was of a greenish brown colour, and measured at least sixteen feet from head to tail. His jaws yawned; and one fat and flabby arm and ponderous paw swung with the motion of the boat, looking horribly human.

The Painter, with an eye to foregrounds, made a bid for him on the spot; but the shabby Inspector was not to be moved by considerations of gain. He pre-ferred his crocodile to infidel gold, and scarcely deigned even to reply to the offer.

Seen in the half-light of a tropical afterglow—the purple mountains coming down in detached masses to the water's edge on the one side; the desert with its volcanic peaks yet rosy upon the other—we thought the approach to Korosko more picturesque than any-thing we had yet seen South of the Cataract. As the dusk deepened, the moon rose; and the palms that had just room to grow between the mountains and the river turned from bronze to silver. It was half-twilight, half-moonlight, by the time we reached the mooring-place; where Talhamy, who had been sent forward in the small boat half-an-hour ago, jumped on board laden with a packet of letters, and a sheaf of newspapers.

For here, where the great caravan-route leads off across the desert to Khartoom, we touched the first Nubian post-office. It was only ten days since we had received our last budget at Assouan; but it seemed like ten weeks.

END OF VOL. I.

PRINTING OFFICE OF THE PUBLISHER.

Ingram Content Group UK Ltd.
Milton Keynes UK
UKHW022301260623
424090UK00005B/239